200 SKILLS

every

FASHION DESIGNER

must have

200 SKILLS
every
FASHION DESIGNER
must have

The Indispensable Guide to Building Skills
and Turning Ideas into Reality

AISLING McKEEFRY

For Gráinne

A QUINTET BOOK

First edition for the United States and Canada published in 2016 by Barron's Educational Series, Inc.

Copyright © 2016 Quintet Publishing Limited

All rights reserved. No part of this publication may be reproduced or distributed in any form or by any means without the written permission of the copyright owner.

All inquiries should be addressed to:
Barron's Educational Series, Inc.
250 Wireless Boulevard
Hauppauge, NY 11788
www.barronseduc.com

ISBN: 978-1-4380-0896-7

Library of Congress Control Number: 2016942773

QTT.TSFD

Conceived, designed, and produced by:
Quintet Publishing
4th Floor Ovest House
58 West Street
Brighton, BN1 2RA
United Kingdom

Co-Author: Matt Pointon
Project Editor: Caroline Elliker
Designer: Tania Gomes
Art Director: Michael Charles
Publisher: Mark Searle
Printed in China by C&C Offset Printing Co Ltd.

9 8 7 6 5 4 3 2 1

CONTENTS

INTRODUCTION

I love working in fashion for so many reasons. The rapid pace that means no two days are ever the same and the passion of the people I collaborate with to make ideas into reality is truly inspiring. Seeing someone wearing something I designed and realizing the influence I can have gives me a real thrill.

I am constantly asked how I made it into the fashion industry. It's challenging but not unattainable, and with the right skills and determination, you can get there too. Fashion is full of real people from normal places. It may appear glamorous—and sometimes it is—but like any profession, there's a lot of hard work involved.

The fashion industry can also appear very daunting; ruthless, elitist, intimidating, and exclusive. This book deconstructs these preconceptions—at its best, fashion is inclusive rather than exclusive, and collaborative rather than cutthroat. All the people I have worked with that have truly inspired me are those that helped, listened, encouraged, and developed me, rather than tried to keep me in my place.

This book is written in the spirit of giving advice and guidance to all those who are interested in working in the fashion industry. While writing it, I've constantly asked myself what information I would have liked to have been given at the start of my career. I've drawn heavily on my experience both as a student and as a professional and thought carefully about how fashion really works. After reading this book, I want you to be raring to go and ready for anything.

There are many different possible beginnings to a career in fashion design and unlimited twists and turns that it can take as it progresses. With so many different disciplines, job roles, and product types, it's impossible to cover everything in exhaustive detail in just one book. With this in mind, the first section of this book contains ten core, overarching skills that crop up throughout the book and are applicable to 99 percent

of roles within the industry. These are the less tangible skills, often behavioral traits or working methods, that give real insight into what it takes to succeed.

Chapter 1 looks at the design process: its principles, sources of inspiration, trends and cycles, as well as practical ways of developing and applying your ideas. Chapter 2 examines illustration skills—vital to being able to communicate ideas and stay ahead of the game. Chapters 3 and 4 cover some of the essential need-to-know elements of fabric and garment construction techniques and are packed with invaluable knowledge.

Selling yourself, your brand, and your product is an increasingly important part of modern fashion, so Chapter 5 looks in detail at marketing, brand building, and business skills to equip and empower you when you need to impress someone in the industry.

Chapter 6 deals with professional skills and provides an enormous amount of information and tips on working in the industry. It offers practical and realistic advice about what your career options might be, how different kinds of work experience can make you a more rounded designer, and how to nurture and manage the essential relationships that will enable you to fulfill your potential. Finally, I have provided an overview of another side of the job that is more hard work and less glamorous than it sounds—shopping!

This book will give you an overview of all of the essential skills you need to be a great fashion designer. It will help you to identify gaps in your knowledge and will explain the processes that fashion designers work with every day. But most importantly, this book will encourage you. As designers it's our duty to be brave and push the boundaries—so get out there, be the very best you can be, and keep pushing fashion forward.

Ashish runway, London Fashion Week, Spring/Summer 2016.

Aisling

CORE SKILLS

1.
CREATIVE FLAIR

Since creative flair is something inherent to fashion designers, it really is the most important core skill. Chances are, if you're seriously interested in being a fashion designer, you will already have it. There are ways in which you can develop and hone this skill to make the most of it.

Having a visual imagination and an ability to visualize are vital. Put simply, this is the ability to imagine things that don't already exist. Most people can do this to a certain extent, but as a designer you need to push these skills to the limit. Don't think within boundaries or parameters—if you can imagine it, you can do it.

There are other ways that you can foster this natural flair. Keep your eyes open and absorb everything around you. Even something as mundane as your daily commute can give you so much customer insight—what bag does she have, what shoes is he wearing? Filter these ideas and remember the great ones—you can fine-tune and apply them when the time is right.

In order to inspire, you need to be inspired, so make time for this. Take yourself to the latest exhibitions. It's your duty to surround yourself with inspirational sources—people, culture, street style, music, films, places, and interiors.

It's also important to realize that possessing creative flair doesn't always mean making flamboyant, eccentric, or over-the-top pieces. It can also be applied through attention to detail and subtlety.

Awareness of context is so important in creating your designs. The idea is not to bombard the customer with ideas but to take pieces of inspiration, allow them to grow, and learn how and when to apply them. Issey Miyake, Japanese fashion designer and fragrance connoisseur, began his fashion career in 1970 in New York City. With his revolutionary style, experimental approach, and technology-driven designs, he is the epitome of creative flair. He is quoted as saying, "Design is not for philosophy—it's for life."

Issey Miyake is synonymous with creative flair and reinvention. Infamous for incorporating technology within his collections, he is a true revolutionary — forever pushing boundaries.

Alexander McQueen—
forever associated with
brave, groundbreaking
design while never
compromising on
construction or
craftsmanship.

2.
BRAVERY

As a designer, your job is to innovate—to inspire people and to create newness. You must strive to get there first and drive fashion forward. You need to be brave and take risks.

This is easy to say, and it's also easy to see how it applies to haute couture fashion houses, which are constantly breaking new ground. But what if you design for a fairly safe contemporary brand with a cautious customer base? Doing something new doesn't always have to be wild, wacky, and out there. As trends trickle down from the runways to the mainstream, you need to pitch runway influences at the right level for your customer. It's your role to know where fashion is going and to push in that direction, even if your buying team ends up sitting on your boldest designs for eighteen months before your customer catches up with the trend.

There may be ways of diluting the wildest ideas to make them relevant to your customer. Even if you know that the customer won't want the latest trend yet, you can take little steps toward educating and challenging them to lead them in the right direction—it doesn't need to be a huge leap of faith. And you may even need to educate those you work with before you can get to the customer.

Whatever you're designing, even if it's a basic item, you should think of reinvention—there is no point in just churning out old designs. Anything that is 100-percent unique will always be a risk because you will be in uncharted waters. But you don't always have to dive in headfirst—ideas can be tested on small scales to gauge reaction.

Until you've had a couple of bestsellers under your belt, or have had a positive press reaction to your range, you might be scared to take risks. Once you have more experience, and more success in the bank, you will gain confidence. Push the boundaries, challenge, and question.

3.
ORGANIZATION

- -

Organizational skills are not necessarily associated with designers or creative people, but they are important skills to have and hone, even if they don't come naturally to you.

In fact, it's hard to think of a design scenario in which you don't have to be organized—from meeting a project deadline to carrying out a lookbook photo shoot, or from flying to the other side of the world and navigating around unknown areas, to hitting deadlines within an industry with millions of dollars' worth of repercussions if you're not ready.

As much as design is about abstract, creative skills, these more practical talents are vital in terms of translating ideas into a tangible end product.

4.
CRITICAL EYE

- -

As a designer, it's your job to produce creative ideas—and lots of them. Not all of these will be winners, but they're all a valid part of the creative process.

Therefore, you really need to master the skill of being critical of your own work. You will need to learn to objectively judge what you have produced. Your concepts will sometimes be very personal, but having a critical eye is about taking a step back and not being too emotionally linked to your ideas.

Review everything you do and challenge yourself. This is not about being negative or self-deprecating, but rather looking at how to improve your designs. It's also not about procrastinating—you need to be decisive. This questioning and reviewing should continue the entire way through the design process until a decision is made and you need to commit. After that, only small tweaks and aesthetic changes should occur.

For most fashion courses, you will be required to critique your own designs. Even established designers must continue to apply this technique all the way through the design process and again at the end of the season after seeing sales performance.

TIPS TO HELP YOU STAY ORGANIZED

- Write lists—check tasks off and rewrite them when something else comes up.
- Be aware of deadlines.
- Break projects down into steps.
- Plan your time—what will you get done when?
- Know when to delegate or ask for help—you won't be able to do it all alone.

USEFUL QUESTIONS TO ASK YOURSELF

- What is the end use? Is it fit for purpose?
- What makes this idea different, new, and exciting?
- Is it feasible?
- Does it fulfill the brief?
- Does it suit my target customer?
- Is my customer ready for it?

5.
DEVELOPING A THICK SKIN

In addition to casting a critical eye over your own work, you need to learn how to accept feedback. An ability to accept feedback is closely linked to being thick-skinned—not letting negative feedback get to you!

ACCEPTING FEEDBACK

In fashion courses you will receive feedback on your projects and individual pieces of art. At the undergraduate level, every project will be critiqued—you need to learn from any feedback and take it with you for the next project. By the time you're working within the industry, it becomes the norm to accept feedback on a design-by-design basis—anything from a flat "no, I don't like it" to a fairly laborious back-and-forth tweaking process. Even if you are in a relatively independent position, such as running your own brand, you will still receive feedback through the reaction to your collection.

Being asked or told to change work should not be taken as criticism—it is part of a collaborative effort to get to the best possible product. Don't take things personally. Instead, you should think about what you, as a designer, can learn from the feedback and how it can improve you.

Fashion is not a precise science, so throughout the design stage there is no right or wrong—it's one opinion versus another. Sometimes it can be hard not to take things to heart—perhaps after a long day at the end of a development trip, or if you feel your buying and merchandising (planning and allocating) teams are more aligned and you're out on a limb. But you also need to be aware of how feedback is delivered to you. It should not be done in an inappropriate forum, such as

in front of a supplier. It also should not be done in an inappropriate way, such as by shouting and screaming. You shouldn't feel belittled, and there should not be a blame culture. My advice is to nip problems like this in the bud and establish what is acceptable.

SALES PERFORMANCE

Sales performance is another form of feedback, and again, something you need to be thick-skinned about. Everyone in your business wants a product to sell, but as the creative force it can be hard not to take it personally when things haven't worked. You need to learn lessons from what has and hasn't worked, but remember, many factors affect sales performance—it's not all your fault.

It all links closely back to the skill of having a critical eye (see page 12). Detach yourself and look at things objectively—does your design meet the brief and will it sell?

6.
RESOURCEFULNESS

Resourcefulness is the ability to find quick and clever ways to solve problems. It's about thinking clearly and using things already available to you. Throughout the book, you will see many skills that include resourcefulness because it's a skill that crops up in many guises. These can broadly be thought of in three main categories: resourcefulness with your finances, resourcefulness with the people around you, and resourcefulness with your thoughts and ideas.

1. RESOURCEFULNESS WITH YOUR FINANCES

This is relevant at every stage of your journey to becoming a fashion designer. Materials are expensive, from art suppliers for your very first project to raw materials and processes for making your final collection. Keeping costs down means always considering alternative paths to get where you want to go. This could include seeking sponsorship, asking a company to sell to you at wholesale price, negotiating better prices, or improvising and getting the most out of materials available to you.

2. RESOURCEFULNESS FROM A "PEOPLE" POINT OF VIEW

This can be done through getting people on board with your creative ideas to help you to execute them. Using the network of contacts you will build up, this skill is about thinking of who can help to get something done at the right time. It can be as simple as pulling in favors when time is tight.

3. RESOURCEFULNESS FROM A MORE CREATIVE STANDPOINT

The third category is all about seeing opportunities through thinking resourcefully. Over the years, you will accumulate ideas and inspiration—the resourceful part is to know when to apply them and how to morph seemingly disparate ideas together.

Synonymous with upcycling, British designer Christopher Raeburn takes resourcefulness to another level by transforming reappropriated military fabrics into innovative designs.

7.
BEING DECISIVE

The ever-evolving nature of fashion means that time is always a critical factor. The imperatives to be the most directional and the first to bring a product to stores ensures the pressure is always on. An ability to be decisive is an essential skill for a designer.

Making a decision quickly and emphatically means that you and those around you can work with maximum efficiency. There's no time to deliberate when your competitors are threatening to get ahead of you.

The sheer volume of ideas you generate will mean that you are constantly selecting and refining them based on elements such as aesthetics, processes, cost, and third-party relationships.

Whether wading through samples and runway images or on shopping trips, you will need to be constantly finding and recognizing key pieces—extracting the gem from the rough. You might have to decide whether to spend thousands of dollars on a sample in an instant because you won't be able to go back for it.

With experience, you will build up confidence in your decision-making, but in the early stages of your development, it's important to follow your instincts.

QUESTIONS TO ASK YOURSELF TO GAIN PERSPECTIVE IN YOUR DECISION-MAKING

- How much is at stake here?
- What impact will this decision have on the final product?
- Will anyone but me notice the difference?
- How will it affect my brand?

8.
THINKING COMMERCIALLY

For an idealist or fashion purist, it can sometimes be difficult to accept an ugly truth—fashion is ultimately an industry. Alongside beautiful innovations and cutting-edge concepts, fashion is driven by the ability to make products that people, on whatever scale, want to buy. There are always targets to meet, investors to please, and rents to pay. The ability to think commercially allows you to turn your ideas into products, into sales, and ultimately into money. One element of this is seeing opportunities.

HOW TO FIND YOUR NICHE

You need to be analytical—to learn lessons from what has and has not worked in the past. How can you apply what you find to influence your future designs?

Understanding trends is essential, too. Your line does not exist in isolation, so how can you apply wider emerging trends to your collection? How can you anticipate trends and, so, demand for your product?

You need to know your customer base, the market, and your product category inside out. There will be a lot of competition going after the same demographic, so you need to know what they will want and when. Where is your customer's taste now and where can you take them? Whatever your customer wants—whether that's something fairly safe or outrageous—you need to deliver it and exceed their expectations.

Thinking commercially is not about giving up your dreams or principles but about compromising when it makes sense to. It's about separating your head from your heart and making sound business decisions.

9.
DRIVE AND AMBITION

The simple fact is this: there are not enough jobs for the number of people who want to work in the fashion industry. Therefore, when studying fashion or starting out on your own, you constantly have to go the extra mile, and to do this you need ambition and drive. These are very hard attributes to teach or learn—they have to come from within you. You need to want it and be hungry for it.

From the offset, the fashion world is competitive. You should think of this as an environment of healthy competition. When studying, you are encouraged to enter competitions and to pitch yourself against your peers and friends. As your career progresses, you will often measure yourself against peers too—are you at the stage you want to be at, or do you need to push yourself more? You will often find yourself interviewing directly against your friends, especially for internships or for new jobs. You need to adjust to what can be an uncomfortable situation and embrace it. It's not about ruthlessness or one-upmanship, but rather doing your best to succeed and having the determination to get ahead.

In terms of motivation, you have to do it for the love of it. It's not easy, and often not as well paid and glamorous as it's made out to be, so you have to love the work and want to do it. There will be plenty of times you don't get the job or win the competition. You have to take the setbacks, bounce back, and keep learning from them.

In terms of ambition, it's good to think about who you look up to. This could be anyone—from an amazingly talented senior designer to a world leader. What qualities do they have and what have they achieved? Focus on what you want to achieve, and work toward these goals. It might help to draw up a list of short-term and long-term goals.

If you do have this innate drive, the key is learning to demonstrate how driven you are to potential employers—which means going the extra mile. This could be anything, such as pulling together a one-page document focused on the company you're applying for to show at an interview, or making sure your portfolio stands out from the crowd.

From a creative point of view, ambition and drive are essential. To realize a creative vision or project, there is no halfway house. Fashion is not a field where you can complete something and check it off; it's never ending. You need the motivation to be constantly striving for better—striving for perfection.

10.
FORGING RELATIONSHIPS

Fashion is a collaborative business. It would be practically impossible to go all the way from a concept to a commercial garment completely alone, and it would certainly be a highly inefficient way of working.

The design stage is often done in isolation. However, the practices involved in setting up your own brand—working within retail, at a supplier's, or freelancing—means you will come into contact with and be reliant on a lot of third parties. You will work with so many people, so it's essential that you learn to forge strong relationships. This will make day-to-day working with them much more pleasant, but there are many other advantages too.

For a global business, at times fashion feels like a very small world. It's amazing how often paths cross, and your reputation will often precede you. Almost any employer is likely to have a contact that knows you, and they will always ask for feedback, so it's important to cultivate a positive professional reputation.

Some relationships will become integral to your everyday role – for example, those with your pattern cutter, key supplier, buyer (planner), and merchandiser (allocator). In other relationships, you may go for months without seeing those people but will need to pick up where you left off—for example, a photographer you work with twice a year, or perhaps a component supplier you occasionally use. Networking skills are important to develop—start chatting with people and remember their names.

When you're really up against it, strong relationships can mean that you can call in favors from people. Similarly, helping people out when you can should get some good karma in the bank for when you need help. This kind of give and take is crucial, so you will need to work on your negotiation skills.

Communication is key too. You need to communicate in an appropriate manner. Be friendly and open, but professional. Treat people, including those in a less senior position to you, respectfully.

In any collaboration there will always be differences of opinion, but you need to deal with these properly. Try to influence people rather than confront them. Look for a solution that realizes your vision, but at the same time, compromise when you have to. Negotiate and choose your battles wisely.

Vetements, Paris Fashion Week, Fall/Winter 2016/17.

1

DESIGN

11.
GETTING INSPIRED

As a designer, anything can inspire you, and often the most unlikely sources can lead to the most exciting ideas. Make it a habit to soak up everything around you and think about how what you see, hear, smell, and read might relate to your ideas and work.

Seek out the things you love and think about why you connect with them. Notice detail. A tiny thing can become the basis for an entire life's work. Inspiration is sometimes direct. A fastener on a gate in Kyoto would make a great fitting on a bag. Or the intangible mood of something can make you stop in your tracks and prompts a release of endorphins.

Also look at the things you hate. Identify what it is about the combination of two particular materials that repulses you. Decide if not liking something is a result of your taste or the fact that it's badly designed.

Interpreting inspiration is a crucial exercise in developing skills that will set your work apart from that of everyone else. Consciously practicing observation, research, interpretation, filtering, and refining will strengthen your ability to be decisive and realize your ideas. Fashion is often about following trends, but at

the heart of fashion design is a need to break with tradition, to innovate and lead. It is how you see and interpret the world that produces originality, that urges you to challenge convention and gives your work a unique twist. We'll explore this more in Finding Your Handwriting (see page 22).

Advances in technology and travel allow easy access to places and influences. Travel can act as a creative reset—a visual lens change. Suddenly, everything is interesting—unfamiliar surroundings give the seemingly mundane new focus.

The Internet means research, imagery, and inspiration are only ever a click away. The volume of information available can feel overwhelming and impossible even to process. Don't try. Just absorb everything that stimulates you, inspires other thoughts, makes you smile, or shocks you; gather, photograph, sketch, pin, and print. Keep these inspirations close by, play with groups, use them as the starting point of a drawing exercise, and let them sit and percolate.

Inspiration can be found anywhere you go — keep a visual record of it.

12.
FINDING YOUR HANDWRITING

- -

Essentially, most sources of inspiration are available to all other designers. We all look at seasonal runway shows twice a year, plus Resort and Pre-Fall collections in between. A lot of us follow the same bloggers, read the same Instagram feeds, subscribe to the same magazines, and are inspired by the same muses. What sets you apart is how you filter the inspiration around you.

You will naturally have your own handwriting—a taste level that is inherent and unique to you. If a group of art students were all given the same brief, you could guarantee that no two final projects or collections would look the same.

French New Wave film director Jean-Luc Godard said, "It's not where you take things from—it's where you take them to." Be creative, challenge the norm, turn things on their head, and question everything, and your natural handwriting will prevail. Use your time spent at college to find and develop your natural handwriting. Maybe all your projects take on a minimal feel? Or is everything worked into, overprinted, embellished, and intricate?

Within the industry, you may be lucky enough to land a job at a brand that is 100-percent true to your natural handwriting. And, of course, if you set up your own label –especially in the early days—your unique selling point (USP) is your brand's aesthetic.

However, there may be times when you are asked to fulfill a project or brief outside of your natural handwriting. For example, you're a womenswear designer but have been asked to design a menswear line, or you're a print designer who specializes in Renaissance-style florals but have been asked to work on a minimal graphic print package. If this is the case, do your research and concentrate on end use. Get into the consumer's head in order to fulfill the brief. But rest assured, even in this case, your individuality will flow through and the final product will reflect your unique handwriting.

13.
PRIMARY SOURCES

When given a brief or beginning a project, one of the first steps is to research in a bid to get inspired. As a designer, it's imperative that you understand the difference between primary and secondary sources and fully utilize both to influence and inspire you.

Primary sources are largely original elements or materials collected by the designer—pieces that you see or create firsthand. They may include sketches and items you work up during the research phase. A typical example of this would be an observational sketch of something you see at an exhibition that you then later use in full or in part toward your final design.

Firsthand research can be a visual image, an environment, or a sound or smell that stimulates you. It can include sketches, photographs, original objects, pieces of clothing, vintage pieces, art, exhibitions, paintings, architecture, interiors, and everyday objects—from street signs to food. Often, it comes in the form of nontangible influences—old films, new films, music, literature and novels, poetry, dreams, random conversations, slogans, slang, cultural events, and environments (such as festivals, drama, theater)… the list is endless.

RECORDING PRIMARY SOURCES

It's a good idea to try to record these primary influences. This gives you the opportunity to incorporate them into future designs or to research them further at a later date. This can be as simple as jotting down a note to yourself on your phone or in your diary, sending a quick voice memo to yourself, taking a photograph, or doing a quick doodle.

The important thing is to capture the moment. A photograph you took may become your color palette. A street sign you saw abroad may inspire the font you use for your brand or business card. A lyric you've heard might be the starting point of your final collection. Your challenge is to make these primary sources feel contemporary and modern in today's fashion world.

Design

14.
SECONDARY SOURCES

So how do secondary sources differ from primary sources, and how do you use them to influence your final designs? Secondary sources interpret, analyze, and comment on primary sources. They often include previously gathered material, such as published images—the most common form of these being magazines, books, and, in an increasingly digital age, blog posts. These sources are one or more steps removed from the event. Secondary sources may have pictures, quotes, or graphics of primary sources in them.

Also included within secondary sources are fashion-forecasting publications, which again can be in a physical form or as part of a website subscription. Here, a wealth of primary research has been gathered and collated into a trend or prediction for upcoming seasons and specific departments. Conclusions about overarching themes for the season; analysis of key shapes, materials, and textures; print direction; and color have been reached by the forecaster, who analyzes primary research and presents those influences in very much the same way as you would when presenting a mood board.

Secondary sources are sometimes frowned upon. A good example of this is how people use the online tool Pinterest. This is a visual discovery tool that you can use to find ideas for all of your projects and interests. If we, as designers and creators, upload original content onto the site, the model works and we, in turn, inspire others. If we simply pillage and repin existing images, the primary sources dry up and there is little originality.

I'm a firm believer in using a combination of both primary and secondary sources at the design research stage. Add to this your natural handwriting and natural eye, as we spoke about within the Finding Your Handwriting section (see page 22). Two people will record very different references from the same source—and you will have research that is unique only to yourself.

Secondary sources interpret, analyze, and comment on primary sources.

15.
UNDERSTANDING CONTEXT

An awareness of context is as important as primary and secondary research. A good understanding of the history of art will allow you to design within the context of a bigger picture. Vera Wang once said, "I go to the past for research. I need to know what came before so I can break the rules."

Fashion has long held a reputation for being frivolous and throwaway. Yet global, political, and cultural factors directly influence fashion and shape the trends of the upcoming season. The greatest example of this is the history of hemlines throughout the 20th century. The rise and fall of hemlines reflected wartime deprivations and postwar indulgence. In 1947 Christian Dior released his first collection, "The New Look." Dior's collection of full skirts and silhouettes made from yards and yards of fabric was a revolt against years of wartime rationing. This collection marked the beginning of the postwar efforts to revive France's internationally acclaimed fashion industry.

Cultivate an understanding of the history of art and fashion, along with an awareness of current affairs and the political, economic, and social climate. Attend exhibitions, go to gigs, notice what's happening around you—street style movements, celebrity influences, and the trends influencing youth culture.

Trend forecasters such as Lidewij Edelkoort anticipate future fashion trends by drawing on global cultural, social, economic, and political changes. They present biannual summaries and predictions of socio-cultural trends to industries such as fashion, textiles, interiors, cars, cosmetics, retail, and food, and in doing so have an enormous impact on the direction that those industries and retailers take.

Make time to research what has inspired the collections shown by designers at Fashion Week. Vogue.com is an excellent starting point.

1980s punks and skinheads in the UK, and a Dior "New Look" model in 1950s France. Both greatly influenced fashion.

16.
REFINING IDEAS

Researching old and new fashion magazines provides much inspiration.

Having received your brief, the first stage of researching should be broad and without perimeters. Explore everything that you associate with the brief and offshoots from those avenues down which you travel.

Once you have done this, start to refine your research. Group your initial research into loose themes. This could be a physical process of printing your research out and grouping your ideas using a sketchbook to help you, or a digital process of creating files or pages around each idea. There will be a number of avenues down which you can go. Later in the process, mood boards (see pages 30–33)—essentially inspiration boards that communicate your theme—can be really useful to convey your message.

Do one or two of your ideas excite you more than others? Are you breaking new ground and pushing the boundaries? There might be ideas within a few groups that you wish to explore more—think about morphing these ideas: what would the outcome be? Think of the mileage in each idea and ultimately the type of product it could lead to. Even at this initial stage, always have the original brief in mind and ask yourself, "Am I fulfilling the brief?"

17.
SKETCHBOOKS

There are many ways to record, review, and refine your research and ideas throughout the design process. There's no right or wrong method, but personally I find sketchbooks my go-to medium when developing ideas. Not only are they a great way to group your findings and see the evolution of your ideas, but they are also portable, meaning you can add to them at any time.

The purpose of a sketchbook is to allow you to develop your ideas. Sketchbooks are intended to be useful tools to help refine your many ideas into a definitive concept around which your project or collection will be based. The book itself can be anything—from a purchased sketchbook to sheets of paper you've made into a book to an actual published book that inspires you—into which you'll stick, paste, and doodle your findings.

The medium by which you record your findings can again be as varied and unorthodox as you like.

Your sketchbook is very personal; it may never be seen by anyone but yourself, or it may be submitted as an additional piece of work alongside your final project and collection. It can also take many forms. Perhaps it's loose and has everything and anything in it, from handwritten thoughts or quotes to sketches and artifacts. Or maybe it's a work of art in itself, with each page beautifully curated.

A research board is essentially the same thing as a sketchbook but in board form—a rough and ever-changing collection of images and artifacts that you've gathered throughout the research stage.

It might take a few goes of compiling a sketchbook before getting into the rhythm of what works for you. If you keep it with you at all times during the design process and try not to be too precious about adding to it, then a natural style of recording research will come to you.

18.
COMMITTING TO AN IDEA

Once you have worked through your ideas and developed them using tools such as sketchbooks (see page 27), it's now time to commit to an idea. The research and development stage can be endless—be careful that you don't run out of time to actually product-develop, design, and create your piece or collection! Of all of the ideas you've explored and recorded, which intrigue and excite you the most? Which feel new and groundbreaking? Fashion, art, and design are all about pushing the boundaries, delving into unchartered territories, and challenging the status quo. As designers, it's our duty to reinvent, inspire, and innovate.

KEY SKILLS FOR COMMITTING TO AN IDEA

Be critical—Not all of your ideas will be amazing ones. They all won't be relevant to the brief set either. Be critical and dispel any ideas that feel weak.

Be analytical—Analysis is not usually associated with designers, but analyze your research so far, always with the original brief in mind, and try to pinpoint what it is that makes one idea superior to another. This will help you to commit to your final idea.

Be disciplined—Set yourself cutoff dates for each part of the process, including the research stage. There's still a long way to go before fulfilling your brief—don't get into the design and making stage.

Finally, employ foresight—Ask yourself questions: "If I go down this route, what will my final collection look like?" "What silhouettes, materials, and finishes will this idea dictate?" All of these ways of reviewing and analyzing your research to date should help you to commit to your final idea.

Gucci pushing the boundaries at Milan Fashion Week, Spring/ Summer 2016.

19.
REVIEWING AND FINE-TUNING

Having settled on your final idea or subject matter, there's one final stage to work through before moving on to mood boards, color palettes, and ultimately designing—and that's reviewing and fine-tuning. It may seem like you've been doing nothing else since starting the research phase; after all, everything you've gathered, collected, sourced, and created at the research and sketchbook stage has been included for a reason. However, now that you've committed to your final idea, it's worth spending a bit of time just fine-tuning it.

Draw on the skills in the previous section, Committing to an Idea (see page 28), in particular being critical and employing foresight to ensure all of the groundwork has been done before moving on to the next stage. Projects and collections come together so much more easily when you have a strong body of research in place.

Are there any avenues within that final idea that you haven't yet explored? Your research up to this stage has been filtered from varied and vast references down to a fairly specific and hopefully original concept. Go back and fill in any gaps around your final idea, again referring back to the original brief to make sure you are meeting the requirements. The next stage of the design process is making mood boards—how we compile and present our research findings back to the viewer.

Grouping images together can give a great overview and allows you to identify any gaps in your research.

20.
MOOD BOARDS: GATHERING IMAGES

MOOD BOARDS

A mood board differs from a research board in that it is a finely tuned edit of images that communicate a final idea, concept, or theme to the viewer. It's a tool through which ideas evolve and percolate—some of them half finished, others simply snapshots of a thought or idea.

Mood boards are integral to getting your ideas across. They are a collection of images and objects that inspire you—some demonstrating mood, theme, product, colors, materials, and textures. In constructing mood boards, the designer works through distinct stages. The process enables the designer to see how ideas and images work together when combined. Mood boards allow you to construct a cohesive idea from a diverse range of influences and channel them into a brand new design. They also serve as a means of communication. Through the careful process of refining and selecting key elements from your initial pool of research, the mood board acts as a visual presentation tool—communicating your core themes, direction, and message.

As soon as you have an idea or brief in your mind, you need to let it take over your thoughts. You can look for inspiration everywhere—from magazines to museums, exhibitions, films, architecture, the Internet, blogs, social media, runways, fabrics, embellishments, trim shops, firsthand research, and found objects . . . Enjoy this part of the process, and allow time to gather inspiration and relate it back to your original idea.

The importance of creating original content cannot be underestimated so, where possible, seek out and generate firsthand inspiration. Take photos, look for original artifacts—this could be an old postcard or a vintage piece of lace—and include these on your board to ensure individuality. If using known or iconic imagery, play around with filters and layers to make the image fit the overall mood of your board. By generating original content you're contributing and giving something back—and in turn may one day see your original images on other people's mood boards. Be inspired and inspire.

COMMON FUNCTIONS OF A MOOD BOARD

- Starting point for a design project
- Seasonal trend board
- Capsule collections
- Shapes and silhouettes
- Demonstrating detail within a category, e.g., heel interest
- Print ideas

TOOLS

- Foam board—a large, thick, white display board that is easy to pin and staple.
- Pins/mini stapler—pins to plan the layout, a stapler to commit it to the board.
- Spray mount—this is an alternative to fix objects to the board; make sure you wear a mask and work in a ventilated area.
- Scissors, paper trimmer, or scalpel for razor-sharp neat edges.
- Ruler—metal-edged is best.
- Cutting mat with right-angle markings.
- Access to a printer, scanner, photocopier— to generate and manipulate images.
- Camera or smartphone
- Computer or table (essential if you are compiling a mood board).

21.
MOOD BOARDS: SELECTION PROCESS

No matter how strong the images you intend to include on your mood board are, if they're not edited and displayed correctly, it can compromise the final board.

Use tonality to pull a mood board together.

THINGS TO CONSIDER WHEN SELECTING IMAGES FOR A MOOD BOARD

1. Relevance—Think about the impact and importance of each image and why you're including each one. Make sure each image earns its place. What mood does that image conjure up for the viewer? What message does it communicate?

2. Detail—Does the viewer need to see the full picture, or is a particular detail or aspect more important to demonstrate your point? If it's the latter, enlarge or zoom into the detail and re-crop. A lot of your time will be spent enlarging or reducing images.

3. Size of images—Proportionally, you want your selection to work together, so stick to images of roughly the same size, albeit with some being detail shots and others not. Likewise, if your mood board is huge, you don't want images the size of postal stamps because your board will be cluttered and confusing.

4. Landscape or portrait—A mixture of both is good.

5. Color—We'll talk about compiling actual color palettes for your project/collection later (see pages 34–35), but within the selection process, it's important to consider coloration of images. Some images may be full color, and others may be black and white. Paying attention to the overall tonality of the images you're selecting will help to pull the mood board together and guide the viewer's eye. Likewise, if your collection is all about Rio Carnival, for example, but your images are black and white, it will make it all the more difficult for your board to depict that mood.

22.
MOOD BOARDS: LAYOUT

Following on from image selection, the layout of your mood board is crucial to its success. You're aiming to convey a mood and message to the viewer through the careful selection and placement of images. Each of the images should complement the other and inspire your audience.

You may need to lay out your mood board a few times until you get the composition right. It can be a painstaking process of lay out, review, tweak, lay out, review, tweak. Bear in mind at each stage why you're including each image and what the importance of that image is in relation to the other images.

TIPS FOR SHAPING YOUR MOOD BOARD

Key images—Position your "key" images—the images that most clearly and succinctly depict the subject of the board—in the top third of the mood board. You want your audience to engage with and understand your theme easily, and by strategically placing your strongest images in the top half, you'll hopefully aid their understanding and win their confidence.

Top row—The top row of images should all be key images. Our eye naturally reads from top to bottom, so make an impact here.

Mixed product—If you are composing a mood board with mixed product—for example, shoes, bags, and jewelry—try not to group images by product type, but instead place different types of product next to each other.

Group examples together—When trying to demonstrate a "fringe" message within a mood board—for example, "bleached denim is a key fabrication within your summer festival mood board"—group the examples of these images together. This allows you to focus the eye on this one area when delivering that message, rather than the viewer jumping from image to image.

Less is more—Allow your images to breathe. When reviewing your board, don't be afraid to remove images to allow those remaining to make an impact. Place images directly next to each other, leaving a border around the edge of the mood board only.

Crop carefully—When cropping images, don't crop too tightly. Leave space around the subject matter to avoid images competing for attention.

Each image on a mood board should complement the other.

23.
ONLINE MOOD BOARDS

Online mood boards do exactly the same job as physical mood boards, only they allow for more spontaneity and offer more tools for image editing. Unlike cumbersome foam board, the main benefit of online boards is their portability. They also win, hands down, when it comes to ease of sharing, updating, editing, and resizing, as well as being eco-friendly.

Once you've collated your imagery, compose your mood board using programs such as Adobe Illustrator and Photoshop. Refer to Selection Process (see page 31) and Layout (see page 32) for help in composing your online mood board.

To a designer, Pinterest, Instagram, and Tumblr are invaluable tools when researching because the breadth of ever-changing content is unrivaled. However, be mindful when using these sources; you need to upload original content and mix the secondary research gleaned from these sites with original and primary research (see Secondary Sources, page 24). If you are using Pinterest, Instagram, and Tumblr as your sole resources, it's likely that other people may also be doing the same. This will inevitably lead to unoriginal, one-dimensional research.

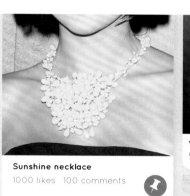

Yellow skirt
500 likes   50 comments

Sunshine necklace
1000 likes   100 comments

Matching yellow

LEADERS IN THE FIELD OF ONLINE MOOD BOARDS

Pinterest—Essentially a dashboard where you can group images, share references, and direct people to the original source of the image.

Instagram—Photo sharing social media app.

Tumblr—Your own unique blog made up of images, videos, quotes, and other people's blog posts. These, in turn, can be shared.

Mix the secondary research gleaned from online mood boards with original and primary research.

24.
COLOR

- -

Color is a science. Unbelievably complicated and formulaic, the topic is a book in itself. Essentially, the human eye detects color through cells in the retina that distinguish between light of different wavelengths. Confused yet? Thankfully, some people have a "natural eye" when it comes to color and color combinations—they instinctively know which colors work together and complement each other. Whether you have that gift or not, below are the basics that all designers should know.

PRIMARY COLORS

There are three primary colors: red, yellow, and blue, or when working with pigments and dyes: magenta, yellow, and cyan. By mixing these three colors, all other colors can be created. Black and white are commonly referred to as the fourth and fifth primary colors.

SECONDARY COLORS

Combining any two of the above primary colors gives you three colors called secondary colors.

Yellow + Red = ORANGE
Red + Blue = VIOLET or PURPLE
Blue + Yellow = GREEN

TERTIARY COLORS

Combining a primary and it's nearest secondary color from the basic color wheel gives you six colors called tertiary colors.

Yellow + Orange = YELLOW-ORANGE
Red + Orange = RED-ORANGE
Red + Violet = RED-VIOLET
Blue + Violet = BLUE-VIOLET
Blue + Green = BLUE-GREEN
Yellow + Green = YELLOW-GREEN

Primary, secondary, and tertiary colors total twelve basic colors, from which an infinite number of colors can be created.

Pantone is a globally recognized provider and communicator of color systems.

25.
SOURCING AND CREATING PALETTES

A color palette is a defined set of colors from which artists or designers work in order to give cohesion to their artwork.

As with many of the stages of design, there is no right or wrong way to compose the perfect color palette. Yes, there are colors that work well together and those that clash—and again there's a science behind it all. For example, complementary colors—colors directly opposite each other on the color wheel, such as blue and orange, or red and green—are great when you want something to stand out, but the same combination of colors make text hard to read.

CONSIDERATIONS WHEN CHOOSING YOUR PALETTE

Deciding which colors to include in your final palette can be based simply on personal preference, but it's also worth considering:

End use—Ensure the colors are appropriate for the product or collection you have in mind.

Range of color—Make sure you include enough colors to accommodate all styles. This is particularly appropriate when designing a collection.

Color weighting and highlight colors—Ask yourself, "Is my palette balanced?" Are there too many tones around one color, or do you need to throw in a highlight color to make the palette pop?

Color trend prediction—If you have access, refer to color prediction companies when creating your palette. In the same way as trend forecasters do, color specialists predict the colors that will be in vogue for the forthcoming season based on a number of social, political, and global factors.

SWATCHES

When putting together a color palette, you will first need physical swatches. Fabric stores are a good place to start when sourcing colors, as you can buy lengths of ribbon and balls of yarn relatively inexpensively. Chain stores selling products such as T-shirts and socks are also a good source for color swatches.

When sourcing swatches for your palette, think about the material from which your final collection will be made. If you're designing leather goods, for example, try to source leather swatches. Note that different materials take color differently—jersey, satins, and grosgrains hold vibrant strong colors well; in contrast, denims are more likely to take on a hue or wash of a certain color.

Cut decent-sized swatches of color and pin them to a strip of foam board. In later sections (pages 54–59), we'll look at briefing designs out to your pattern cutter, supplier, or factory. You will also need to send them color swatches to source from or match to. If it's not possible to send physical swatches, you can match to Pantone swatches and utilize this as a reference.

TIP: **Note that when composing a digital palette, colors can look different on screen than when printed out.**

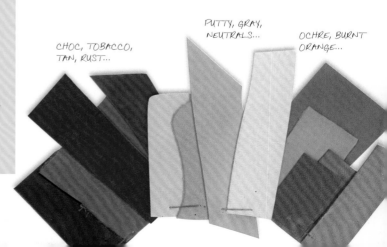

PUTTY, GRAY, NEUTRALS...

CHOC, TOBACCO, TAN, RUST...

OCHRE, BURNT ORANGE...

26.
TREND CYCLES

Part of your responsibility as a fashion designer is to be aware of trends and trend cycles. Trends are generated from many diverse sources, including global cultural, social, economic, and political climates and subsequent reactions to these (see Understanding Context, page 25). An example of this is the rebellious, revolutionary, and military references that meant pessimistic tones were woven through so many Fall 2015 collections as a reaction to recent years of political unrest and conflict.

Current global cultural, social, political, and economic climates influence—knowingly or unknowingly—both the designer and the customer. From this climate, trends are born. Trends can take years to surface, and when they do, there's a definite cycle through which they migrate. The example opposite shows an item from point of conception through to the end of its life cycle and the parallel influences that affect that product.

PROGRESSION OF TREND CYCLES

Trends and the subsequent speed at which customers adopt them can also vary from country to country and within countries. Trends tend to be conceived, germinate, and spread from capital cities before filtering out to surrounding cities, towns, and areas.

In 2012, I can remember being openly mocked by a doorman of a pub in a small town for wearing jeans with ripped knees. Fast forward to 2015, and the busted-knee jean was hands down the best-selling silhouette on denim. Not everyone wants to be a trend maker or early adopter. Some are happy to be trend aware, while others—trend followers—need to see a trend around for a while before embracing it.

STAGES OF TREND CYCLES

1. Conception—Products are conceived out of a reaction by influential design houses to trends generated by the current climate.

2. Fashion week collections—These products are then showcased at quarterly collections, and stocked in high-end department stores or designer stores.

3. Contemporary chain stores—These are influenced by design houses and react to their shows within their own collections (see Runway Analysis, page 38).

4. Mainstream department stores—These are typically slower to react to both trends and key trend items than chain stores. They often dilute both to cater to their customer.

5. Discount mass retailers—These further dilute trends and key items. They offer mass-produced products at the lowest possible retail prices, in most cases compromising designs.

6. Market stalls—These are trend graveyards! Garments arrive here as the result of retailers having canceled orders due to poor sales; this is a reflection of declining customer demand and an indication of the end of the product life cycle.

ZEITGEIST

A challenge to traditional trend cycles, the influence of the *zeitgeist* (the "defining spirit of the time") is on the rise. Designers need to look everywhere for these trends and work out how to develop them into something original.

2 QUARTERLY FASHION WEEK COLLECTIONS

3 CONTEMPORARY CHAIN STORE REACTIONS

4 MAINSTREAM DEPARTMENT STORES

5 DISCOUNT MASS RETAILERS

1 SOCIAL/POLITICAL & ECONOMIC CLIMATE

6 MARKET STALLS

Bubbling under

Dead & buried

27.
RUNWAY ANALYSIS

Fashion weeks are quarterly showcases where the most influential and directional fashion houses launch their new collections. These have a significant impact on which trends are adopted and, in turn, influence the products that other brands offer their customers.

Fashion weeks happen twice a year—Fall collections are showcased in February, and Spring/Summer collections are held in September. The four main host cities are New York, London, Milan, and Paris, but there are 150 fashion weeks worldwide each year. In between resort and pre-Fall collections drop. Rather than concentrated weeks of back-to-back shows, resort and pre-Fall collections are usually photo shoots of looks, uploaded over a six- to eight-week period in June/July and December/January, respectively.

There are also hundreds of designers showing "off schedule," and additional International Fashion Weeks to inspire you.

REACTING TO RUNWAY TRENDS

Your job as a designer is to absorb, digest, and forecast how the collections you see will influence the fashion industry, and in particular the market you're designing within. It's also about identifying key items—the absolute must-have pieces within collections. These are the pieces that you forecast will be big either in terms of sales or because they capture the essence of the season. You then apply these observations to your brand. The first question to ask is will your customer want to buy into this aesthetic or piece?

It's categorically not about producing runway copies—that's lazy designing and it rightly has serious legal implications. Make the time over those crucial four weeks to immerse yourself fully in every style that comes down the runway. Do your homework—identify what inspired that collection and its context. Be a visionary—make the trends; don't follow them.

Vogue.com is a free and effective way to keep up-to-date with all things fashion week.

Start identifying overarching themes and key items that you'd like to respond to, and add your own research. Look at the trends you have already pulled together for the relevant season and see what twist the latest collections give to them. Remember, it's about designing for your brand and customer.

Add all of these factors and influences into the mix and you'll have a unique product that reflects the seasonal trends.

Immerse yourself fully in every style that comes down the runway.

28.
UNDERSTANDING AND INTERPRETING A PROJECT BRIEF

Your first experience of fulfilling a project brief will more than likely be while you are studying. Creative briefs, like many briefs, are spoken or written instructions asking you to fulfill a project or body of work around a chosen subject by a specified date.

WHAT IS A PROJECT BRIEF?

Creative project briefs come in many guises. Some may be prescriptive, while others may have a single word—they'll be purposefully broad in order to inspire you. In some cases, you'll be asked to set your own brief with little or no direction—a blank canvas! The most common project briefs, however, are usually a title, followed by a descriptive paragraph, a directive of the amount of work and format expected, and the delivery deadline.

APPROACHING A PROJECT BRIEF

The most important step in meeting a brief is making sure you fully understand what's being asked of you. Read it, reread it, and read it again. If anything is unclear, just ask for clarification.

Even at an early stage, a project brief will conjure up endless ideas and key words; try to think about the mileage in your favorite ideas. Decide if there is enough scope in your idea to generate the work asked of you.

Once you've settled on an idea, plan your time. A critical path—essentially key stages and cutoff dates—is indispensable to ensure you meet the final deadline. This can be done simply by printing off a weekly planner and working backward from the deadline date. Forecast how long each part of the design process will take: research and sketchbook stage, mood boards, color palette, design development (including thumbnailing and fabric manipulation/experimentation), final illustrations, and final garment construction.

Consider your audience—is it womenswear, menswear, or unisex? Think about the end use of your product or garment and consider the cost up front. Your idea may be leading you toward a collection made from beautiful, soft Italian Nappa leather, yet you're a student on a budget. Try to think of all of these things before trying to fulfill your brief to avoid having to start over or compromise your final project.

AN EXAMPLE OF A PROJECT BRIEF

"Discarded Objects"

Every day we discard thousands of objects intentionally or unintentionally. Using found objects as your starting point, pull together the following:

• 1 sketchbook showing research
• 1 mood board
• 1 color palette showing material direction
• Evidence of thumbnailing/working sketches
• Fabric experimentation/manipulation
• Illustrated collection of 6–8 outfits, can be womenswear, menswear, or accessories
• Final garment or accessory

Deadline:

29.
UNDERSTANDING AND INTERPRETING A COMMERCIAL BRIEF

- -

Understanding and interpreting a commercial brief within the industry employs quite a different skill set from understanding and interpreting a project-based brief as a student. A commercial brief will certainly be more prescriptive—there are more parameters in which to work and more analysis employed at each stage of the design process, essentially to ensure the final product sells and is profitable. You must consider the end use and customer at every step of the way.

WHAT IS A COMMERCIAL BRIEF?

Again, commercial briefs are spoken or written instructions asking you to fulfill a project or body of work. This body of work will include many of the same processes involved in a project brief (see page 39): research, mood boards, color palettes, design development, etc., but the end product will be a specified number of designs, commonly referred to within the industry as "options."

Your designs will be influenced by a trend or trends and created by yourself or as part of a design team. They will be true to brand and designed with your target customer in mind.

You will be given a deadline—a date when all of your design packs are due at the supplier. This date will be part of a bigger critical path ensuring that the product is designed, developed, booked, and delivered within the specified period.

APPROACHING A COMMERCIAL BRIEF

Approach the research and inspiration stage of the design process just as you would a project brief. You are aiming to produce a trend board—essentially exactly the same as a mood board. Give yourself complete creative freedom and take time to be inspired. Think about all of those primary and secondary sources (see pages 23–24) of research that you can tap into. Push the boundaries.

Next, analyze. Consider the season; consider the brand you're designing for, the target customer, what the trend forecasters are predicting, what you've seen from the influential design houses on the runways. Also look at sales history—this is covered in the Analyzing Sales History section (see page 42). From all of this, build your trend board. Your trend board may be multiproduct and used by all of the designers in the team, or it might be department specific—for example, containing footwear references and design details only.

When approaching color and fabric direction, again, consult with forecasters and sales history. What worked this time last year and why? Finally, get your option counts from buyers and merchandisers so you know how many designs are needed, and look at your critical path to identify your design "packs-out date" (this is the date your pack/spec/design needs to be sent to the supplier).

AN EXAMPLE OF A COMMERCIAL BRIEF

"Design a directional, fashion-forward line of footwear for SS16 for our twenty-something going-out customer. No. of options: 30. All design packs must be sent out by. . ."

30.
DEVELOPING IDEAS

Once you've done your initial research, pulled together mood or trend boards, and have a rough idea of the type of product or collection you want to design, it's time to put pen to paper and start developing your ideas. This is a really exciting and liberating part of the design process.

Start by thumbnailing (see Thumbnailing, page 85). These tiny drawings are ideal for developing a single idea through a series of iterations. The method allows you to get lots of ideas down relatively quickly. Thumbnailing produces inaccurate scribbles—maybe of the whole garment or a detail within the garment—and you should use them in this stage of the design process as a tool to get your creative juices flowing and explore ideas.

Don't spend too much time on your thumbnails. They're a means to an end; they're not meant to be works of art.

Thumbnailing allows you to visualize a concept in various iterations.

31.
ANALYZING SALES HISTORY

When developing new ideas, it's not necessarily all about starting from scratch, especially within retail, where you have the benefit of sales history to steer you through the forthcoming season. What were your best sellers last season? Just as importantly, what didn't work and why? What are your "flow lines"—products that sell season after season and need little, if any, update. It's important to reflect and analyze the previous season's sales in order to both develop the product further from a design point of view and to give customers what they want.

Analyzing sales history is a science. It's about harnessing all that was good about the best seller, then redesigning it to make it current. Your aim is to design something that will be just as profitable—if not more profitable—than the previous best seller, while moving it on enough to make the customer buy it.

TIP: Moving successful ideas forward is no easy task. It's best to keep a constant: if you're trying out a new silhouette, offer it in a color or material you know the customer loves. Likewise, if you're using a new material, test it out on an existing shape. This will give you a true read as to what the customer likes or dislikes.

QUESTIONS TO ASK YOURSELF ABOUT LAST YEAR'S BEST SELLER

Was it the silhouette? If so, maybe update it with this season's print.

Was it the material? Think about other shapes that you could use that same material on.

Maybe it was the color? Did one color far outsell the other? Consider using that color again.

Was it something less tangible? Maybe the timing was just right and everyone who's anyone just had to have a wide-legged flare in his or her wardrobe that summer.

Was it price? Did you offer exceptional value for money?

Or was it the fact that you were first to market? Well done!

32.
SOURCING PACKS WITHIN INDUSTRY

As part of the development process, you will invariably need to source materials, yarns, trims, and components with which to experiment and make your final garment or collection.

At the undergraduate level, you need to be resourceful. You'll be on a budget and will need to keep in mind the ever-increasing cost of your project or collection. Fabric shops are an excellent starting point, but it's also worth sourcing from more unusual places. Perhaps you're a jewelry design student—think about hitting the secondhand vintage markets for components that you can break down and remodel into new designs. It's also worth contacting companies or suppliers that are of interest to you to outline your project and seek sponsorship.

At the industry level, unable to travel to international material markets as often as we'd like, we use sourcing packs to acquire the latest and most innovative materials and components. Essentially, a sourcing pack is a physical or digital collection of images or references from which your supplier can source. It's a way of communicating your requirements clearly.

Send out your sourcing packs as early on in the design development stage as possible to give your suppliers ample time to respond. Seasonal sourcing packs can be issued as soon as you've built your trend boards for the season, meaning materials can be available even before you put pen to paper, allowing you to be reactive and first to market.

TIP: Be specific—communicate clearly and give as much direction as possible. Material markets are enormous, so help your supplier to focus in on what you're looking for.

Fabric swatches in a sourcing pack communicate requirements to suppliers.

SOURCING PACKS SHOULD INCLUDE

Mood boards—These share your vision with your supplier (see pages 30–33). They are more likely to "get it" if they can see your starting point.

Material swatches—Samples of the types of material you're looking for, e.g., lurex, lace, organza. These should be as large as possible.

Color direction—Swatches of color or your palette (see page 35) from which to source materials and yarns.

Components—Physical examples of the type of zipper or trim you require.

Print direction—Be specific. Don't just ask for florals; include imagery around the type of floral prints you're looking for.

Lists—Key materials, trims, components, etc. Sourcing packs should be fully annotated.

YARN SOURCING

DATE:

PLEASE SOURCE SIMLIAR QUALITIES TO THE ATTACHED.

PLEASE SOURCE A SIMILAR LOOKING YARN

YARN CONTENTS: BRUSHED ACRYLIC / MOHAIR

PLEASE SOURCE AND SUBMIT FOR REVIEW.

YARN INFORMATION/CONTENTS

CONTENTS: 72%, ACRYLIC 28%, NYLON

GAUGE: PLEASE SOURCE HAND FEEL AS CLOSE AS POSSIBLE TO ENCLOSED SWATCH

33.
SOURCING FIRSTHAND

Throughout your career as a fashion designer, travel will play an integral part. One element of traveling for your job will be to source materials firsthand—leathers from Italy, embellishments from India, synthetics from China. There are hundreds of materials, trims, and component outlets from which to source, with each containing hundreds of vendors. Your supplier will accompany you to source for samples and, once the order has been placed, return independently to buy in bulk for production.

The idea is to find the latest, most exciting materials and trims from which to design, but the suppliers can be overwhelming. Follow the tips on the left to help you to navigate and get the most out of your trip. Note that yarn sourcing is done at the major trade shows, not from material markets; see Yarn Sourcing and Trade Shows (page 147).

TIPS FOR SOURCING TRIPS

Take a translator—Take your supplier, when possible, to communicate and negotiate.

Take local currency—This is especially important at markets, the majority of which are cash only.

Pick the right floor(s)—Specific floors in stores are split up by material type, e.g., faux fur, denim, lurex. You won't get around it all, so choose areas to tackle. Materials are numbered and displayed on swatch cards.

Take three—You'll need one sample or swatch card to attach to your spec, one to retain for cross-referencing, and one for your supplier to keep.

Info—Ask for the minimum order quantity (MOQ): the smallest amount you would have to commit to at the bulk order stage. Also get the price per unit.

Business card and photo—Take a photo of the trims you buy at the time of purchase with the business card in shot. Staple the business card to your samples to avoid confusion at the briefing-out stage.

Above: *A typical swatch card from a fabric market.*
Right: *Fabric can often be purchased by the yard off a roll.*

34.
TESTING IDEAS AND TECHNIQUES

Once you've sourced all of your materials, trims, and components, you'll be itching to get started. The experimentation stage of the design process is another really enjoyable, highly creative phase. Rarely do you end up with the product that you envisioned at the start of your journey. You make discoveries, learn from mistakes, and amalgamate processes in the pursuit of designing something unique.

Remember the cost implications throughout. The more detailed, intricate, and time-consuming the process is, the more expensive it becomes and the less likely it is to be mass produced. Alternatively, you may be a bespoke design house, unconcerned with mass production.

Each of the materials used within each design will also carry a minimum order quantity (MOQ), so beware when using lots of different materials within the one product, as you may struggle to meet the MOQ for each of the materials you're using. Send the swatch, prototype, or flat artwork, plus the details of where to source the trims from with your design spec.

FORMS OF EXPERIMENTATION

Producing a fabric swatch showing material manipulation—Processes include—but are not limited to—hand- or machine-stitching, dying, bleaching, distressing, shredding, layering, printing, laser cutting, and embellishing. This may be a process that you intend to apply to the material before the pattern-cutting stage, or, within retail, the swatch and an explanation of the process is attached to the design spec for the factory to emulate. Throughout the process, record the techniques and processes in your sketchbook—anything from dye lab recipes to the grade of sandpaper used to distress that denim jacket.

Swatching—Producing a fabric or paper swatch to indicate the layout, embellishment components, and techniques you wish the artworker to follow. See the Embellishments section (page 193).

3-D experimentation—A great way of checking and communicating positioning and scale. Use an existing block—a shoe, a bag, or a template—to work directly onto. For speed, glue or double-sided tape can be used to position and affix your embellishment or fabric directly onto the product or garment.

CAD—Use computer-aided design (CAD) to experiment with proportion of print or color within your garment (see CAD, page 53).

35.
COLLECTION BUILDING AND OVERVIEW

Having "thumbnailed" (see Developing Ideas, page 41) and recorded as many ideas and design details as you have, or as time allows, the next stage of the design process is to refine those ideas. You may have produced in excess of 200 thumbnails yet only have the budget or been briefed for a collection of just six outfits. You'll need to be your own critic, employing skills of selection, refinement, and downright ruthlessness without compromising the brief or your creative vision. This evolution stage is as important to the end product as your initial ideas.

Sketch out the ideas that you feel are the strongest. At this stage, you should make the sketches larger than the thumbnails in order to get an overview of the collection. You could simply enlarge your chosen thumbnails, but redrawing them allows you to further refine each piece, while also adding more detail.

Now simply start grouping your sketches into outfits and your outfits into collections. This process can be done physically by cutting and positioning your sketches next to each other.

STEP BACK AND REVIEW

Take time to reflect on how the collection is looking. The brief you're working toward will influence the questions you ask yourself, but consider things such as:

- Silhouette—Do you have a mix of shape, dress length, heel height?
- Material and print—Use Pantone pens to block areas of print or color to ensure it's weighted correctly.
- End use—Is there something for every end use or occasion, as specified within the brief?

IDENTIFY GAPS

Have you selected too many of one product type and omitted another in the selection process? For example, if you're designing an ethereal boho collection but have only drawn dresses, think about including separates, or maybe even a wide-legged jumpsuit. Go back and fill in the gaps and then repeat the review process until you're 100-percent happy with your final lineup.

36.
COMMITTING TO YOUR FINAL DESIGN

Having refined your ideas from a myriad of thumbnails to an edited collection of sketches, it's now time to make any changes or add any additional details before finalizing your design spec and sending it to the pattern cutter or supplier for sampling.

In essence, this is the final stage of the design process—any tweaks from receipt of first sample onward should be minor aesthetic or fit adjustments, so it's really worth investing the time at this stage to ensure every piece is the ultimate piece before committing it to a spec and prototype.

Make every piece earn its place. It's a common misconception within the industry that the fewer options you have to design, the easier it is. Not so! When options are limited, every single option must work hard to drive sales.

Think about the technicalities—openings, fastenings, construction. Your design must be both wearable and production friendly. Also, pay attention to detail— what makes this the ultimate white shirt? Why will someone fall in love with this pair of shoes over your competitors' shoes? Likewise, don't overdo it. Some of the most beautiful designs succeed through their simplicity.

Consider the cost and retail price, particularly when deciding on materials and components (see Pricing a Garment, page 202, and Undertaking a Supplier Costing Exercise, page 210).

Redraw your sketch in pencil, ensuring that it is technically and proportionally accurate, before penning it in. This is the drawing that you'll fully annotate and brief out (see Spec Sheets, pages 54–55).

37.
KEY ITEMS

When developing and planning your collection, you need to identify your "key items"—the pieces for which you anticipate high demand and those you hope will become next season's best sellers. These are the products that independently sum up the essence of the collection or season, making them integral to the line. Think of key items as the headlines of a collection—items that your brand must absolutely carry and your customers will expect you to have.

Key items can include peacock pieces (see Peacock Pieces, page 206)—flamboyant, often impractical products specifically designed to attract the attention of both press and customers to lure them into taking a closer look at the full collection. A key item must have enough broad appeal to drive sales while still being current, directional, exciting, and on trend.

IDENTIFYING YOUR KEY ITEMS

Using your mood or trend board as a starting point, try to identify your key items, and list or thumbnail them. Imagine if your collection could consist of only five pieces, and identify which five pieces they would be.

CONSIDER THE FOLLOWING:

The brand—Your key items must reflect and be true to brand.

The customer—Who is your target customer? Is he or she edgy, grungy, minimal, or directional? Do your key items cater to that?

The end use—Going out, casual day, occasion, festival—where will the product be worn?

You've now identified your key items around which the rest of the collection will form.

Right: *Examples of key items in a Womenswear Spring/Summer collection. Top left clockwise: embellished dress, distressed denim jacket, patch and motifs, and embellished strappy sandal.*

38.
APPLYING KEY TRENDS AND DETAILS

Aside from reacting to seasonal trend cycles, another way to develop a product is to take the trend for the season, or one of the key details from within that trend, and apply it to an existing product… then add a little bit of magic!

HOW TO APPLY KEY TRENDS

Let's imagine that you have identified an emerging 1970s trend. Identify where you could apply a 1970s aesthetic in key departments within womenswear, menswear, footwear, or accessories. Not all trends are relevant to all departments.

Let's say you choose dresses, denim, and footwear. Now, using sales history (see Analyzing Sales History, page 42), identify the key items and best sellers within those departments and redesign them, each with your 1970s hat on. Look for ways to reinvent and move on while anchoring your design on something that the customer recognizes and is familiar with.

Now here's the magic part—when you do all of this and throw your brand identity into the mix, you're giving the product an unexpected twist. It's a potent mix of influences, but the result will be reinvented products unique to your brand.

USING KEY DETAILS

The same process can be applied to key details within a trend. Maybe you had amazing sales reactions to a flat shoe with a pom-pom on it that was inspired by a carnival trend. Use this nugget of sales history—your customers love a pom-pom—and apply it to other product types. What would that pom-pom look like on a heeled shoe, an ankle boot, or an athletic shoe? Likewise, update the best-selling flat shoe with a new pom-pom, in a different color or size. What would pom-poms look like in other departments—on bags or as trims on tops or playsuits?

Mix it up, challenge the norm, sprinkle on some of that magic dust, and you'll set yourself apart from your competitors.

Use sales history to reinvent best sellers through key trends.

39.
REINVENTING SAMPLES

One method of developing a product is through the aid of purchased samples. As part of the design process, designers scour the globe for inspiration from which they develop their ideas. This inspiration can come in many forms—a beautiful Persian rug could inspire a print story, or a detail on a military uniform could be the beginnings of a pocket design on a piece of outerwear. A designer sees something—be it a finished garment or a detail—buys or photographs it, and from that sample, he or she can develop a brand-new garment.

INSPIRATIONAL SHOPPING

It's a common misconception that designers buy samples on inspirational shopping trips and then simply copy them. That should never be the case. The clue is in the title, "inspirational shopping." Our job as designers is to inspire, and while we look to the past for future ideas, to simply copy is lazy. Furthermore, blatant plagiarism should not be tolerated within the fashion industry—it is, in fact, a criminal offense.

When shopping for inspiration samples, you'll need to be selective. You can't buy everything. Look for pieces that make you stop in your tracks—those that are innovative and exciting. At the same time, basic blocks—that hero T-shirt that fits like no other—can form the foundation of your ideas and save you hours going back and forth with your pattern cutter or supplier to tweak the pattern.

ADAPTING A PURCHASED SAMPLE

Source both vintage and new season—amalgamate the two to reinvent. Remember, the fact that it's vintage doesn't make it permissible to copy it. Copyright can protect a design or designer for years—don't be tempted.

Use the feature of the garment that inspires you, but give it your own twist. Thumbnailing (see page 85) is an excellent tool to use when designing from a purchased

sample, enabling you to ensure your design has changed enough before briefing it out.

Thumbnail sketches of original ideas inspired by a bought sample.

40.
HAND DRAWING

Despite the increasing influence of technological innovations in the fashion world, it's still really important to learn to be able to hand draw your designs. We will cover the alternative to this, computer-aided design (CAD), in the next section (see page 53).

One of the many reasons to recommend hand drawing is its flexibility. I've been able to design in so many places—on planes, on the train, in the middle of supplier meetings—either to hit a deadline or just whenever and wherever inspiration took hold.

TIPS FOR MASTERING HAND DRAWING

- **Tracing and templates (see page 80)**—It is absolutely fine to use these. They will give you a much better chance of getting your drawings proportionally accurate.
- **Materials**—A mechanical pencil is often the preferred choice here—it's precise, reliable, and simple! If you do want to color them, Pantone markers are excellent.
- **Detail**—Just include a basic level of detail. There's no need to shade, and you're not aiming for something photo realistic, just something that communicates all of the key features clearly. Add stitch lines to give a sense of construction and any details such as zippers or pockets. Hint at the type of materials used by adding details such as a crease or drape, but there's no need to add texture to the whole sketch. Keep it simple.
- **Annotation**—See Spec Sheets (pages 54–55) for the kind of notes to include.
- **Practice makes perfect**—Putting in the hours will give you the confidence to create a fabulous drawing when the pressure is on (or if your boss is leaning over your shoulder!).

The materials needed for hand drawing are portable, allowing you to capture ideas whenever inspiration strikes.

41.

CAD

As the name suggests, computer-aided design (CAD) is a way of using technology to help with the design process. There are two ways in which this can be done:

1. HAND-DRAWING METHOD

This method begins with a hand-drawn sketch (see Sketchbooks, page 27). This can be scanned into your chosen design program, and then you can apply CAD features over the top of your original. A common application of this method is to use CAD to apply color to the sketch. If you convert the scanned image into a two-color black-and-white image, the program will recognize the lines as boundaries and you can use fill tools to drop colors in. This is great for trial and error.

2. COMPLETE CAD METHOD

In this process, the design is created from scratch within a computer program. This is often done using a tablet and stylus linked to a computer. The surface of the tablet relates to the screen, and designers use the stylus to depict points and lines to build up an image.

PROS AND CONS OF CAD

CAD is great for building up libraries of components that you can use time and time again. This can save an enormous amount of sketching time. For example, a denim designer will always use buttons and zippers, so they can just save these elements and drop them in when they need to. Or a jewelry designer could have each type of chain set up as a brushstroke.

Colorizing images is much faster in CAD, and images are quicker to amend without having to start all over again. Copying and pasting can be a great time saver too. You can drop in textures to get a realistic view of a garment in various finishes and check the scale and placement of a print design very easily.

When reviewing your collection as a whole, it's really useful if you have everything on CAD, as you can very quickly and easily see everything together and make any necessary amendments. For example, you can check the proportion of colors used across your entire line and instantly make any tweaks you feel are required.

Another benefit is that you're working in a digital medium that's all set to be emailed. If your supplier or factory uses the same software as you, CAD files can be swapped so that you can work collaboratively and tweak as you go.

The main drawback of CAD is that it's not always possible to have the equipment with you—that's why there will always be a place for hand drawing.

Hand-drawn sketch that can be scanned into your design program before applying CAD features.

42.
SPEC SHEETS

A spec (specification) sheet is a tool used industry-wide to instruct your supplier or factory on how to make a prototype or "first sample." Spec sheets are usually US letter paper documents, or electronic versions of the same size, containing a hand drawing or CAD of the product, detailed measurements, and all key details associated with the design, materials, and construction of the prototype. Additional information, e.g., fabric swatches and components to source, can be attached and sent with the spec sheet. The designer should retain a copy of the spec sheet and all information sent with it to cross-reference upon receipt of the prototype from the factory.

INFORMATION REQUIRED ON A SPEC SHEET

All spec sheets should contain the following information:

- **Company or brand name**—Plus the word "Copyright" and the copyright symbol, ©.
- **Supplier name**—Name of supplier being briefed.
- **Style name and style number**—This helps when referring to the style internally and with suppliers.
- **Brand**
- **Department**—For example, skirts, dresses, etc.
- **Date**
- **Season**—Fall/Winter (F/W), Spring/Summer (S/S).
- **Designer**—Name and signature.
- **Specify material**
- **Specify lining material**
- **Fastening**—Details of buttons, zippers, fastenings.
- **Callouts**—Any other details not covered above that need specific attention.
- **Supplementary images or samples**—Visuals or purchased samples that the supplier needs to reference or to help explain shape, detail or technique.

Right: *Womenswear spec sheet.*

STYLE NAME: TUNSTALL BIKER JACKET	BRAND: XXXXXXX	TREND: HELL'S BELLES
	SUPPLIER: XXXXXXX	SEASON: XXXXXX
STYLE NUMBER: XXXXXXX	DATE: XXXXXXX	DESIGNER: XXXXXXX

PLEASE SAMPLE IN BLACK BUFFALO LEATHER

DEPT: WW COATS + JACKETS

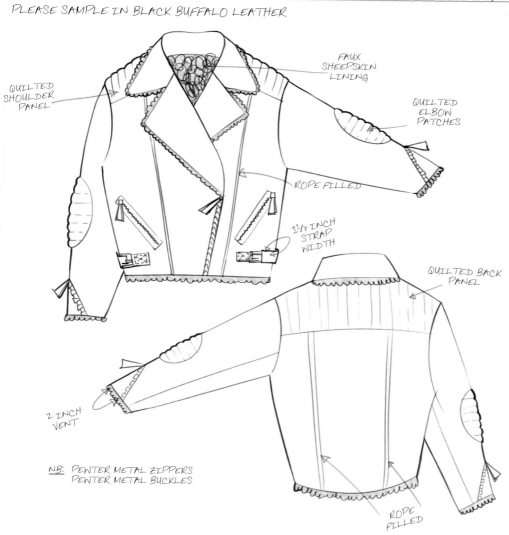

QUILTED SHOULDER PANEL

FAUX SHEEPSKIN LINING

QUILTED ELBOW PATCHES

ROPE FILLED

1 1/8 INCH STRAP WIDTH

QUILTED BACK PANEL

2 INCH VENT

NB: PEWTER METAL ZIPPERS
PEWTER METAL BUCKLES

ROPE FILLED

	M'MENT POINT	SIZE INCH
A	Length SNP— Hem Back	22
B	Bust	20
C	Waist	20
D	Top Hip	/
E	Low Hip	/
F	Hem	19
G	X Shoulder	16
H	Shoulder Seam	5
I	X Front	12
J	X Back	15
K	Slv Length	22
L	Armhole Straight	9
M	Bicep	7
N	Slv Opening	5
O	Back Neck Width	7
P	Front Neck Drop	3
Q	Back Neck Drop	6

43.
BAG SPEC SHEET

Bag spec sheets are used in very much the same way as clothing spec sheets (see page 54 for information to be included in a spec sheet). A technical drawing of the product is annotated with key aesthetic, material, and construction details. Where necessary, bag spec sheets are accompanied by paper patterns.

COMPULSORY INFORMATION REQUIRED ON EVERY BAG SPEC

BODY FABRIC:
- Leather, polyurethane (PU), or textile.
- Swatch of material from a swatch card that you would like the supplier to source with retailer information, or swatch attached for the supplier to source from and submit similar material to.
- Pantone reference if using a generic material, e.g., pig PU to match Pantone ref. 13-2805 TPG.

LINING:
Leather, PU, or textile. Contemporary and mid-range fashion use PU or textile for cost purposes. Canvas, cotton, or grosgrain linings are common linings.

BINDING/PIPING:
- Specify the binding/piping material.
- Binding is when material, usually up to ¼ inch (5 mm) wide, is wrapped around the body seams to conceal the raw edges. The stitch line runs along the edge of the binding.
- Piping is approximately 1–2 mm material that is sandwiched between the body seams. Body material is turned to establish a neat edge, and the stitch line runs along the edge of the body material.

STRAP:
- Specify material.

FITTINGS:
- Specify metal finishes—brass, antique brass, pewter, silver, gold, antique silver, antique gold, rose gold, or coated.

EDGE STAIN:
- Specify color of edge stain paint.

STITCH:
- To match or contrast. Specify when stitch is a feature, e.g., saddle stitch.

ZIP POCKET ON INTERIOR:
Specify size of pocket and type of zipper.

CELL PHONE POCKET ON INTERIOR:
- Width 3 x 4½ inches (7.5 x 11.5 cm).

Attach any imagery or samples that will help the supplier when making the first sample or help illustrate points within the spec more fully.

ADD ANY ADDITIONAL CALLOUTS ON THE SPEC SHEET ITSELF

- Bags are usually drawn at a three-quarter angle and not to scale. To scale, paper patterns are sometimes included within the spec pack to show measurements to scale, similar to a paper pattern. A half paper pattern is sufficient, which the supplier will then flip and mirror.
- For greater accuracy, all measurements may be given in centimeters (cm).
- Terminology of parts of the bag, e.g., slip pocket.
- Drawing of the strap or details where more info is required.
- The construction of the bag—formal bags usually contain cardboard boarding sandwiched between the upper and lining to give structure.

© BRAND NAME HERE

copyright all rights reserved

STYLE NAME: MARTHA GRAB	BRAND: XXXXXXX	TREND: WOODSTOCK NIGHTS
HANDLE SADDLE BAG	SUPPLIER: XXXXXXX	SEASON: XXXXXXX
STYLE NUMBER: XXXXXX	DATE: XXXXXX	DESIGNER: XXXXXX

BODY FABRIC:
A = TAN SUEDE
B = TAN LEATHER
MATCH TO SWATCH ATTACHED

TRIM FABRIC: 1/4 INCH BINDING AS BODY FABRIC

LINING:
CANVAS - TO MATCH BODY FABRIC

FITTINGS:
ANTIQUE BRASS

EDGE STAIN: EDGE STAIN GRAB HANDLE TO MATCH SUEDE

STITCH:
REGULAR TOPSTITCH TO MATCH SADDLE STITCH DETAIL SHOWN

FASTENING:
CONCEALED MAGNETIC DOT UNDER FLAP

ZIPPER POCKET ON INTERIOR:
N/A

CELL PHONE POCKET:
(WIDTH 7.5 x 11.5 CM)
YES

COMMENTS:
PLEASE SOURCE CHUNKY METAL RING FITTINGS

STRAP
1 INCH PLAITED STRAP
1 INCH PLAITED STRAPS TO BE PADDED
3/4 INCH
3/4 INCH
5/8 INCH
SADDLE STITCH

SADDLE STITCH
GRAB HANDLE EDGE STAINED + INSERTED INTO FLAP
1/8 INCH ANTIQUE BRASS POINT STUDS
PLEASE SOURCE CHUNKY ANTIQUE BRASS RING
GUSSET
BINDING
4 3/4 INCH
8 INCH
1 1/2 INCH
1/4 INCH BINDING
FLAP OF BAG
SADDLE STITCH
8 3/4 INCH
ADD BOARDING TO BODY OF BAG FOR STRUCTURE
BODY OF BAG
1 1/2 INCH
1 1/8 INCH
9 1/2 INCH
SLIP POCKET
SADDLE STITCH
PLEASE SOURCE CHUNKY ANTIQUE BRASS RING
1/4 INCH
1/4 INCH
3 1/8 INCH GUSSET
MAGNETIC DOT UNDER FLAP

SLIP POCKET
SUP POCKET FOLDED + STITCHED
FOLDED + STITCHED TO BODY OF BAG ALONG HIGHLIGHTED STITCH LINE ONLY

4 INCH TASSEL

TASSEL
RAW EDGE LEATHER TASSEL
- PLEASE USE COW LEATHER + CUT BOTTOM AT ANGLE
1/4 INCH

SIDE TAB
BOX STITCH TO ATTACH TO BODY GUSSET
1 1/2 INCH
1 1/8 INCH
3/4 INCH

44.
FOOTWEAR SPEC SHEET

Footwear spec sheets are also widely used throughout the industry to communicate key information and instructions between the designer and the factory.

COMPULSORY INFORMATION REQUIRED ON EVERY FOOTWEAR SPEC

KIT:
- The construction on which the prototype will be made.
- The kit is the main components that determine the style of the shoe—a) the shape, as determined by the last (see Footwear, page 138) it has been molded around, b) the sole or platform, and c) the heel.

UPPER:
- Leather, polyurethane (PU), or textile.
- Swatch of material with retailer information that you would like the supplier to source.
- Pantone reference if using a generic material.

LINING:
- PU or textile. Contemporary and mid-range fashion use PU or textile for pricing purposes. Canvas, cotton, or grosgrain linings are common linings.

TOP SOCK:
- Textile or PU. Specify the color of the top sock and give details of any branding artwork—known as the sock stamp—here, providing artwork as a JPEG where necessary. Typical sock stamps are printed, embroidered, or embossed and then overprinted.

INSOLE BINDING:
- The insole board is wrapped in a material before inserting the top sock. Specify insole board material.

BINDING/PIPING:
- Specify the binding/piping material.
- Binding is when material, usually up to 5 mm wide, is wrapped around the topline (top edge) to conceal the raw edges of the upper and lining material. The stitch line runs along the edge of the binding.

- Piping is 1–2 mm material that is sandwiched between the upper and lining. Upper and lining materials are turned to establish a neat edge, and the stitch line runs along the edge of the upper material.

COMPONENT FINISH:
- Specify metal finishes—brass, antique brass, pewter, silver, gold, antique silver, antique gold, rose gold, or coated.

FASTENING:
- Zipper—full, three-quarter, inside leg or back zipper, laces, buckle, hook-and-loop fastening, inside leg elastic on fixed straps.
- Give details or photo references of fastenings to source, or give information of retailers if requesting that the supplier use a specific fastening.
- Specify finish when using metal fastenings.

SOLE:
- Resin outsoles are common for mid-range fashion, in black, natural, or color. Beware of red—Christian Louboutin owns the license for all red soles!
- Leather soles are used within high-end lines.
- Athletic shoe outsoles are used for casual styles and are most commonly in black, white, and gum.

ADD ANY ADDITIONAL CALLOUTS ON THE SPEC SHEET ITSELF

Shoes are usually drawn to scale, and a side view is most common with additional info as below:

- For greater accuracy, measurements may be given in millimeters (mm).
- Terminology of parts of the shoe—inside quarter, feather edge.
- Detail further any hardware, trims, details.
- Top view of the toe shape.
- Top piece of the heel.

EDGE STAIN:

- The edge of the sole can be stained to match the upper, or as a contrast detail. This is done by painting the edge of the sole.
- Specifiy the color required.

HEEL/WEDGE/PLATFORM:

- Specify the covering required for the heel, wedge, platform—to match the upper or a contrast.
- Natural stack gives a wood effect—faux natural stack is a synthetic price-pointed version of natural stack.

© BRAND NAME HERE	STYLE NAME: ANTILL HEELED BIKER BOOT	BRAND: XXXXXX	TREND:
copyright all rights reserved		SUPPLIER: XXXXXX	SEASON: XXXXXX
	STYLE NUMBER: XXXXXX	DATE: XXXXXX	DESIGNER: XXXXXX

UPPER:
BLACK KID LEATHER
- PLEASE ADD PADDING TO TONGUE

LINING:
2 INCH PADDED COLLAR LINING IN BLK KID LEATHER INTO BLACK TEXTILE TONGUE. BLK KID PU LINING

TOP SOCK:
BLACK TEXTILE
-SEE SOCK ARTWORK ATTACHED

INSOLE BINDING:
N/A: FULL TOP SOCK

BINDING/PIPING:
N/A: UPPER TURNED + STITCHED, LININGS RAW EDGED + STITCHED

COMPONENT FINISH:
SHINY PEWTER SQUARED OFF RINGS

FASTENING:
INSIDE LEG ZIPPER - PEWTER ZIPPER VELCRO STRAPS

SOLE:
BLACK CLEATED OUTSOLE BLACK RAND + BLACK SADDLE STITCH

HEEL/WEDGE:
BLACK POLISHED STACK HEEL

PLATFORM:
BLACK POLISHED STACK PLATFORM

SHAPE OF TOP PIECE

SQUARE CUT THROAT

INSIDE LEG ZIPPER ON INSIDE QUARTER

TOE SHAPE + RAND + SADDLE STITCH

LACE FACINGS: BLACK KID PU

2 INCH

3/4 INCH

TONGUE

INSIDE VIEW

2 X STRAPS FINISH AT INSIDE LEG ZIPPER

3/4 INCH

BLACK ROLLED WAXED LACES

3/4 INCH

SQUARE CUT THROAT

LINING FACING

HEEL TOP PIECE SEE ABOVE

ALL AREAS MARKED A TO BE PADDED

BLACK RAND + SADDLE STITCH

CLEATED COMMANDO SOLE OUTSOLE

59

45.
3-D PRINTING

3-D printing is as futuristic and mind-blowing as it sounds. In this rapidly developing technology, instead of printing ink onto paper, other materials are used to build up an item layer by layer. It's a computerized technology where objects are designed through 3-D modeling software. The program then slices the design into thousands of cross sections and then prints these layers one at a time.

At the moment, materials such as plastics, glass, metals, polymers, wax, and even edible food and human tissues can be used. The most common uses are for prototyping, architectural scale models, and medical applications, such as prosthetics.

Typically, the fashion world has embraced this new technology. There are many different types of 3-D technology and advances are being made on a monthly basis, so we won't dwell on the details. We will instead focus on existing uses in the fashion world and look at the potential.

EXAMPLES OF 3-D PRINTING

3-D printing has enabled innovative designers to create unique, weird, and wonderful garments. However, at the moment they are all made of rigid materials that are not comfortable or breathable enough for everyday clothing. The next giant leap in terms of fashion 3-D printing will be to use more comfortable and wearable items, and scientists are working on how to print using silks, cottons, and natural fibers.

Until those developments take place, 3-D printing already has practical uses within the fashion industry. Some companies are already using 3-D printed insoles to mold sports shoes exactly to the wearer's feet. They are ideal for creating prototypes to show exactly how an idea will turn out, and in turn to communicate this to a production team. They can also be used to make molds—for example, a studio could create a mold for sunglasses exactly as they want it and then send this over to a manufacturer to mass produce.

3-D CAD model

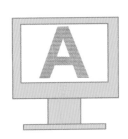

Slicing

Layer-wise assembly

Complete part

3-D PRINTING AT HOME?

Some say that one day we will all have 3-D scanners and printers in the home so we will be able to scan our bodies, download designs, and print new clothes that fit perfectly. If this does happen, it will have far-reaching implications:

Advantages

- Production lead times could be much shorter.
- Smaller production runs will be possible.
- Environmental benefits—Less shipping, transportation, and packaging.
- Less waste of materials—Items are created one layer at a time very specifically.

Challenges

- Impact on the manufacturing industry—Could this become obsolete?
- Legal issues around copyright laws.
- Could cause problems with authenticity and forgery.
- Equipment is currently very expensive.

Who can say what the future holds, but this is definitely a field to be aware of and one to watch.

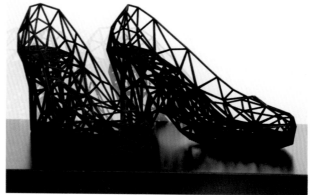

Above: *Chromat Adrenaline Dress with 3D printed panels by Intel Corp.*
Right: *3D printed shoes.*

46.
ACCESSORY PROTOTYPES

When designing accessories, sometimes the most effective way of communicating your design is to produce a mock-up or prototype. This is unrealistic for shoes, bags, and sunglasses because these products are so technical and go through a lot of processes requiring expensive machinery during the production stages. For accessories and jewelry, however, prototypes let you see exactly how the product will look, allowing you to iron out any issues around scale and construction before briefing it out to your supplier (see Jewelry Prototypes, page 63).

PROTOTYPES FOR DIFFERENT PRODUCTS

The majority of accessory prototypes are produced as physical 3-D prototypes rather than flat paper artworks. There are many techniques and processes adopted depending on the product type:

Structured hats—For example, caps or felt hats. Patches or trims can be glued or sewn directly onto an existing block to indicate placement and types of components to source.

Knitted hats, scarves, and gloves—A knitted swatch, either by hand or machine, accompanying your spec can help to show yarn type, knit stitch, technique, or process such as felting or brushing the yarn.

Neckwear—Collars, bibs, corsages, boot lace ties. Source the components and mock up the prototype, again either stitching or gluing them into place before briefing the supplier. Include details of any trims and components to make the job of resourcing easier.

Embellished product—Socks, hosiery, skinny scarves. Approach either by making a paper pattern as you would an artwork (see Embellishments, page 193), or physically stitching or gluing the components onto an existing product.

With all of the above, include as much information as possible when sending your prototype to the manufacturer. Detailed descriptions and instructions on key methods used to make the prototype, as well as information on where to source the components, all help.

MAKE BREAK AT BACK OF NECK AND INSERT 1-INCH-WIDE BLACK ELASTIC FOR HEAD ENTRY

1 IN
2 IN

SECURE ELASTIC WITH DOUBLE ROW OF STITCHING

TOTAL NECK CIRCUMFERENCE = 14 INCH TO INCLUDE ELASTIC INSERT

PLEASE SOURCE SIMILAR PATCHES TO PROTOTYPE

REDUCE WIDTH OF SCARF TO 5 INCH THROUGHOUT

5 INCH

BOW TO BE FIXED AND NON-FUNCTIONING. BACK ELASTIC ALLOWS HEAD ENTRY

SECURE FLOWERS BY STITCHING AROUND OUTSIDE IN BLACK COTTON

REVERSE OF SCARF = BLACK POLYESTER AS PROTOTYPE

A handmade physical accessory prototype. Typically, this is sent to your supplier, along with annotations. From this they source components, and produce and submit a first sample.

47.
JEWELRY PROTOTYPES

The role of a jewelry designer is multifaceted—much like a precious cut stone. It can take on many guises, but it's certainly one of the most hands-on design roles because it involves physically making and creating 3-D pieces or elements from scratch. The easiest way to brief a design to a supplier or factory is through producing a prototype. Here's how!

Being resourceful and having foresight and vision are just some of the integral skills that jewelry designers must possess. Prototypes are often made completely from scratch, so you have to seek potential components in all things. Source from trim markets and vintage markets; buy samples to break down for components; consider mechanical components, fabric trims, corsages—the options are unlimited.

Prototypes are usually made either in a designer's workshop or at their desk. Similar to the process of an artworker (see Embellishments, page 193), artworks can be created on paper.

A sketch of the finished product is created through a combination of gluing components and hand drawing directly onto the paper. If all of the components are available, complete prototypes can be made using tools such as pliers, soldering iron, and a glue gun, and this sample is then sent out to the factory to make.

When designing and prototyping fine jewelry, the process is considerably different. Designs are created using computer-aided design (CAD) for accuracy. Jewelry designers often have an extensive digital library of components that they use time and time again. The finished artwork is intricately carved out of wax, from which the prototype is then cast and approved before going into bulk production.

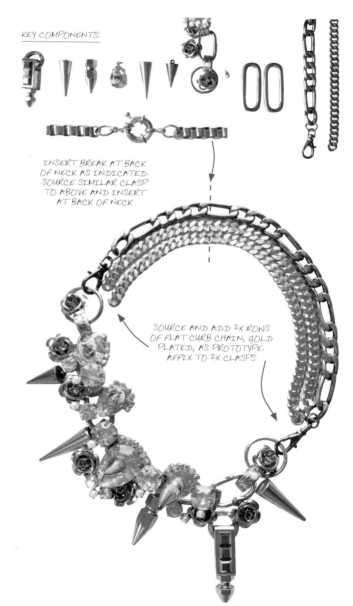

KEY COMPONENTS:

INSERT BREAK AT BACK OF NECK AS INDICATED. SOURCE SIMILAR CLASP TO ABOVE AND INSERT AT BACK OF NECK

SOURCE AND ADD 2X ROWS OF FLAT CURB CHAIN, GOLD PLATED, AS PROTOTYPE. AFFIX TO 2X CLASPS

A handmade physical jewelry prototype, including a component key.

48.
DESIGNING WITHIN COST RESTRAINTS

Whether you're trying to keep down the cost of a project or having to work toward a target garment cost, learning to design within cost restraints is very important. Fashion design is a field of freedom and limitless imagination, but cost is one of the boundaries that you will often have to respect when creating commercially viable products.

As you gain more experience, you will know very quickly, from the retail price you are aiming for, whether the item will need to be, for example, leather or synthetic.

You will also have the benefit of knowing previous adjustments you've made to products and whether they affected the customer appeal. This experience allows you to get the majority of your designs within or close to the cost budget the first time. In the meantime, here is a breakdown of some of the things to consider to make sure you're designing cleverly:

CONSIDER EACH DESIGN DETAIL

Do you need it? Is each feature integral to the essence of the design, or are there some superfluous features that can be removed? With this in mind, clever design means being realistic about the features you need and aligning them with your budget.

It's much better to start with a simpler design and realize you can afford to add more elements to it than to start with a convoluted design that you gradually have to strip back, feature by feature—it's easier to add than take away! If you do need the feature, be sure to think about the most cost-effective way of getting it.

FAMILIARIZE YOURSELF WITH THE PRODUCTION PROCESS

There are costs associated with every stage of the production process. When less experienced in the differences in cost, it is often easier to imagine you were constructing the project on your own. Consider how much time each process will take; the time taken at every stage impacts on unit cost.

For example, on a sandal with multiple straps, each of the straps has to be cut, finished, and attached separately. This will be a more expensive process than having one or two larger straps, and more labor-intensive than a simple leather ankle boot. Think about deconstructing your ideas.

The difference in cost of different production techniques can also be seen through the higher cost of "fully fashioned" knitwear—which requires each piece to be knitted in its individual shape—compared to "cut and sew," where larger pieces of knitted fabric are cut to shape and then sewn together (see Womenswear, page 133).

Having to color-match diverse components may involve getting them sprayed with the same finish —e.g., matte black—so it would also add extra expense.

MATERIAL CONSUMPTION

To keep cost prices down, you need to minimize material wastage. One way to do this is to add seams. If you think about a leather knee-high boot, most low- and mid-priced examples will feature a lot of panels stitched together—usually with front, back, and two side seams. The reason for this is that smaller individual pieces of leather mean more flexibility when Lay Planning (see page 168) the cuts of fabric, which means fewer pieces of waste will end up in the trash.

In contrast, a high-end boot might have fewer seams, meaning fewer larger pieces of leather have been used—hence more wastage. Understanding this can also help you to appreciate the quality and reasoning behind the pricing of high-end fashion.

Another example would be a dress where the design requires the fabric to be cut "on the bias" so that it drapes in a particular way, which will lead to additional waste through a large single cut that must be done in a certain direction.

NUMBER OF MATERIALS

The more complex your design is in terms of different materials, the higher the cost will be. This is because each material used will have a minimum order quantity (MOQ). So if a sandal has a number of different-colored straps, the supplier will have to purchase the MOQ in each of the colors and pass this cost on to you. If they're the same color, there will be just one MOQ and fewer excess materials.

QUALITY OF MATERIALS AND COMPONENTS

If you're clever with materials, you may be able to retain design details by downgrading the components without significantly affecting the quality. For example, suede is perceived to be more expensive than leather, but they cost the same.

Suppliers in the Far East have created a rapidly growing industry specializing in incredibly convincing synthetic leathers and suede. Similarly, cow hide has very similar qualities to pony skin but costs a fraction of the price. Plastic zippers are much cheaper than metal ones, so they can often be used, unless a metal zipper is a real feature.

DON'T WORK TOO LITERALLY WITH COSTS

It's impossible to get a complete breakdown of the cost that each component brings to your design, so you shouldn't think in that amount of detail. Replacing a 20-cent component with a 10-cent component won't always save you 10 cents per unit. It's much more complicated than that, and don't forget that suppliers will still have to charge you for labor and add a mark-up to make a profit.

It's not your job to work in this kind of detail or to be hunched over a calculator—instead you should consider what steps in the right direction you can take to push costs down.

WORKING WITH COST RESTRAINTS

- Consider every design detail.
- Know the basic production processes and costs.
- Design with target cost price in mind.
- Be clever about material choice.
- Be savvy about material consumption.

2

ILLUSTRATION

49.
LINE TECHNIQUES

- -

Drawing is the core method of researching, recording, investigating, developing, and communicating your ideas. Possessing strong drawing skills allows you to easily sketch ideas onto paper, kick-starting the creative process.

Before you begin, determine which artists and techniques you like. You might enjoy the expressive line drawing of Gustav Klimt, or the more minimal sketches of David Hockney. Be influenced by their techniques, but aim to develop your own unique style.

TOP TIPS FOR DRAWING

REPRESENT MATERIALS
Create your own line techniques to represent those materials you're using, e.g., knit, fur, linen, and drape, the latter of which we will deal with in a later section (see pages 86–89).

UNDERSTAND THE BENEFITS OF SPACING
Appreciate the importance of gaps between lines and the different effects of the spacing.

THINK TACTILE
Appreciate the difference between surfaces—hard, smooth, rough, and soft—and consider how light is reflected or absorbed within each. A great tip is to "think tactile"—if a surface is rough, approach it in a rough way with rough materials and a rough technique.

CONVEY THE LIGHT SOURCE

Choose how you will convey the light source—you can use an eraser to pick out highlights or perhaps add a layer of white crayon or paint.

USE THE WEIGHT OF YOUR PENCIL

Practice using the weight of your pencil on the paper. Try drawing light, medium, and dark lines as shown.

SIX CORE LINE TECHNIQUES

Develop and practice the following line techniques in order to understand when to use them to apply tone and texture:

1. Short dashes
2. Hatching
3. Cross-hatching
4. Stippling
5. Smudges
6. Scribbles

50.
DRAWING MATERIALS

PENCIL

Perhaps the most portable, convenient, and low-cost medium, the pencil is the most common drawing material for most artists. Pencils are available in a full spectrum of graphite grades for different effects—H means "hard," B means "black." A 9H pencil has the hardest graphite, producing light marks and staying sharp the longest. A 6B pencil is the other extreme; its softer graphite produces heavier marks and needs to be sharpened more frequently.

The full range is mentioned below, but owning a 2H, HB, 2B, and 4B is an adequate range for most fashion illustrators. Sharpening pencils with a scalpel is preferable because it gives more precision than a pencil sharpener. Mechanical pencils ensure precision and are good for technical drawings, whereas a range of pencils is useful to create texture and depth in a fashion illustration.

PEN

Second to the pencil in terms of convenience and portability, the humble pen can create incredible results, although beware: it's an unforgiving medium! The most popular types of pen for drawing, mark making, and illustration are graphic, drafting, ball point, and fountain pens. The quality and thickness of line desired will determine your choice, as will the fluidity and control of the line you are hoping to achieve.

Nib sizes range from .005 through to 08 (thinnest to thickest). Again, a moderate selection of 0.5, 02, 05, 07, and a marker should suffice for most illustrators. Adding water to pen and ink can achieve some dramatic effects when illustrating fashion drawings and is a particularly useful way of creating shadows and shading.

CHARCOAL

Charcoal is a burnt organic material that can give a much broader range of marks than graphite. Charcoal traditionally comes in stick format, but in more recent years, it has become available in pencil form, allowing you to sharpen as you would a graphite pencil.

Charcoal sticks come in two types: vine or compressed. Vine charcoal is softer and produces lighter marks, whereas compressed charcoal is more concentrated, producing darker marks. Charcoal is an excellent medium for life drawing, as it is quick and easy to apply to paper and can be erased when applied lightly—for example, when creating your drawing or composition or when completing quick ten-second sketches of poses.

MARKERS

Available with a wide variety of tips and a full spectrum of colors, markers create a broad range of lines. You have to be decisive and deliberate when making your marks because this medium cannot be erased. Nonpermanent markers can be mixed with water in the same way as ink to create striking effects.

Within the marker category, Pantone pens are an excellent medium for shading and coloring both fashion illustrations and technical drawings. The pens correspond to 300 colors within the Pantone system. Nibs are available in fine, medium fine, or broad. Pantone pens differ from markers because you can build up layers of color and use them almost like watercolor paints.

TIP: Sealant sprays are useful to fix all of the above mediums to paper once your drawing or illustration is complete. This stops your creations from smudging!

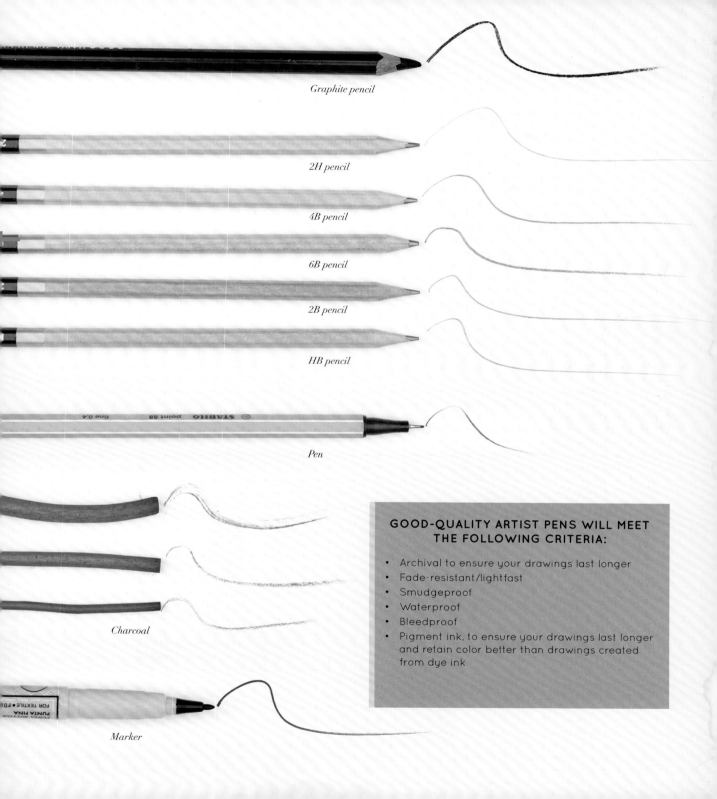

Graphite pencil

2H pencil

4B pencil

6B pencil

2B pencil

HB pencil

Pen

Charcoal

Marker

GOOD-QUALITY ARTIST PENS WILL MEET THE FOLLOWING CRITERIA:

- Archival to ensure your drawings last longer
- Fade-resistant/lightfast
- Smudgeproof
- Waterproof
- Bleedproof
- Pigment ink, to ensure your drawings last longer and retain color better than drawings created from dye ink

51.
LIFE DRAWING

Life drawing is taught as a core skill within any design course. It's an integral skill to hold in order to understand the body and how clothes hang on it, and also to communicate design ideas through fashion illustration, which we will go into more detail about in this chapter.

TIPS FOR LIFE DRAWING

1. DRAW FROM REAL PEOPLE WHENEVER POSSIBLE

There are many options available to you—hopefully this is an option offered to you within your course. If not, sign up for a night class if possible, or use your friends to pose for you, and you in turn for them. Quick ten-second sketches of poses you see on the TV are another great source to gain experience.

2. PRACTICE

As with a lot of skills, it's imperative to practice regularly. Through sketching often, you'll really see improvements. It's also important to warm up through a series of short sketches before tackling your final drawing.

3. LOOK AT WHAT YOU'RE DRAWING

This sounds silly, but one of the key skills when life drawing is to draw how things actually look, not how you think they should look.

4. PAY ATTENTION TO DETAIL

Record shapes accurately. Observation is key here—your eyes should constantly be flitting from paper to object and back again. This should become second nature when life drawing.

5. PAY ATTENTION TO PROPORTION, PERSPECTIVE, AND VANISHING POINTS

We'll go into more detail on this in the sections on Understanding Perspective (see pages 72–73) and Understanding Proportion (see pages 74–75).

6. PAY ATTENTION TO SHADOW, TEXTURE AND DETAILS

Refine those skills taught in Line Techniques (see page 66).

7. CHOOSE THE RIGHT MEDIUM

When life drawing, the circumstances may mean that time restraints are imposed, so you need to be practical (see Drawing Materials, pages 68–69).

52.
UNDERSTANDING PERSPECTIVE

An understanding of perspective—essentially communicating an impression of depth—is an essential skill of drawing technique. Knowledge of the basics of perspective will help when designing, illustrating, and completing technical drawings.

When learning about perspective, note the following key points:

HORIZON LINE

This is the viewer's eye level—anything above that level is taller than the viewer. Anything below that level is shorter than the viewer.

VANISHING POINT

Any set of parallel lines appears to the viewer's eye to meet on the horizon. The simplest example of this is train tracks. The two tracks don't actually meet in reality but get so far away that the distance between them can't be perceived. All lines showing depth converge to a vanishing point.

ONE-POINT, TWO-POINT, AND THREE-POINT PERSPECTIVE

Any image or drawing containing parallel lines will have perspective points and vanishing points. This is less so in natural scenes. However, an understanding of one-, two-, and three-point perspective will help you to depict and master the art of drawing them.

ONE-POINT PERSPECTIVE

Length lines meet at a single vanishing point; height lines stay vertical and parallel to each other, and width lines stay horizontal and parallel to each other.

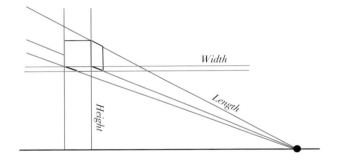

TWO-POINT PERSPECTIVE

Length lines meet at one vanishing point; width lines meet at a second vanishing point; and height lines stay vertical and parallel to each other.

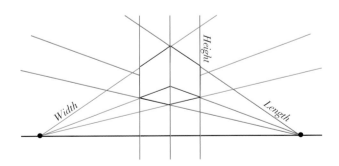

THREE-POINT PERSPECTIVE
The length, width, and height lines all go to three separate vanishing points.

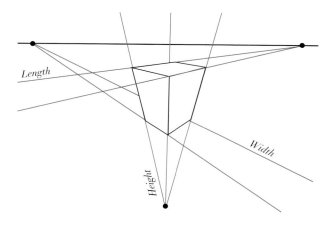

Length

Width

Height

USING PERSPECTIVE
As with all types of drawing and illustrating, it's not enough simply to understand perspective; the key is to observe perspective in everything around you and practice drawing perspective to refine the skill. You are aiming to create a sense of depth and lead the viewer's eye around the page.

Place objects, or limbs when practicing fashion illustration, in front of each other and notice the change in perspective. Observe the relationship between the two objects. Shadows also help when reading and drawing perspective; the length of the shadows gives the viewer clues on the distance between the objects.

TIP: When tackling perspective, keep your head completely still and only move your eyes. This will give a consistent horizon line around which everything you see is centered.

53.
UNDERSTANDING PROPORTION

Proportion is the discipline of ensuring objects within a composition are the correct size in relation to each other. Measuring the size and position of one object in relation to another and the negative space between objects is critical to understanding proportion. Proportion and perspective go hand in hand—you must get the scale of objects correct as they recede into the distance or background. If the proportion of one element is wrong, it can skew the rest of the composition. The tips below can really help in understanding proportion.

PENCIL AND THUMB TECHNIQUE

This technique involves using your pencil as a ruler to measure the height and length of your object and transferring those measurements onto paper.

- **Step 1:** Lock your arm and hold it out in front of you so your arm is horizontal.
- **Step 2:** Close one eye.
- **Step 3:** Line up the top of the object you wish to measure with the top of the pencil.
- **Step 4:** Place your thumb on the pencil at the bottom of the object you are measuring.

You now have your first measurement—your base measurement—that you can mark on your paper or scale up or down, depending on the scale of your drawing. Now every time you go to draw something else within that composition, use the base measurement to compare the length of that object to all other objects within your drawing.

TIP: Your base measurement can be on the vertical or horizontal; it is just to get a relative size. What matters is the proportion, not the actual measurement.

GRID METHOD

This method is particularly effective if your are enlarging or reducing proportions. For example, if you want to enlarge an object you are drawing by two and a half times, draw the squares on your paper or work surface two and a half times larger than the squares on your reference photo—in the example below, this would be 2.5 x 2.5 inches.

- **Step 1:** Draw a grid over your reference photo, ensuring all squares are perfect squares measuring exactly the same, e.g., 1 x 1 inch. These are known as your grid lines.
- **Step 2:** Draw a grid of equal ratio onto your paper or work surface.
- **Step 3:** Now simply draw what you see in each square of your reference photo into the correlating square on your paper.

TIPS ON TACKLING PROPORTION

Try both methods and go with whichever suits you. The simplest way to tackle proportion is to try to be aware of the entire drawing even before you have drawn it. Sketch out the entire drawing, really loosely, before filling in any details. This will give you boundaries within which to work and will ensure your drawing will be correctly positioned on your paper and won't fall off the page at a later stage. You're now free to go back and work on each specific area.

The pencil and thumb technique can help you to tackle proportion.

MEASUREMENTS

You need measurements to determine:

- The center line of an object
- The distance between objects
- The relationship between the sizes of objects
- Where the edge of an object lies

54.
EXAGGERATING PROPORTION

In addition to the importance of mastering life drawing and being able to sketch ideas realistically, there are some very different conventions of fashion illustration. They are used to communicate the concept and essence of a design and differ greatly from the reality of how a garment and a figure will look (see Fashion Illustration Versus Technical Illustration, pages 78–79). The essence of this convention is "longer and leaner," therefore arms become elongated and waists and torsos become much narrower.

These conventions are inevitably linked with the use of mostly very tall and very thin models within the industry, which is in turn criticized for creating a set of unrealistic and unhealthy ideals. What these conventions add, however, is a sense of elegance, and the long limbs in particular introduce a feeling of movement and energy. Whether you choose to go along with these conventions or not is up to you, but you should understand them.

In regular, realistic life drawing, there is a set of conventions about proportion. Typically, a figure is drawn as eight heads high and two heads wide. In fashion illustration, this is more like nine or ten heads high (in extreme cases, eleven) and only one-and-a-half heads wide. Normally the additional height from these "additional heads" goes into the legs.

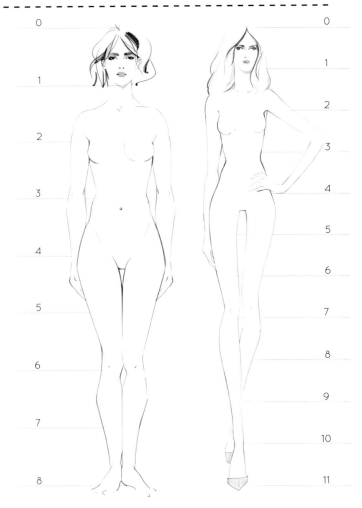

Above left: *A realistic life drawing with a conventional proportion of eight heads high and two heads wide.*
Above right: *A fashion illustration with a proportion of eleven heads high and one-and-a-half heads wide.*

«THE FEMALE FIGURE:

The diagram opposite shows a fashion illustration of the female body. Note the elongation of the limbs and the proportions within the illustration.

- Head is from 0–1.
- Neck is from 1–1½.
- Shoulders are at 1½.
- High point of the bust is at 2 and the bust line is at 2¼.
- Waist and elbows are at 3.
- High hip is at 3½.
- Hips are at 4.
- Crotch is at 4¼.
- Fingertips are at 5½. (generally midthigh).
- Top of knee is at 6½.
- Widest part of calf is at 7½.
- Ankle is at 10.

THE MALE FIGURE: »

The diagram to the right shows a fashion illustration of the male body. Note how proportionally different it is from the female illustration.

- Head is from 0–1.
- Neck is from 1–1½.
- Shoulders are at 1¼–1½.
- Pecs are at 2¼.
- Waist and elbows are at 3¼.
- High hip is at 3½.
- Hips are at 4.
- Crotch is at 4½.
- Fingertips are at 5¼.
- Knees are at 6½.
- Widest part of calf is at 7½.
- Ankle is at 9.

TEMPLATES FOR "FASHION ILLUSTRATION" PROPORTIONS

"Fashion illustration" proportions have been used on both of the above diagrams—limbs are elongated and the width of the body is reduced. This may be useful as a template when illustrating lineups or indeed modifying proportions. Experiment with adding movement to these proportionally exaggerated figures until you find your own style of fashion illustration.

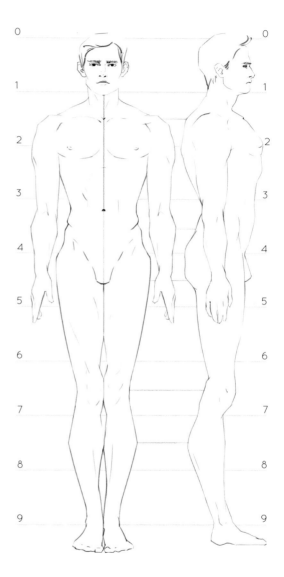

A fashion illustration of the male figure.

55.
FASHION ILLUSTRATION VERSUS TECHNICAL ILLUSTRATION

As a designer, you will need to master the art of fashion illustration and the skill of technical illustration. Both are completely different in style and execution but are essential for translating your wildest ideas for clothing into the finished article.

FASHION ILLUSTRATION

Fashion illustration is all about capturing the feel of a garment—that is to say, the conceptual and idealized feel of a garment. Garments have to look their best—often even better than they ever could in real life! Proportion is exaggerated—figures can be improbably tall and impossibly thin, with razor-sharp bone structure. Clothes look at their best with a sense of drama.

The purpose of these drawings is to capture the essence of an idea. Fashion illustrations can be useful if you need to sell your ideas, whether to an investor, for a private commission, or when working with a brand or retailer; it could be the buying and merchandizing teams that you need to win over to make sure they back your ideas with cash. However, if you were to send these ideas over to a pattern cutter, manufacturer, or production team, you are likely to get vastly different interpretations of your idea, and the end product will not work—this is where technical illustration comes in.

Fashion illustration.

Technical illustration.

TECHNICAL ILLUSTRATION

Technical illustrations are sometimes referred to as "flats" because they are often drawn as though the garment was laid flat on a table. They are an essential way of communicating the reality of your ideas to a whole team so that everyone gets a consistent message.

Technical illustrations are accurate representations of the garment and can serve two purposes:

Visual aid—using computer-aided design (CAD) the designer can, among other things, drop color or textures into the "flat" which can help when visualizing both individual pieces and whole collections. (See CAD, page 53.)

Technical specifications—once annotated, technical illustrations are the blueprints that show how the garment needs to be made and assembled. Each industry and company will have different standards

and requirements about specifications needed, but essentially they should contain all of the relevant information to allow a pattern cutter to make the garment without any more input from the designer. (See Spec Sheets, pages 54–55 for detail of the information commonly found.) Technical illustrations can be hand drawn but are increasingly originated using CAD.

The illustrations above show the difference between a fashion Illustration (left) and an un-annotated technical illustration or "flat" (right).

56.
TRACING AND TEMPLATES

As we've discussed, it's important to master many drawing skills on the way to becoming a great fashion designer. But when you need to come up with a new concept, or capture technical elements of a garment, you won't have time to commission a life model and spend a day creating a masterpiece! Instead, you need to know how and when to apply tracing and use templates. Let's be clear: this is not cheating and it doesn't mean you can't draw; it's about speed and efficiency. Tracing and templates are used throughout the industry.

TEMPLATES FOR FASHION ILLUSTRATION

In fashion illustration you can create your own suite of templates easily and use them time and again. Start with an image from a runway or photo shoot and notice details about the figure—e.g., where the hipbones sit and where the elbows hang. Look at how that particular fabric behaves too, so that you can use it as a basis for other fabrics. Now trace over those essential elements, and you have a basic template that you can trace over again and again to quickly get an impressive effect.

TEMPLATES FOR TECHNICAL ILLUSTRATION

The images below show a variety of typical templates for technical illustration (see Fashion Illustration Versus Technical Illustration, pages 78–79). Use a proportionally accurate figure as your template (see Understanding Proportion, pages 74–75) and draw basic garment blocks over the top. These blocks act as a base for you to draw clothes onto, reflecting key details such as sleeve length, cut, pockets, and so on.

Templates for footwear and accessories are less useful because these are designed in close-up detail and off the figure. With shoes, there is much more variation of pitch—flat shoes, high heels, and athletic shoes. Tracing could definitely be employed across a line of shoes in the same shape where you have different colorways or embellishments.

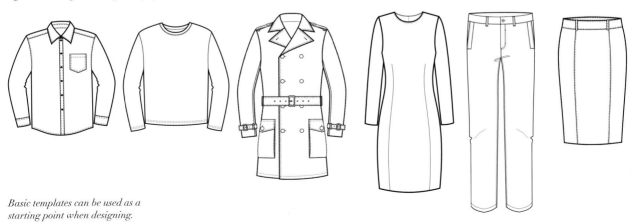

Basic templates can be used as a starting point when designing.

57.
CHOOSING THE RIGHT MEDIUM

At various stages of the design process you need to illustrate your ideas and designs. This can range from a quick thumbnail sketch in pencil on the back of an envelope to a technical drawing using computer-aided design (CAD), see page 53.

You must first decide if what you're communicating is nonrepresentational—meaning it is supposed to convey a feeling or impression—or technical. Is it a beautifully emotive fashion illustration or an accurate technical spec from which an accurate prototype must be produced? Ask yourself, what does the viewer need to know? Do they need technical information and direction, or are they looking to be inspired? Or both? Select the right medium for the right part of the process.

CHOOSING YOUR MEDIUM

You will need to be able to turn your hand to different mediums depending on the situation you're in. When working within the fashion retail industry, you may develop CAD skills when working at your desk but will still need strong drawing skills when at supplier meetings or on development trips where CAD is not available. To meet deadlines within the industry, there may not be time to use CAD for your sketches or have the luxury of coloring them in.

Circumstances will often influence your choice of medium. The choice you make will sometimes come down to time restrictions, which could be caused by either the pressure of a deadline or by the need to take a fleeting opportunity. Sometimes you might only have seconds to impress someone with an idea—in that case, use a quickly sketched outline to create an impression and secure the deal!

On that note, it takes confidence to work under pressure and often under the spotlight or in front of an audience. Again, this comes with practice and experience, but take your time and don't feel pressured. Often all of those people are staring at you in disbelief at what you can do, rather than judging you.

The medium that you select must be fit for purpose in relation to the environment, time available, and end use. Sometimes the choice of medium is made for you by the situation or environment. For example, if you were on your way to Paris for a research trip and needed to get some ideas down to meet a deadline, the likelihood is that you would opt for pencil or pen and paper over CAD.

GUIDE TO SELECTING THE RIGHT MEDIUM

TECHNICAL DRAWING

Thumbnailing/sketch stage—Pencil or pen to get the idea down simply.

Drawing up—Pencil to allow for corrections and changes before committing your drawing to pen.

Final design—Pen, if hand drawing, or CAD.

Color up—Pantone pens or CAD. Both can be used for shading or to show proportion of color within the design (see CAD, page 53).

FASHION ILLUSTRATION

There is a wider range of materials available to you when drawing nonrepresentationally, as the fashion illustration is, after all, a form of art. Experiment drawing with pen and ink; painting with watercolor, gouache, or oil; using collage, or a mixture of all of these to find your unique way of illustrating.

58.
ILLUSTRATING FOLDS

Accurately portraying how clothes hang on the body is crucial when both designing and illustrating your final fashion designs. Learning the principles of fold construction can really help to bring realism to your fashion illustrations. Folds show depth, volume, and perspective, and can also suggest movement, so along with practicing line techniques to suggest texture, it's important to practice illustrating folds to accurately communicate your designs.

THE SEVEN MAIN FOLDS

1. PIPE FOLDS
These are the simplest and most common types of folds. The two main pipe folds are:

Relaxed Pipe Folds (1a)
A common fold, most noticeably when fabric falls freely from a condensed area, e.g., a skirt waistband. Note how pipe folds are a direct result of gravity, and how heavier fabrics will hang and fold differently with more lightweight materials.

Irregular Pipe Folds (1b)
The gathering is more irregular and, as a result, so too are the folds. Think of a tulle tutu.

2. SPIRAL FOLDS
These are most commonly seen when rolling up the sleeve of your sweatshirt.

3. ZIGZAG FOLDS
These are most visible at the back of the knee, when someone has been sitting for a long time. Notice "planes" within zigzag folds—horizontal diamond shapes formed by fabric folding from all directions—and how the light falls on the different planes of the zigzag folds.

1a *Relaxed Pipe Folds*

1b *Irregular Pipe Folds*

2 *Spiral Folds*

3 *Zigzag Folds*

4. DIAPER FOLDS

These are historically seen within any drawing of saints or Grecian dress. More contemporary silhouettes include a cowl neckline.

5. DROP FOLDS

Another fairly common fold, drop folds are evident when hanging fabric from a point, e.g., hanging a coat off a hook.

6. INERT FOLDS

These are visible when a mass of fabric drops or crumples on the ground, e.g., in a pile of laundry. Inert folds can also suggest the direction from which a figure has come.

7. HALF-LOCK FOLDS

These are evident when a tubular piece of cloth is bent at a sharp or unnatural angle, e.g., sharply bent legs.

TIPS FOR DRAWING FOLDS

Drawing folds can feel like an art form in itself and at times can seem a little overwhelming. Keep it simple and don't detract from the design itself. Include only those folds that add something to your illustration. As with all drawing skills, practice is key.

Create, observe, and draw folds—Notice how your own clothing drapes, folds, and hangs. Take photos of interesting folds that you see to later use as references from which to draw. Look for how parts of fabric can be grouped into horizontal, diagonal, or vertical planes.

Experiment with light—Shine a desk lamp onto material to exaggerate shadows, and notice how light falls on the different planes within folds.

Think tension—Where does the tension come from, and what is the form around which the fabric folds?

Gravity—Note the effects of gravity and any points of support.

Notice how the same fold can look different on different fabrics—Thinner materials fold and crease more easily; thicker materials have fewer folds.

Pay special attention to volume—Is the material skin-tight or does it sit away from the body? Sketch the outline roughly until you're happy before getting into the detail of illustrating the folds.

5 *Drop Folds*

4 *Diaper Folds*

6 *Inert Folds*

7 *Half-Lock Folds*

59.
ANIMATION

Adding a sense of dynamism and motion to your drawing breathes life into your fashion illustrations. As with life drawing, this is a skill that needs to be practiced. Remember to warm up and loosen your hand by drawing a quick series of poses before tackling your final illustration.

TIPS FOR DRAWING MOVEMENT

1. APPROACH YOUR ILLUSTRATION LIKE AN ANIMATION
Within every movement there is a beginning, middle, and end point—for example, the position of the leg when walking down the runway. Notice where the three points are, and illustrate each point using lighter weights of line for the beginning and end point and heavier lines for the middle point.

2. NOTICE HOW THE BODY BENDS AND MOVES
Practice by studying sports people or animals, as well as the human form. Notice what happens to the arms when walking, as opposed to when running. What happens to the feet when dancing? Where do limbs sit at the start, middle, and end points of these movements? Is the object or person that you're drawing leaning? If so, note where their frame is positioned in relation to if they were upright.

3. EXAGGERATE MOVEMENTS
When we walk, we don't necessarily swing our arms, but by drawing the arms at the most extreme point in a range of motion, we can imply movement to the viewer.

4. EXPERIMENT WITH DIFFERENT LINE QUALITIES
Single lines, double lines, wiggly or frenzied lines, and thick lines all imply different phases of movement, from static to frantic. The speed at which you physically apply the line can also convey movement.

5. DRAW LINES AROUND THE IMAGE
This is a quick and simple way of implying movement.

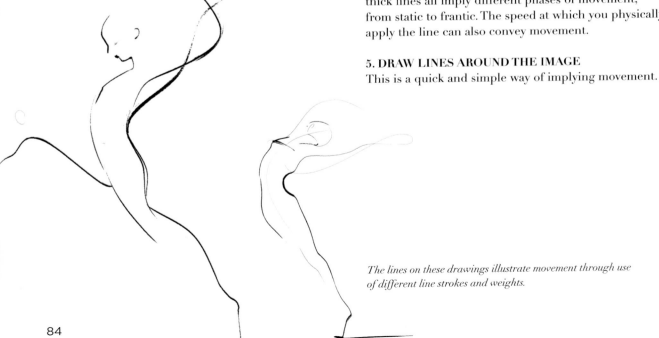

The lines on these drawings illustrate movement through use of different line strokes and weights.

60.
THUMBNAILING

Thumbnails act as tools to explore multiple ideas quickly (see Developing Ideas, page 41). Usually created with pencil on paper, they are miniature versions of a picture, usually no bigger than a couple of inches in size—hence the name. The essence of a thumbnail is speed and abbreviation and an absence of corrections. Try to get into the habit of thumbnailing frequently and quickly. Use it as a memory aid, as well as a design tool. Carrying around a small notebook and pencil is the simplest way of achieving this because it will encourage you to record impressions that will later evolve into designs.

Designers produce thumbnails at various stages of the design process, such as at the inspiration stage to capture an idea or when designing to experiment with shape and detail. At the line-building stage, it's useful to thumbnail every piece to check proportion and end use across a final collection, ensuring that there is a variety of silhouettes and not too much repetition.

Remember, thumbnails are not intended to be finished pieces of work, although they can be beautiful works of art in their own right. Think of them as blueprints for a sketch—a way of recording and working through ideas before the sketch and spec stage.

Likewise, don't be picky about the materials you have on hand when thumbnailing. A quick sketch on a napkin or an idea illustrated in lip liner on the back of a receipt might go on to be a best seller!

Templates can be used for speed when thumbnailing. Simply reduce and repeat a basic version of your intended block, e.g., a T-shirt block, onto paper, and roughly sketch variations of sleeve length, pocket detail, or collars over the top. However, I'd recommend you create freehand thumbnails, and—as with many stages of the design process—practice makes perfect!

HOW TO DRAW A THUMBNAIL SKETCH

1. Strip out all of the detail—Get the basic outline of your idea down as quickly and as simply as possible. Outline the key shape—most people draw freehand when thumbnailing, but you may wish to draw over a template if you find this easier.

2. Start to add key details only—For example, if you have the outline of the shirt, loosely draw in the collar, the sleeve length, and any pockets or fastenings.

3. Try out a number of different ideas and styles before committing to your final design(s), and try to solve any problems—the design needs to be both aesthetically pleasing and functional. At this stage, you may wish to add notes to the thumbnail—such as things to remember at sketch stage or potential construction issues. You may even wish to produce additional thumbnails of key details in isolation, e.g., the collar.

4. Now think about color—either by coloring up your thumbnail or by simply blocking out areas in black and white to indicate proposed proportion of color.

3

UNDERSTANDING FABRIC

THE FOUR TEXTILE DISCIPLINES

Embarking on courses in art and design provides the opportunity to explore many varied disciplines, from graphics to 3-D design to textiles. Having made the decision to go down the fashion route, you'll be exposed to the four main disciplines that sit under the fashion design umbrella: fashion design, knitwear, weave, and print. This skill is all about making an informed decision about which of those you'll choose to specialize in, the key skills associated with each, and the type of career that each could lead to.

FASHION DESIGN

The most glamorous of the four, fashion design is both a 2-D and 3-D craft, from designing and pattern cutting to garment construction and realization.

KEY SKILLS

- Garment design
- Pattern cutting
- Technical ability
- Fashion illustration
- Good material knowledge

TYPICAL CAREER PATHS

- Establishing your own brand
- Designing within retail for a brand or supplier
- Freelancing

KNITWEAR

Knitwear is a 3-D craft and one of the most technical disciplines of the four. Check out Gudrun & Gudrun and Lalo for innovation within knit design.

KEY SKILLS

- Technical ability
- Yarn and material knowledge
- Fashion illustration

TYPICAL CAREER PATHS

- Becoming a knitwear designer, either your own label or for a brand or supplier
- Freelancing
- Working for a swatch company, combining yarn and stitch to develop new knit techniques

WEAVE

Another 3-D technical discipline, woven materials are made by interlacing two (or more) sets of yarns or threads—a process that, along with knitwear, requires patience and precision. Moa Hallgren is currently pushing the boundaries within the wonderful world of weave.

KEY SKILLS
- Technical ability
- Yarn and material knowledge
- Fashion illustration

TYPICAL CAREER PATHS
- Career paths are centered around inventing new materials, textures, or patterns within materials for designers to then use.
- Typical end uses include formal wear and tailoring products, accessories—hats and scarves—and interiors, as well as the option to design for swatch companies.

PRINT

Print is a 2-D craft, so it is deemed the least technical of all four disciplines, but is highly skilled in other ways. Check out Mary Katranzou for inspirational print and placements and Ashish for bringing artworking and embellishing into the 21st century.

KEY SKILLS
- Drawing skills
- Good eye for color, pattern, and placement skills
- Visualization and realization of a print or design from scratch

TYPICAL CAREER PATHS
- Setting up your own print label
- Designing within retail for a brand or supplier
- Working for a swatch company
- Print designers also tend to make good artworkers as they're skilled in both all-over and placement design

A mixture of any of the four disciplines could lead to an exciting end product. And remember, you never really close the doors to the disciplines you don't necessarily specialize in. My degree was in knitwear, but I'm now a footwear designer and specialize in all things accessories. Many of the core skills and processes that you learn are transferable across fields, and the disciplines influence each other.

Above: *Woven fabrics are produced on a loom.*
Below: *A print designer at work.*

62.
NATURAL ANIMAL FIBERS

Fibers are the root of the textile chain from which materials are created and clothes are made. Fibers fall into two categories—natural and synthetic. In the next two sections, we'll look at the most common natural animal and plant fibers.

SILK

Silk is made of protein from the cocoon of the silkworm, which is spun into strands. Most of the world's silk is produced in China and India. Silk is an extremely strong fiber, and its composition means that it refracts light, giving it a shimmering appearance.

Silk has a smooth, soft texture; excellent drapability; and luxurious feel—which means it is often used for dresses, blouses, ties, scarves, lingerie, and pajamas. It is relatively expensive and needs to be handled and washed carefully to avoid damage. Silk can be blended with other fibers to add sheen.

WOOL

Wool is the processed natural fiber from the fleece of an animal, most typically sheep. In addition to sheep, wool can be made from the coat of goats (Mohair, Kashmir), rabbit (Angora), and even llama and alpaca. The fleece is shorn from the animal and then cleaned.

The crimped, wavy construction of the fiber means that when it is spun, individual pieces cling to each other to create a yarn. The texture also means that wool traps air, helping it to retain heat and making it relatively bulky. Yarn is most commonly knitted or woven into fabric for use for clothing—typically knitted sweaters, scarves, thermal socks, and warm coats.

The quality of wool is measured by how fine it is, ranging from ultra-fine merino wools to the coarse wools used in household carpets. Most wool is produced in Australia, China, the US, and New Zealand.

Above: *Silk bias-cut maxi dress.*
Below: *Natural wool knitted sweaters by ELEVEN SIX.*

63.
NATURAL PLANT FIBERS

Cotton and linen are the most common plant fibers used within manufacturing.

COTTON

Cotton comes from the soft, fluffy fiber that grows on cotton plants. This is harvested and then spun into yarns or threads, which are in turn woven or knitted to create fabrics. Most cotton is produced in China, India, and the US.

Cotton is soft and breathable. It doesn't irritate the skin, so it's very comfortable, and it is machine washable and easy to care for. The fact that it's absorbent and highly versatile makes it very good for printing on. The properties of cotton fabrics depend on their construction.

LINEN

Linen is made from the fibers of the flax plant. These are separated, processed, and then spun into yarns that can be woven into fabrics.

Linen has a smooth, cooling feel, so it's often been used for clothing in warm climates. It can be prone to creasing and wrinkling. Typical linen garments include crisp summer shirts and casual trousers.

Above: *Woven cotton fabric homeware.*
Below: *Woven linen close-up.*

64.
MAN-MADE FIBERS

- -

Synthetic fibers have existed since scientists began experimenting with ways to improve on natural fibers in the late 19th century. Since then, many innovations have been made. Each of these has their relative strengths and weaknesses. Man-made fibers tend to be cheaper to produce because they are reliant on laboratories rather than a farming and harvesting process. This means that a lot of the cheapest and truly "disposable" fashion is made from synthetic fibers.

Synthetic and natural fibers are most commonly blended. For example, polyester and cotton are blended together in shirts to combine the cool feel of cotton with the crease resistance of polyester. Lycra or spandex can also be blended with cotton in a denim weave to make your skinny jeans really stretchy and figure hugging.

RAYON/VISCOSE

Both of these are very similar and are most commonly used as a substitute for silk, as they have a similar luster. It feels comfortable because it's breathable, but it has to be washed carefully, as it is not very durable and can crease easily. These are often used for shirts, dresses, and lining garments.

POLYESTER

Polyester is very strong and resistant to creasing, so garments keep their shape well. It's easy to wash but can be damaged by heat. Polyester is not breathable and is sometimes associated with a "cheap" shiny finish. It is nonabsorbent and dries quickly, so it can be used in raincoats.

ACRYLIC

Acrylic is used as a man-made alternative to wool. It is durable, soft, colorfast, and easy to clean; however, it's not as warm as natural wool and can irritate the skin. Acrylic is often used for sweaters.

NYLON

Nylon is tough, lightweight, and elastic. It is resilient and easy to care for, but prone to conducting static electricity. It is sometimes used to imitate silk, and one of the first popular uses was to replace silk in the manufacture of stockings. It is often used to make waterproof jackets, sportswear, or swimwear.

LUREX

This is a type of yarn with a metallic appearance that is used to add glamorous shine to garments.

SPANDEX/LYCRA

This has great elastic qualities, meaning it can be used to make figure-hugging garments that still allow you to move. Lots of sportswear, underwear, and swimwear will contain spandex or lycra. It is lightweight, strong, and durable, but it isn't breathable. It can also be very unforgiving to wear.

Rayon/Viscose

Polyester

Acrylic

Nylon

Lurex

Spandex/Lycra

65.
IN DEPTH: LEATHER

Leather is a treated animal hide that gives a very durable and flexible fabric. In addition to cow leather, it can be made from the skin of deer, goats, ostrich, pig, snake, and even fish. Leather has an iconic place in the fashion world—few menswear images are as memorable as the sight of Marlon Brando or James Dean in a leather jacket!

Leather production begins with the rawhide, which is the skin of an animal, most commonly cattle. The prepared hide is put through a process called tanning. Chemicals are used to stabilize the skin to make sure it remains flexible and doesn't decompose.

Most leather is produced in Italy, India, Brazil, or China, but most countries have tanneries, as humans have used leather for clothing and footwear for over 5,000 years.

QUALITIES OF LEATHER

Leather is most commonly used for shoes, hats, jackets, belts, and luxury handbags, but also for trousers and skirts.

FULL GRAIN

This is the highest quality. The skin keeps its original grain so it has a lot of individual character, almost like a fine piece of timber. It's breathable and extremely strong, flexible and durable, and ages very well, developing even more character over time. A lot of footwear is made from full-grain leather.

TOP GRAIN

The surface of top-grain leather is sanded and buffed, and then a finish coat is added. This gives a more uniform finish with less individuality. It is thinner, more pliable, less breathable, and less durable. A typical use might be a smooth and soft leather handbag.

CORRECTED GRAIN

This has been sanded and dyed to hide imperfections, and then an artificial grain is applied to the surface to make it look more like full-grain leather.

OTHER KEY TYPES OF LEATHER

Nappa—Very soft and pliable and comes from kid, lamb, or sheep skin. It is often dyed.

Patent—This has a very shiny finish that almost looks like glass, due to the plastic or lacquer coating. Often used for shoes, especially formal men's shoes, or for accessories, such as clutch bags.

Suede—This is made from the underside of the skin and has a napped finish, which means it's slightly raised and fuzzy. It's less durable but softer than leather and can become dirty and absorb liquid. Common uses are shoes, boots, and jackets.

Nubuck—This is top-grain cattle leather that has been sanded or buffed to create a nap similar to suede. Since it is still made from the outer part of the hide, it is more durable, stronger, and thicker than suede.

Box leather—Rigid, coated leather that is very tough. It is often used for work boots, biker boots, and satchels.

66.
IN DEPTH: DENIM

DENIM

Denim is a fabric made from using cotton in a twill weave. This gives the fabric its diagonal ribbing. For a typical pair of blue jeans, only the warp threads are dyed and the weft threads are white. This is why the outside of your jeans is a different color from the inside.

Another key consideration when working with denim is the dying and wash. "Raw denim" is prone to shrinking and color bleeding, so the majority of jeans bought in shops have been prewashed and dried a few times so the level of color is more stable.

The darkest washes are known as rinse washes. Other effects include stone wash and acid wash, along with other techniques to create distressed effects, such as sandblasting and abrasion.

The versatility of denim means that it can still be seen everywhere, from worksites to red carpets. In addition to jeans, denim can be used for almost any garment, including shirts, skirts, and jackets.

THE HISTORY OF DENIM

The name of denim comes from the French phrase "de Nimes," meaning "from Nimes"—the French city where it was originally produced. Denim originally found popularity for workwear due to its durable qualities.

In 1853, during the Californian gold rush, Levi Strauss began importing denim to make the sturdy, solid trousers that would become jeans, which were ideal for both miners and cowboys. These were appropriated by rock'n'rolling teenagers in the 1950s and have never been out of style since, being constantly reinvented as trends change.

The most obvious way that jeans can adapt to and even come to define trends is the cut and fit, from 1950s drainpipes to 1970s flares, baggy jeans in the 1990s, or skinny jeans in the 2000s.

Stacked denim jeans in various rinse washes.

WORKING WITH KNITTED FABRICS

Due to their construction techniques, knitted fabrics behave very differently from woven fabrics (see Woven Fabrics, pages 104–105). Woven fabrics are made by interlacing vertical (warp) and horizontal (weft) yarns. This technique gives the fabric a good degree of stability in both directions.

Knitted fabrics are made from rows of interlocking loops and stitches, which means each of these loops is able to maneuver and the fabric is able to stretch. This variation in properties between woven and knitted fabrics means you need to know whether the garment you are creating is best suited to a woven or to a knitted fabric.

Since knitting is a 3-D discipline (as opposed to the very flat construction of a woven fabric), garments are often created by the way stitches are combined. This makes knit extremely versatile, especially for small pieces and garments. Think about how a pair of socks is knitted and how many small pieces of woven fabric you would need to make that shape—and even then you wouldn't be able to get them on without the stretch of a knitted fabric.

SEWING WITH KNITTED FABRIC

Understanding the grain of fabric is important when pattern cutting (see Understanding Grain Lines, page 159). It is very important to check the grain when working with knitted fabrics because directional stretch is more noticeable.

Most knits are two-way, meaning they stretch width-wise. In this case, you need to make sure that the stretch will run across the garment horizontally too. This is because this is the direction in which you need "give" in the garment—for example, to stretch a sweater over your head. It also gives added stability to the length of the garment—you don't want gravity to cause you to go home in a longer sweater than you left the house in!

A ballpoint needle needs to be used when sewing knitted fabrics. The rounded tip means the needle will push in between the knitted loops, rather than piercing through the strands of yarn. Zigzag stitches rather than straight stitches are needed, as the stitches need to move and stretch with the fabric to avoid tearing.

Knitted fabric should be washed and dried before sewing them together to preshrink the fabric. It should then be allowed to rest before cutting. This is to ensure the integrity of the fabric before you use it—otherwise it will become misshapen. Ready-made knitted fabrics will have already been treated in this way, but it's an important process if you have knitted a fabric yourself.

Areas such as shoulders, which take a lot of the weight of the fabric below them—and are key joins in the garment—are often stabilized with the addition of some tape or clear elastic.

Above left: *Chiara Ferragni modeling knitwear during Paris Fashion Week.*
Below left: *Interlocking loops and stitches of knitted fabric.*
Bottom right: *Alpaca knitted cardigan by ELEVEN SIX.*

PROPERTIES OF KNITTED FABRIC

- **Simplicity**—There is often no need for zippers, buttonholes, or other closures, as the fabric has enough "give" to stretch when dressing.
- **Stretch**—Allows freedom of movement, meaning knitted garments can be particularly comfortable. It also allows for figure-hugging designs, and many "activewear" garments are constructed through knit.
- **Resilience**—Knitted fabrics are much better at snapping back into shape, with an element of elasticity (although this does have a limit, as garments can become unshapely if stretched too much).
- **Easy care**—The spaces created between the fibers as a result of the construction method means that knitted fabrics crease much less than woven fabrics, so they can be easier to care for.
- **Warmth**—The construction naturally creates space for warm air to be held in the fabric, giving it a layer of insulation.

68.
KNITWEAR BASICS

Knitting is a method used to produce fabric for a garment with interlocking loops of yarn, either by hand using knitting needles or by machine. These loops—known as stitches—create a number of consecutive rows of interlocking stitches. As each row progresses, a newly created loop is pulled through one or more loops from the previous row, placed on the gaining needle, and the loops from the prior row are then pulled off the other needle.

Using two needles, the handknitter knits from right to left on one side of the fabric—the "knit stitch"—then turns the work over and moves right to left back to the starting position—the "purl stitch." The purl stitch is effectively the reverse of the knit stitch.

The key stages of knitting are, in summary, to create a slip knot and "cast-on" to begin a row of stitches. A combination of knit stitch and purl stitch is then used to knit rows of stitches before "casting off" to secure the final row and prevent unraveling.

INCREASING AND DECREASING

To alter the width of your pattern and make interesting knitted shapes and pattern pieces, you need to increase and decrease stitches. Increasing stitches adds an extra stitch to your needle, therefore increasing the width.

Decreasing stitches removes a stitch from your needle, therefore decreasing the width.

TENSION OR GAUGE

Tension or gauge within knitwear simply means stitches per inch. It refers to the number of stitches per inch you create horizontally and the number of rows per inch vertically. Gauge, abbreviated as GG, ranges from finest to chunkiest: 12 GG, 7 GG, 5 GG, 3 GG, 1.5 GG, and handknit.

Interlocking loops of a knitted fabric.

69.
MACHINE KNITTING

The dometic knitting machine was invented in the 1870s, and by the 1970s, no crafty household was complete without one. Today there are numerous types of knitting machines, ranging from simple single-bed domestic machines to highly complex electronic mechanisms. Brother, Silver Reed, and Passap are some of the companies producing machines.

Domestic and industrial knitting machines work by passing yarn first through a tensioning mechanism and then through the knit carriage or cam, before feeding it to needles as they knit. The carriage is passed across the bed of needles, causing the needles to move, and producing each next stitch.

PATTERNATION AND STITCH TYPES

Patterns and stitch types are created within knitwear by selecting and deselecting certain needles on the knitting machine. Buttons, knobs, and levers on the carriage are moved to different positions, or mechanical punch cards, electronic pattern reading devices, or computer controls are used in order to make the stitch pattern—essentially made by selecting needles to leave out of work. Common stitches are tuck, slip, lace, Fair Isle, and intarsia (see Ten Basic Knit Stitches, pages 144–146).

TYPES OF KNITTING MACHINES

Single Bed/Flat Bed
Most highly available, single-bed machines work with the most common yarn thickness and produce a number of versatile stitches. Standard single beds use one bed of needles to produce different gauges of knit—a fine- or standard-gauge machine can knit fine yarns up to a good jersey/T-shirt weight, while mid-gauge or bulky knitting machines are better for thicker yarns.

A standard-gauge, single-bed machine has 200 needles on the bed, measuring 4.5 mm between needles, which equates to a 5 GG machine. A fine-gauge machine has 250 needles on the bed, measuring 3.5 mm between needles/7 GG. A mid-gauge machine measures 6–7 mm between needles/4 GG, while a chunky machine measures 9 mm between needles/3 GG. The gauge measurement is taken from the center of one needle to the center of the adjacent one. All machines have a tension range adjusted by a dial on the carriage.

Double Bed
This machine has two beds of needles fixed together, allowing you to knit among others, rib stitches, plain stitch, stop stitch, or tuck.

Circular Machines
These machines knit continuously, allowing you to form a seamless tube.

Passap
Passap machines boast inbuilt patterns and are primarily used for patternation (see above) within knitwear.

Dubied
Double-bed dubied machines are available in a variety of gauges—most commonly 10 and 12 GG. As with domestic machines, the bottom bed can drop away, allowing you to produce both single and rib fabrics. Dubieds can produce much finer fabrics than domestic machines.

70.
HAND KNITTING

All stitches are comprised of knit or purl. Understand these and you're well on your way. All that remains is to pick up your needles and yarn, and follow this step-by-step guide to hand knitting.

MAKING A SLIP KNOT

1. Make a loop as shown, ensuring that the tail of the yarn is running down the center of the loop and lies behind the loop.

2. Next pull the tail slightly through the loop and insert one of your needles.

3. Finally, pull the yarn tightly around your needle. You have created your slip knot, and are ready to cast on your first row of knitting.

CASTING ON

1. Take the needle with your slip knot on it in your left hand, and picking up the other needle with your right hand, push it behind the other needle through the slip knot. Wrap the yarn around the right needle and between the needles.

2. Now pull the yarn you just wrapped around the right needle through the slip knot—this can be tricky, but apply a little pressure and pull the yarn through, as shown.

3. Now you should have one loop on each needle—the slip knot on the left-hand needle and another loop on the right-hand needle. Transfer the loop on the right-hand needle to the left-hand needle, resulting in two loops on the left-hand needle.

4. To create the next loop, insert the right-hand needle between the two loops on the left-hand needle. Wrap the yarn around the right-hand needle.

5. Pull the yarn through the loop closest to the end of the needle so that you have one loop on the right-hand needle.

6. Finally move the right-hand loop to the left-hand needle—you should now have three loops on the left-hand needle. Continue this process until you have cast on as many stitches as you require.

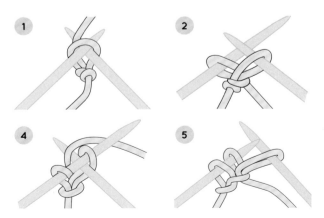

71.
SWATCHING

Before starting out on any piece of knitwear, it's a really good idea to first produce a knitted swatch. This is a small sample of the knit, and it's especially important in knitwear since you are effectively creating the fabric and garment at the same time, unlike when working with woven fabrics.

The primary purpose of swatching is to measure the gauge (see Understanding Tension, pages 100–101) and to check the needles and yarn specified knit to the correct size and scale. It also gives you an idea of the handle of the fabric you're about to create and a chance to practice before you start on the real thing.

HOW TO USE A SWATCH TO MEASURE GAUGE

Most knitting patterns will give you a target gauge. For example, 20 stitches and 22 rows = 4 inches (10 cm) with size 8 needles. Follow the recommendations of needle size, yarn, and stitch type to knit a square. If knitting freehand, it's still a really good idea to swatch first, as it lets you check and tweak the gauge before starting on your garment.

The most accurate way to measure gauge is to knit a swatch larger then the recommended stitches and rows specified. Use a standard measuring tape or ruler to measure both vertically and diagonally somewhere in the center of your square—this will give a more accurate measurement. Gauge swatches should always be measured off the needles because the needles distort the fabric. Finish the swatch as you intend to finish your garment—cast off.

Hopefully your measurements are spot-on and you're ready to start your final piece. If not, simply adjust your needle sizes—smaller/thinner needles to tighten up the stitches, bigger/thicker needles to loosen your knitting.

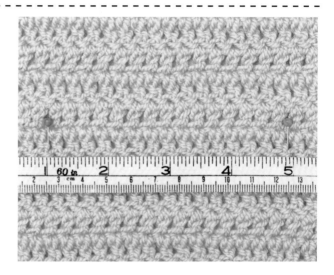

TIP: Consider gravity. If you are knitting a garment that will ultimately hang off your body, e.g., a sweater, try to emulate the hang when measuring. Pinning the swatch to a corkboard and allowing it to hang is the simplest way to do this. This is not necessary for items such as socks or throws.

72.
UNDERSTANDING TENSION

The key to becoming a skilled knitwear designer lies in understanding tension, or gauge, as it's more commonly referred to. Gauge, technically abbreviated GG, simply means stitches per inch—it is the number of stitches per inch you create horizontally and the number of rows per inch vertically. Gauge is used in both hand and machine knitting and is one of the key specifications to consider when choosing a knitting machine.

Whether hand or machine knitting, it's really important to consider the gauge of your pattern or swatch before starting to knit, because this determines not only the size but also the behavior of the fabric created and the way it handles. Most knitting patterns will tell you the target gauge. If you are freehand knitting, it's advisable to knit a swatch (see page 99) and measure the gauge before starting.

FACTORS AFFECTING GAUGE

STITCHES
Different stitch types produce a different number of stitches over an identical width. Cables and ribs "pull in" and give more stitches per inch than, say, a simple seed stitch.

YARN
Thicker yarns generally produce larger stitches than thinner yarns and, as a result, reduce the number of stitches per inch.

NEEDLES
Thicker knitting needles, or knitting pins, produce larger stitches, reducing the number of stitches and rows per inch. Needle diameters range from 2 to 25 mm (roughly $1/16$ to 1 inch). The diameter affects the size of stitches, which affects the gauge of the knitting. In general, the thicker the yarn, the thicker the needle you should use with it.

KNITTER'S TENSION
No two knitters knit the same. Given the same size needles, the same yarn, and using the same stitch, one might knit seven stitches per inch, while the other may knit nine stitches per inch, thus affecting the resulting tension. Indeed, your own mood can affect how tightly you knit, which in turn affects the gauge.

CHEAT SHEET FOR UNDERSTANDING GAUGE

- The THICKER the yarn, the FEWER stitches per inch.
- The THICKER the needle, the BIGGER the stitches.
- The BIGGER the stitches, the FEWER stitches per inch.
- The THINNER the yarn, the MORE stitches per inch.
- The THINNER the needle, the SMALLER the stitches.
- The SMALLER the stitches, the MORE stitches per inch.

NEEDLE SIZES AND CONVERSIONS

METRIC SIZE (MM)	US SIZE	UK SIZE	JAPANESE SIZE
0.7	000000		
1	00000		
1.2	0000		
1.5	000		
1.75	00		
2.0	0	14	
2.1			0
2.25	1	13	
2.4			1
2.5			
2.7			2
2.75	2	12	
3.0		11	3
3.25	3	10	
3.3			4
3.5	4		
3.6			5
3.75	5	9	
3.9			6
4.0	6	8	
4.2			7
4.5	7	7	8
4.8			9
5.0	8	6	
5.1			10
5.4			11
5.5	9	5	
5.7			12
6.0	10	4	13
6.3			14
6.5	10 ½	3	
6.6			15
7.0		2	7 mm
7.5		1	
8.0	11	0	8 mm
9.0	13	00	9 mm
10.0	15	000	10 mm
12.0	17		
16.0	19		
19.0	35		
25.0	50		

73.
KNITWEAR AND SOCIAL MEDIA

The importance of social media within the fashion world cannot be underestimated. We'll talk about the role it plays when launching your own line in later sections (pages 236–237), but why is it important for knitwear designers to embrace social media? What are the benefits of mixing an ancient craft with modern technology?

The world of knitwear seems to inhabit it's very own social media landscape. Pinterest, Instagram, and Twitter all play a role, not to mention YouTube and blogs—check out www.yarnharlot.ca. However, there are dedicated knitwear platforms that all knitwear designers should engage with to be inspired, in turn to inspire and for all things brand related.

RAVELRY (WWW.RAVELRY.COM)

Ravelry is the number-one knitting and crochet community site online, with over four million registered users in 2014. It is the single place to be online if you want to succeed as a knitwear designer—a targeted platform to find potential business, sell pattern downloads, and generally advertise your work.

I'd really recommend setting up a designer profile and a group for your work—from here you can link your designs to your group and invite your contacts or fellow Ravelry users to join the group and get conversations going. Join other groups that interest you, and you'll soon have your very own online knitwear community.

Check out https://www.ravelry.com/groups/designers; it's a great starting point for general design conversations, covering topics such as being a designer on Ravelry, copyright and infringement issues, and all elements of design and pattern making and publishing patterns.

ETSY (WWW.ETSY.COM)

Etsy has been described as crafty cross between Amazon and eBay." It's a peer-to-peer e-commerce website, championing handmade, unique, and individual design along with some great vintage pieces. Not only is it the number-one creative platform to sell from, but you can also scour the globe for materials, yarns, and incredible vintage inspiration samples without leaving your house.

At the start of 2015, Etsy had 54 million users, connecting 1.4 million active sellers with 19.8 million active buyers. It's really easy to register and buy or sell on Etsy. Simply create a username and you also have the option to create a shop name—be careful, though, the username cannot be changed once created! Creating a shop on Etsy is free; however, there is a small listing fee and Etsy takes a small percentage of any listings sold.

74.
REINVENTING TRADITIONAL KNITTING

MISSONI

Founded in 1953 by husband and wife Ottavio and Rosita, Missoni is perhaps the most famous knitwear brand on the planet. Based in Italy, the high-end Italian brand is famous for it's zigzag, stripe, and wave knits in an array of colors.

Championed by Anna Piaggi, former editor of Italy's *Arianna* magazine, and Diana Vreeland, former editor of American *Vogue*, Missoni held mass influence in the early 1970s. Over the years the brand has developed over 25 sub-lines, including diffusion line M Missoni and Missoni Home, and there are rumors of Hotel Missoni on the horizon. In 2014, Rossella Jardini, former creative director of Moschino, was hired as a consultant.

SONIA RYKIEL

Sonia Rykiel is as synonymous with knitwear as she is with the "Swinging 60s" and London's Kings Road. In the early 1960s, she reinvented knitwear—transforming it from largely shapeless, clumsy sweaters into skinny-rib, finely knit, brightly colored hero pieces. Never before had anyone put seams on the outside of garments or emblazoned sweaters with slogans. A celebrity following ensued, including Audrey Hepburn and Brigitte Bardot.

Having previously only stocked in her husband's boutique Laura, in 1968 Sonia launched her own fashion house. She has more recently collaborated with contemporary market giant, H&M, and has inspired a whole generation of designers, from Comme des Garcon to Yohji Yamamoto.

KAFFE FASSETT

Another love child of the 1960s, Kaffe Fassett is best known for colorful craftwork—be it knitwear, needlepoint, or patchwork. His one-man show at London's Victoria and Albert Museum in 1988 was the first time a living textile artist had exhibited there.

Having met Scottish fashion designer and long-term collaborator Bill Gibb in the late 1960s, Fassett's work initially concentrated on teaching the design and, in particular, the color stages of his craftwork. Missoni commissioned his early collections.

In conjunction with Oxfam, Kaffe works with local communities in India and Guatemala, advising on designs that sell in developed countries. He is fabric designer for Rowan Patchwork and Quilting and the primary knitwear designer for Rowan Yarns.

Models walk the runway during the Missoni fashion show as part of Milan Fashion Week Spring/ Summer 2016.

75.
WOVEN FABRICS

Woven fabrics have been around for a very long time. Early examples have been discovered from most cultures around the world, and the oldest woven fabric ever found dates from 7000 B.C. in what is now Turkey. Originally, woven fabrics were made from flax (linen), silk, wool, and cotton. Now, many synthetic fibers are also woven. The Industrial Revolution in the late 18th century brought the innovation of using machines to spin thread and also the mechanical loom. Mass production of woven fabrics was born, and many towns in northern England built their economies around their new textile factories.

THE PRINCIPLES OF WEAVING

On any scale, the principle of weaving remains the same. Two (or more) sets of yarns or threads are interlaced. Each of these threads has a name and is shown in pink below:

WARP

This thread is stretched across the loom, running along the length of the fabric.

WEFT

This goes across the warp at a right angle and is passed above and below the warp threads to interlock.

SELVAGE

This is the edge of the fabric where the weft wraps around to loop back in the other direction across the weft. This stops the fabric from unraveling.

The most basic weave is shown opposite, where the weft passes under one warp strand and over the next and continues to alternate like this; however, there are many weave variations (see pages 106–107).

ADVANTAGES OF WOVEN FABRICS

Woven fabrics are typically more stable than knitted fabrics, which stretch more because they are produced by a series of intertwined loops that can expand and contract under force (see Working with Knitted Fabrics, page 94). In a woven fabric, the warp stretches less than the weft because this has already been stretched during the weaving process.

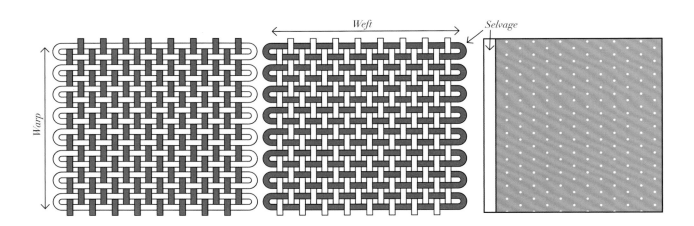

Above: *This very simple equipment shows the principle of weaving. Here, the warp is stretched across the frame, running vertically, and the weft is threaded through above and below strands of warp.*

An industrial mill capable of using many threads to create intricate patterns (see Woven Patterns, page 108 and Woven Jacquard and Tapestry Patterns, pages 120–121).

105

76.
TYPES OF WOVEN FABRICS

PLAIN WEAVE

As the name suggests, this is the simplest and most common type of weave. Weft yarns alternate passing over and under single warp yarns ("one to one"). Fabrics as diverse as calico, muslin, gingham, cheesecloth, percale, voile, chiffon, and taffeta are all plain weaves; the weight of yarn, material used, and the spacing of the weave determine their characteristics. Plain weaves are relatively inexpensive, strong, durable, and extremely versatile and are often the base for printed woven fabrics due to their even surface.

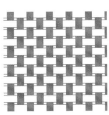

Plain Weave

BASKET WEAVE

A variant of the plain weave, where the weft threads pass over two warp threads then under two ("two to two"). This gives a more textured finish and a checkered effect. Oxford cloth, commonly used for making shirts, is an example of basket weave.

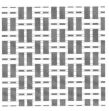

Basket Weave

TWILL WEAVE

These fabrics have a visible diagonal grain running through them caused by offsetting the weave. The weft passes under and over two or more warp threads each time. Each following row begins with the next stage of the progression to make the pattern.

Twill weave fabrics have more drapability than plain weave fabrics, meaning that they hang straighter under their own weight. Tweed, denim, and garbardine are all examples of twill weave fabrics.

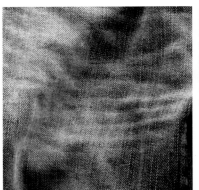

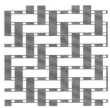

Twill Weave

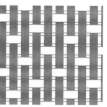

SATIN WEAVE

With a satin weave, the majority of either the warp or weft is on the front side of the fabric. In the example to the right, the weft pops over the warp for one thread and then ducks back under for four threads, meaning that we see four warp threads uninterrupted.

Seeing more continuous runs of a single yarn gives satin weave fabrics a shinier appearance, allowing them to reflect more light than plain weaves, where overlapping threads interrupt this.

Satin—commonly woven from silk, polyester, or nylon—is soft and smooth and has incredible drape, so it's often used for luxurious items like prom dresses. It is less durable and snags easily, since the construction means the threads are less interlocked and stable than more simple weaves.

Satin Weave

Pile Fabrics

PILE FABRICS

Velvet, corduroy, and other pile fabrics are made using a more complicated weaving process in which an extra set of warp threads is looped over wires that are then removed. For velvet, the remaining wires are then cut, which gives it a fine, bristly surface.

The most luxurious velvets are made from silk, but these are very expensive. Cotton, wool, and viscose velvets are all more affordable and have differing qualities.

An example of a pile fabric where the loops are uncut is terrycloth (toweling).

77.
WOVEN PATTERNS

In addition to the many different types of weave construction, there are almost limitless types of woven pattern that can be created with the use of different colors and configurations of thread. Below is a selection of the most common types of woven pattern. Woven patterns in garments are an alternative to printed patterns (see Repeat Print Design, page 118).

Herringbone

Ticking Stripe

Plaid or Tartan — The difference here is that tartans are officially registered to a Scottish clan, whereas plaid patterns are similar in construction but have no familial ties.

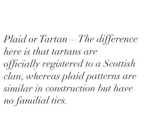

Plaid or Tartan

Gingham

Houndstooth

78.
WORKING WITH MODERN FABRICS

Research and development of new materials and fabrics is a field that is constantly moving forward. Many of these new fabrics make the jump from the laboratory to the runway via designers with an eye for innovation and unlikely juxtaposition. Many designers are embracing these modern fabrics, which are increasingly used in functional clothing, as a way of reinventing and reinvigorating a collection.

EXAMPLES OF MODERN FABRICS

NEOPRENE
This synthetic rubber is usually used for wetsuits but has been adapted here by Alexander Wang.

POLAR FLEECE
Brushed warp knit polyester is traditionally used for practical fleece jackets, but DKNY used luxe fleece in new shapes for their Fall/Winter 2015 collection.

TINSEL YARN
Tinsel yarn has long been used to add sparkle to knitted garments. Recent innovations have used long strands of the yarn to give great festival looks with a glam-rock edge. This tinsel yarn, chevron-fringed jacket is by Tim Ryan, a London-based knitwear designer with an innovative, visionary approach. Tim specializes in handcrafted limited-edition knitwear.

SEQUINS
Sequins come in a range of shapes and sizes, such as flat, multifaceted, reversible, and oversized paillette. Here, Ashish uses sequins onto voile for a sportier end use in London Fashion Week, Spring/Summer 2016.

Neoprene

Polar Fleece

Tinsel Yarn

Sequins

LUREX

This striking Ferragamo Fall/Winter 2014 head-to-toe lurex dress features ombré pleats.

THERMOCHROMIC FABRICS

These respond to heat by changing color. This Alexander Wang, Fall/Winter 2014 New York outfit features layered laser-effect fabrics that also appear to be heat sensitive.

THE ADVANTAGES OF TECHNOLOGICAL INNOVATIONS

Technological innovations can help to reduce the environmental impact of the fashion industry. It's not something many people would realize, but fashion manufacture uses enormous volumes of water. This can lead to water scarcity, pollution of water supplies, and high energy usage through water treatment and pumping. For example, once you factor in the water needed to grow cotton and apply dyes, approximately 10,000 liters of water is consumed in making a pair of jeans.

Manufacturers are developing technologies such as AirDye and DyeCoo that don't use water or hazardous chemicals. By embracing technologies such as these, designers are able to lessen the impact on the environment through creating sustainable products, but they also add another selling point by appealing to environmentally conscious customers.

Lurex

Thermochromic Fabrics

Emma Watson in a recycled Calvin Klein dress at Met Gala, 2016.

79.
CROCHET AND MACRAMÉ

These two traditional handmade techniques have had a resurgence, making appearances on the runway, not just at the local church fete! They are examples of how once-unfashionable techniques can inspire designers to create something new.

CROCHET

Crochet is derived from the French word for "hook," due to the hooked needle used during the process. The technique has similarities to knitting in that loops of thread or yarn are interlocked to create fabric. The fabric typically has an open, web-like pattern and the appearance of a coarse lace. Traditionally, crochet has been used for tableware, such as doilies and table runners, as well as sundresses, but modern designers have increasingly reimagined the use of the technique.

MACRAMÉ

Macramé uses knotting techniques, rather than knitting or weaving, to create a decorative fabric. It has traditionally been used for homewares—for example, to make plant holders—but more recently, designers have co-opted it for use in clothing and footwear.

Above: *Julie Eilenberger macramé dress, Berlin Fashion Week Spring/Summer 2011.* Left: *Balmain crochet dress, Paris Fashion Week Spring/Summer 2016.*

80.
SCREEN PRINTING

Screen printing is the most traditional form of printing a design onto fabric. It is a type of stencil printing where one color at a time can be printed. More sophisticated designs can feature multiple colors, each printed at a separate stage and building in layers to create the final pattern.

THE SCREEN-PRINTING PROCESS

1. A screen-printing stencil is made by painting a photosensitive emulsion onto a mesh screen, often made of silk. This is done in a darkroom to avoid activating the emulsion.
2. A stencil of the design is then placed on top of the silk screen, in the areas where you want ink to pass through to the fabric. This is traditionally done by cutting a stencil out of card, but is now often done by printing the design onto a transparent acetate.
3. A bright light is then shone onto the emulsion. The emulsion sets hard where it is exposed to light, but the areas masked by the design remain soft and wash away when blasted with water. This creates gaps in the mesh through which the ink can pass, applying your design onto pieces of fabric.
4. Ink is forced through the gaps by running a squeegee over the mesh.

ADVANTAGES OF THE SCREEN-PRINTING PROCESS

The beauty of screen printing is that once a screen has been produced, it can be used again and again, so it's great for mass production of items such as T-shirts. Andy Warhol really popularized the use of screen printing in the art world during the 1960s, using it to reproduce his iconic images.

It's a very versatile process that can be used on an industrial scale but can also be carried out at home. It's this DIY accessibility that led to screen printing being used a lot during the punk scene of the late 1970s, allowing bands and fans to print outrageous T-shirts independently and in small batches. Most colleges will have screen-printing equipment that you can use.

INDUSTRIAL-SCALE SCREEN PRINTING

Screen printing is also carried out on an industrial scale to produce rolls of printed fabric. This is often done using a rotary screen-printing machine that uses successive rollers to apply the design's colors to build up the multicolored pattern.

APPARATUS NEEDED

- **Wooden screen**—Used to stretch silk over, similar to the way a canvas is stretched for painting.
- **Silk or mesh**—This "screen" is pulled tightly over the wooden frame.
- **Photosensitive emulsion**—Applied to the screen in a darkroom.
- **Stencil**—Placed on top of the screen in a darkroom.
- **Bright light**—Used to set the exposed emulsion.
- **Shower or power hose**—To blast away the emulsion where ink needs to pass through the mesh onto the fabric.
- **Ink**—Used to commit the design to fabric.
- **Squeegee**—Used to force the ink through the mesh onto the fabric.

Soo Joo Park is seen outside the DKNY show wearing a DKNY sweater during New York Fashion Week, Women's Fall/Winter 2016. Screen printed by hand in NYC in a limited run of 150 pieces.

81.
HEAT-TRANSFER PRINTING

- -

Heat-transfer printing has become a very accessible technique. It is most often used for small runs of printing, such as T-shirts. While the method is easy, results can be mixed, with colors lacking vibrancy. It is important to follow heat and timing instructions carefully.

THE HEAT-TRANSFER PRINTING PROCESS

1. In its simplest form for home use, a design can be printed out onto a special type of paper using a computer and printer.

2. The paper is then placed onto fabric, and, commonly, a household iron is then used to heat the paper and transfer the design onto the fabric.

INDUSTRIAL-SCALE HEAT-TRANSFER PRINTING

As with most printing techniques, heat transfer is also applied on an industrial scale with increasingly complex, expensive, and efficient machinery. Local print shops will often have a heat press that applies pressure more evenly than the humble iron, and that automatically times the heat application to perfection.

PRINTING IN REVERSE

It's important to print the design in reverse (mirror image) so that any text and any other features are correctly oriented.

82.
DIGITAL PRINTING

- -

Digital printing is a relatively new technology that is being used increasingly within the fashion industry, both for printing onto garments (known as DTG, or "direct to garment" printing) and for the production of rolls of printed fabrics to construct clothing from. It is a form of ink-jet printing, so in principle the technology is similar to that used in a lot of home printers.

ADVANTAGES OF DIGITAL PRINTING

VERSATILITY

Digital printing technology has developed ways of printing onto a wide range of textiles through the use of different combinations of chemicals. This means that it has become very versatile and can often deliver similar results across very different fabrics.

NATURAL DRAPE

The printed design is also much less tactile than that on screen-printed fabrics, so the drape is not affected.

COMPATIBILITY

The direct integration with computer technology means that digital printing is particularly good for printing patterns or designs that have been produced using graphic design software programs.

COLOR AND DEFINITION

There is an almost limitless range of colors and combinations. Image definition is very good, so printing photographic images is possible.

SIMPLICITY

In terms of set up, digital printing is very simple when compared to screen printing: most changes can be done very quickly using computer software. Compare that to the DIY screen-printing process (see page 112) and consider how long it would take you to tweak a design when using that method!

SMALL PRINT RUNS BECOME FEASIBLE

There are many companies that offer a fabric-printing service, often through websites. These allow any designer to upload a design and order a print run of fabric, however small the scale—something that would be prohibitively expensive if working with an industrial screen-printing company, as the majority of cost in that instance would be in setting up the screens.

DISADVANTAGES OF DIGITAL PRINTING

The drawback is the high cost of both the printing equipment and the materials, such as ink. This means that for mass production, there is very little gain through economies of scale—a very large print run would have a relatively similar cost per item when compared to the increased value of a large-screen printing run.

Above: *Photographic image printed onto a silk dress.*
Right: *Industrial digital printer.*

83.
PLACEMENT PRINTS

Placement prints are elements of print that appear in a specific place on a garment. A classic example of this is a graphic T-shirt, where the design would be placed on the chest and would be in the same position on every item in the production run. A typical placement print could be an image, a block of text, or a brand logo that is to feature in the same place on every garment.

THE PLACEMENT PRINT PROCESS

AFTER CONSTRUCTION

Because of the importance of positioning in a placement print, the printing process is often done after a garment has been constructed. So in the printed T-shirt example, a plain T-shirt is made and the print is added afterward using one of the printing techniques we have covered (see pages 112–115). This allows you to carefully position the print onto the garment, confident that the image will sit exactly where you want it to when the garment is being worn.

BEFORE CONSTRUCTION

Alternatively, a placement print can be printed before a garment is constructed. This is often done if a print needs to flow across a seam or join. In this instance, the print is applied to fabric first. It is vital at the lay planning and pattern-cutting stage to ensure that the correct part of the print will end up in the right place on the garment.

OVERSIZE PLACEMENT PRINTS

Occasionally, a designer will use an oversize placement print design that appears all over a garment and gives the impression that it's an all-over, repeated print. The placement can still be very intentional and identical on every item made.

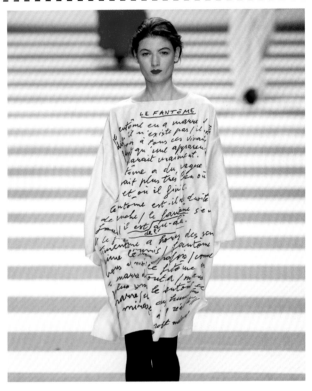

Above: *Oversize placement print used by Jean-Charles de Castelbajac.*
Right: *Standard placement print on a graphic T-shirt.*

84.
REPEAT PRINT

The alternative to placement printing is the use of a repeat print. This is where a pattern is created that appears continuously and seamlessly, over and over on a piece of fabric. When this fabric is cut and stitched into a garment, it doesn't usually matter to the designer where each individual element of the pattern ends up.

Repeat patterns can be designed either to give a very uniform feel, where the repetition is really obvious, or to give the impression of the print being random, where it is more difficult to discern where each instance of the repeat begins and ends.

As with many of the skills in this book, print design is another area that you may choose to specialize in. Most design houses, labels, and retailers will employ people in the role of print designer.

THE REPEAT PRINT PROCESS

Unlike a placement print, a repeat print is always committed to fabric before garment construction. Sometimes a designer will source fabric that has already been printed and use it in their garment. Alternatively, you may wish to create something completely unique by designing your very own repeat print.

COMMON EXAMPLES OF REPEAT PRINT

1. Floral
2. Stripe
3. Animal
4. Geometric
5. Polka dot

COPYRIGHT

Like many elements of fashion, print designs are subject to copyright, so it's important to get clearance if there is a particular image or design you want to use. Similarly, print designers sell licenses for their prints and for a higher fee will grant you exclusive use.

85.

REPEAT PRINT DESIGN

When designing repeat prints, there are some basic configurations that you will need to understand, each of which results in a different effect.

TILES AND TESSELLATION

There are more complex types of pattern, but here we will deal in terms of tiles. In this way of thinking, a repeat pattern is built up by fitting square tiles together to give a continuous repetitive design.

Tessellation is a really key principle here. This is a mathematical term that deals with the idea of shapes fitting together neatly, without any gaps. Since we are looking at perfectly square tiles for these examples, we can safely assume that each of the tiles will fit next to

each other. So if a single design element is placed in the center of our tile and then multiple tiles are placed next to each other, we build up a simple block repeat pattern.

CENTER REPEAT/BLOCK REPEAT/SQUARE REPEAT/STRAIGHT REPEAT

These are names for the simplest type of repeat pattern, where the design is centered within a square and each of the squares fit together adjacently like tiles. The grids in the illustrations below show tile positioning.

Other pattern configurations are less simple than the block repeat. If a design is cut off on the side of a tile, the truncated image must be completed by meeting its "other half" where it joins the tile beside it.

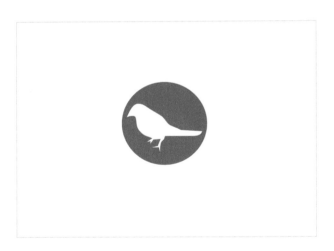

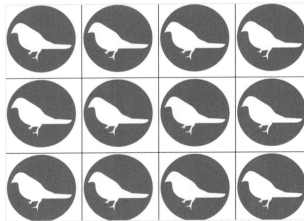

HALF-DROP REPEAT

This is a very common pattern type within textile design. The recurring motif is repeated halfway down a tile vertically.

BRICK REPEAT

Similar to the half-drop repeat, but instead the recurring motif moves half a tile horizontally on each row.

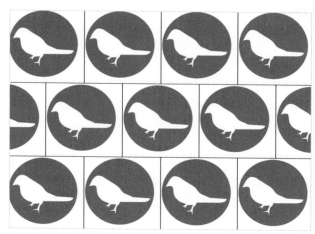

MIRROR REPEAT

This is based on the center repeat pattern, but with the recurring motifs horizontally facing each other in a mirror-image design.

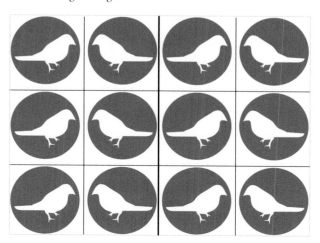

86.
WOVEN JACQUARD AND TAPESTRY PATTERNS

In addition to the fairly simple woven repeat patterns we looked at on page 108, weaving techniques can create incredibly intricate patterns. These patterns give the complexity of printed patterns without fading, washing out, or wearing out as easily because they are intrinsic to the fabric.

These techniques might not be something that you will end up doing hands-on, but it's important that you are aware of the processes and fabric options since you are likely to select and use these fabrics in your work.

JACQUARD FABRICS

The Jacquard loom, invented in 1801 by Joseph Marie Jacquard, allows individual warps to be manipulated during the weaving process, giving an extra dimension of control. In regular weaving, the warp remains still. Jacquard fabrics are commonly used for decorative upholstery, but can also be used to create clothing with a luxurious feel.

BROCADE

These lavish fabrics feature a raised design, typically in gold or silver thread.

DAMASK

Damask weave patterns contain two colors—one for the warp and one for the weft. The fabric is reversible, with each side being the negative of the other.

TAPESTRY

Tapestry has its origins as an art form used to create pictures and scenes. It's a form of weaving where only the weft shows on the surface. Usually a neutral warp thread is used because this is hidden. The weft threads do not run from selvage to selvage; they start and end where the specific color is needed. For this reason, the reverse of handmade tapestries look really messy.

As with most production techniques, tapestry has gone through technological advances, with computerized tapestry machines available since the 1990s. This technology allows for elaborate designs to be produced quickly.

Above left: *An example of a brocade dress from Burberry Fall/Winter 2016 collection. Luxe materials including brocades, damasks, jacquards, and tapestries were a key message for this season from many of the powerhouse designer brands.*
Above right: *Damask fabric.*
Below: *Tapestry fabric used on accessories in the Tempracha by Sanele Cele collection, 2014.*

4
GARMENT CONSTRUCTION

An essential set of skills for any designer is to have an understanding of how garments are constructed and knowing the names of their various elements. Most types of clothing and accessories have their own sets of terminologies that have their origins in the traditional construction crafts such as shoemakers, tailors, and milliners. It's impossible to give exhaustive lists of these terms, but the following set of skills shows examples of garments labeled with the names of their constituent parts. Think about how each part fits together to create a three-dimensional shape from flat fabric. Compare these examples to your own clothes—how do they differ in style, cut, and construction?

From crop tops to tunics, and camisoles to roll necks, tops comes in many guises. Most popular of all is the simple T-shirt—cap, short, or long-sleeved, like this one on the right—it's a wardrobe staple.

87.
TOPS

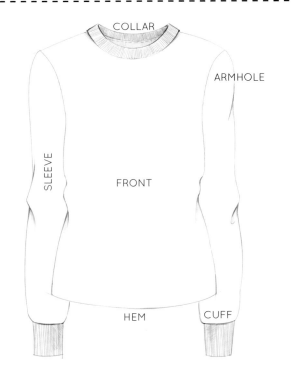

COLLAR

ARMHOLE

SLEEVE

FRONT

HEM

CUFF

88.
DRESS

- -

Easily the most exhaustive garment in terms of constructions, the dress warrants a book of its own to cover its many silhouettes. Variations across necklines, bodices, sleeve lengths, and hemlines make for an ever-evolving garment that can single-handedly sum up an entire season.

NECKLINE

ARMHOLE

BODICE

DART

SLEEVE

WAIST

CUFF

SKIRT

HEM

BACK BODICE

BACK ZIPPER

BACK SEAM

89.
PANTS

Pants are another wardrobe staple whose silhouette varies according to their fit. Baggy, chinos, culottes, flares, jeans, leggings, suit pants, track pants—there are many types. Variations are also determined by the "rise" (where the trouser sits on the hips), details such as pleated or flat front, and pocket and waistband interest. The illustration here shows classic five-pocket jeans.

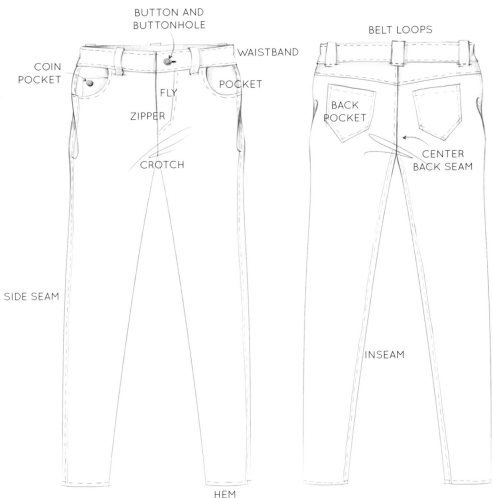

BUTTON AND BUTTONHOLE

WAISTBAND

COIN POCKET

POCKET

FLY

ZIPPER

CROTCH

SIDE SEAM

HEM

BELT LOOPS

BACK POCKET

CENTER BACK SEAM

INSEAM

90.
SHIRTS

Most variations of shirt and blouse styles are in two areas. First is the collar (see page 175)—the shape of it and whether it has buttons to keep it in place or not. Second is the silhouette—for example, slim fit or blouson.

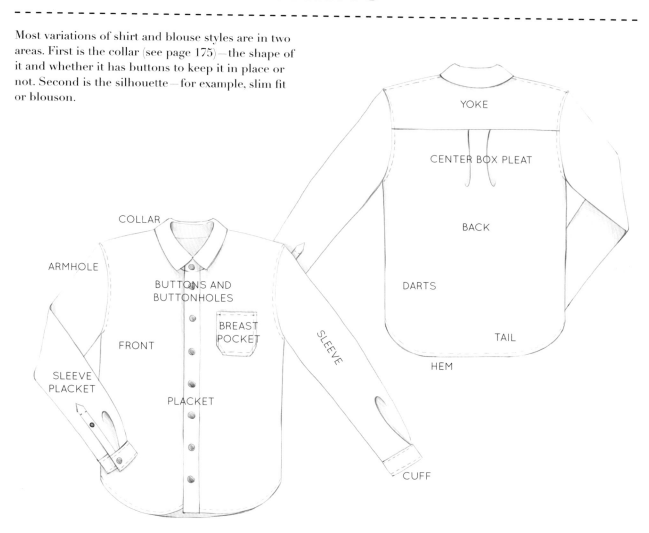

YOKE

CENTER BOX PLEAT

BACK

COLLAR

ARMHOLE

BUTTONS AND BUTTONHOLES

DARTS

BREAST POCKET

FRONT

SLEEVE

TAIL

SLEEVE PLACKET

HEM

PLACKET

CUFF

91.
SKIRTS

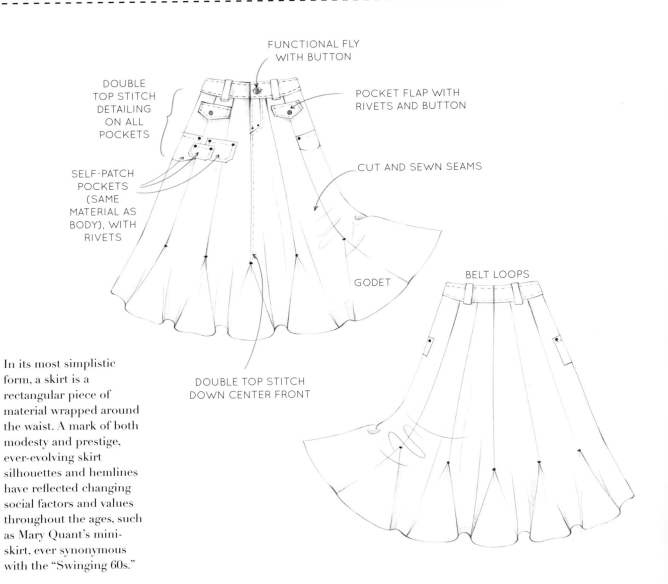

FUNCTIONAL FLY
WITH BUTTON

DOUBLE
TOP STITCH
DETAILING
ON ALL
POCKETS

POCKET FLAP WITH
RIVETS AND BUTTON

SELF-PATCH
POCKETS
(SAME
MATERIAL AS
BODY), WITH
RIVETS

CUT AND SEWN SEAMS

GODET

BELT LOOPS

DOUBLE TOP STITCH
DOWN CENTER FRONT

In its most simplistic form, a skirt is a rectangular piece of material wrapped around the waist. A mark of both modesty and prestige, ever-evolving skirt silhouettes and hemlines have reflected changing social factors and values throughout the ages, such as Mary Quant's mini-skirt, ever synonymous with the "Swinging 60s."

92.
COATS

The illustration shows a double-breasted trench coat. From bikers, bombers, and parkas to overcoats and peacoats, this garment can be either casual or formal, depending on its cut and fabrication.

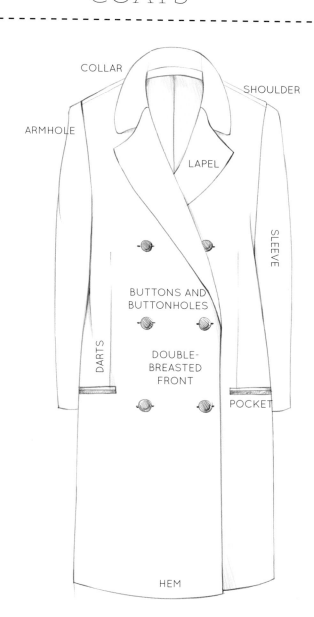

COLLAR

SHOULDER

ARMHOLE

LAPEL

SLEEVE

BUTTONS AND BUTTONHOLES

DARTS

DOUBLE-BREASTED FRONT

POCKET

HEM

93.
JACKETS

- -

The illustration shows a single-breasted jacket.
A double-breasted jacket differs in that the fabric
overlaps at the front when fastened and has an
additional set of buttons.

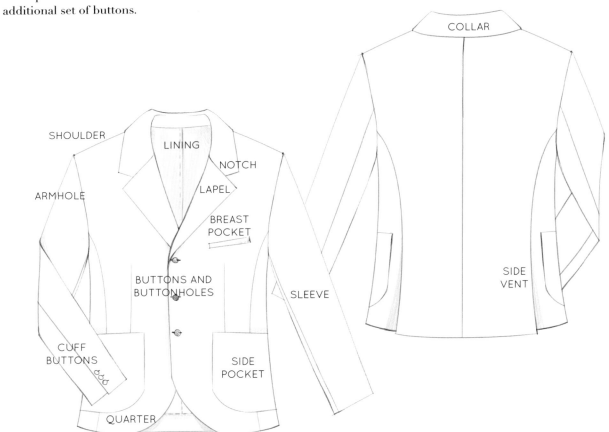

SHOULDER

LINING

NOTCH

LAPEL

ARMHOLE

BREAST
POCKET

BUTTONS AND
BUTTONHOLES

SLEEVE

CUFF
BUTTONS

SIDE
POCKET

QUARTER

COLLAR

SIDE
VENT

94.
LINGERIE

Bras in particular are very technical in terms of their construction, consisting of over 25 components per garment. They must be well made and fitted correctly to ensure they are comfortable to wear.

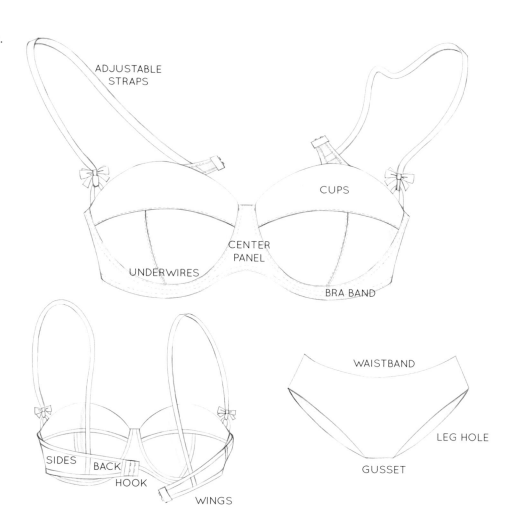

ADJUSTABLE STRAPS

CUPS

CENTER PANEL

UNDERWIRES

BRA BAND

SIDES   BACK

HOOK

WINGS

WAISTBAND

LEG HOLE

GUSSET

95.
FOOTWEAR

The illustration shows an Oxford brogue, which contains lots of interesting technical details. There are many different types of shoe, one of the major variants being heel height.

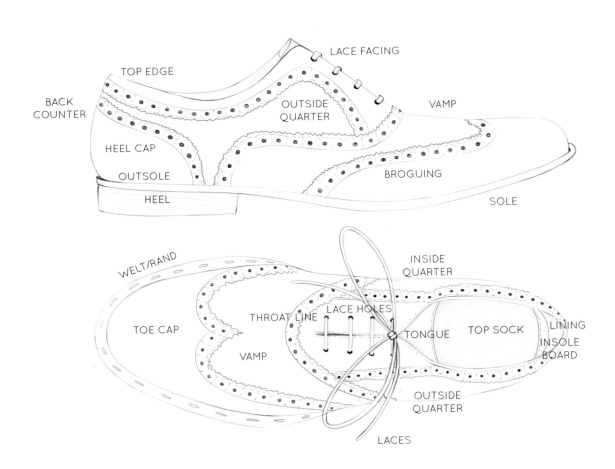

TOP EDGE

LACE FACING

BACK COUNTER

OUTSIDE QUARTER

VAMP

HEEL CAP

OUTSOLE

HEEL

BROGUING

SOLE

WELT/RAND

INSIDE QUARTER

TOE CAP

THROAT LINE

LACE HOLES

TONGUE

TOP SOCK

LINING

INSOLE BOARD

VAMP

OUTSIDE QUARTER

LACES

96.
BAGS

From the practical need to carry everyday items around, bags have evolved to be synonymous with prestige and social status. In the late 1990s, premium brands such as Mulberry, Fendi, and Chloe gave birth to the "It Bag"—a must-have, season-defining item—which seemed to overshadow anything else that the owner was wearing. These bags became known only by the name of the design, such as the Bayswater, the Baguette, and the Paddington.

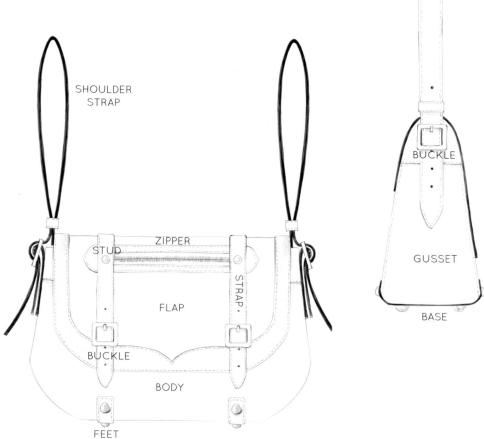

SHOULDER STRAP

ZIPPER

STUD

STRAP

FLAP

BUCKLE

BODY

FEET

BUCKLE

GUSSET

BASE

97.
SWIMWEAR

Here are some of the most common female swimwear shapes. Male swimwear keeps it very simple with either a swimming short or a brief-shaped trunk!

HALTER

ATHLETIC

TRIANGLE

BANDEAU

TANKINI

RASH VEST

COVER-UP

UNDERWIRE

BIKINI

MONOKINI

SWIMDRESS

ONE-PIECE

SHORTS

SKIRT

98.
WOMENSWEAR

The construction and structure of garments varies so greatly that it is impossible to cover every likely element in a book such as this. There are, however, a number of stages of the design and creation process that many garments will have in common. Also, in principle, the production process will have similarities.

END USE

In addition to garment type, a really key consideration when creating womenswear or menswear is end use. A designer should know who a garment is for and where it will be worn. Many brands structure their design teams around end use rather than garment type. Typical categories include:

- Casual wear
- Formal wear
- Work wear
- Loungewear
- Outerwear
- Sportswear and activewear
- Occasion wear (including prom, wedding, and evening dresses)

THE PROCESS

DESIGN AND SPEC SHEET

After the initial design has been completed, the designer fills out a spec sheet (see pages 54–55) with measurements, other technical details, and practical considerations, such as fastenings. Fabric samples are considered and suitable fabric is sourced.

PATTERN MAKING

When working on the pattern, 3-D considerations—such as how to use seam lines and darts to create the correct silhouette, the weight of fabric and how it drapes, and whether any areas such as collars or shoulders will need to be stiffened—are made.

TOILING

A toile is a prototype made in a fabric similar to that intended for the end product. It is then adjusted on a stand or fit model (see Making Alterations, page 192). Industry standard for toiling is US size 6 (UK size 10).

From this process, a final pattern is produced and then a first sample is made, which then leads to the fit process (see page 185).

COUNTRIES OF ORIGIN

HONG KONG AND CHINA

A vast production base for outerwear, tailoring, and dresses, from casual to occasion. Structured and premium knit skirts, blouses, tops, jumpsuits, knitwear, denim and casual/cargo pants, casual jackets, lingerie, and swimwear. Woven production.

INDIA

More specialized in woven and cotton products, such as sundresses, madras checked casual shirts, playsuits, beachwear, embroidered tops, and skirts. Indian producers are skilled in beautiful crafts such as cutwork, different varieties of embroidery, appliqué, sequin handwork, ribbon work, and surface decoration.

MAURITIUS

Jersey knits and denim for high-volume production.

BANGLADESH

Bangladesh is the second largest exporter of garments after China. Both woven and knitted fabrics are produced, and many brands use factories in Bangladesh to manufacture jersey T-shirts, sweatshirts, and denim.

EASTERN EUROPE

Eastern Europe has factories for short lead-time products for the UK market. Product types include dresses, tops, skirts, trousers, jackets, and coats.

TURKEY

Great for garment washing, such as denim, jersey/knits, and casual pants. Knitwear can be produced here through "cut and sew" manufacture (see Accessories, page 142). Also great for knits/jersey, including lace, as used for lingerie. Jersey T-shirts, and leggings are also key.

GREECE

Great for knitted jersey. Casual wear, skirts, leggings, sleepwear, jersey beachwear, sweat tops, and T-shirts.

ITALY

Famous for its premium factories, Italy offers high-end production to premium designer brands.

PORTUGAL

Jersey.

US/UK

The vast majority of clothes for the US and UK are made overseas. However, there is a resurgence in local production within those territories, particularly where a short lead time is required to allow quick reaction. Los Angeles is home to a number of "cut and sew" factories and premium denim brands. Many companies use L.A. manufacturers to sample their designs and then switch to South America for production.

SOUTH AMERICA

A lot of denim production has moved to South America as a result of increasing production costs in Asia. Many L.A.-based companies have second factories in Mexico or Guatemala.

WOMENSWEAR TRADE SHOWS

- **Première Vision**—Print and fabric fair; Paris: February and September.
- **Texworld**—International textile trade fair, New York: January and July, Paris: September and February, Istanbul: March.
- **Denim Première Vision**—Leading premium denim supply show; Barcelona: May.

Swimwear and Lingerie

- **Interfilière**—International sourcing event for lingerie and swimwear; Paris: July.
- **Mare di Moda**—Beachwear and underwear; Cannes: November.

Brand Trade Shows

Showcasing the newest brands:

- **Who's Next**—Paris: January and September.
- **Première Classe**—Paris: January and September.
- **Revolver**—Copenhagen: February and August.
- **Scoop**—London: January, July, and September.
- **Capsule**—Las Vegas, February.
- **Coterie NY**—February and September.
- **Magic Las Vegas**—February and August, New York: January and July.

Note: all dates are subject to change. See also Trade Shows in Handbags (page 141) and Yarn Sourcing and Trade Shows (page 147).

99.
MENSWEAR

COUNTRIES OF ORIGIN

See Womenswear (pages 133–134) for product type by country.

- Hong Kong
- China
- Bangladesh
- Pakistan
- Burma
- Vietnam
- Cambodia
- Egypt
- Morocco
- Romania
- Turkmenistan
- India
- Mauritius
- Greece
- Turkey
- Italy
- Portugal
- UK
- US

MENSWEAR TRADE SHOWS

- **Pitti Uomo**—Florence: January and June.
- **Capsule**—New York, Paris, and Las Vegas: January and February.
- **Project**—Las Vegas: February and August, New York: January.
- **Magic**—Las Vegas: February.
- **Tranoi**—Paris: January, New York: February.
- **Jacket Required**—London: February.
- **Première Vision**—Paris: February and September.
- **Texworld**—New York: January and July, Paris: September and February, Istanbul: March.

The majority of menswear processes—from concept to customer—differ very little from those of womenswear. The inspiration, design, creative, and production processes are essentially the same across both—it's the end product that is different, although in recent seasons even those differences are diminishing.

The line between womenswear and menswear design is becoming increasingly blurred. Unisex is emerging as a third market to sit alongside these traditional categories. Everyone from Stockholm-based, über-cool brand Acne, which released a capsule collection of transgender denim back in 2010, to BOY London is getting in on the androgynous vibe.

Although end use is pretty much split the same as womenswear, the popularity of Kanye West's brand Yeezy—known for their long-line tees, drop-crotch sweatpants, and blanket wraps for men—is further proof that the menswear customer appreciates directional silhouette, color, and material base as much as their womenswear counterpart. Menswear and womenswear consumers do differ when it comes to brand loyalty; men are seemingly more brand driven.

SIZING

The industry standard is a 40-inch chest, medium top, 34-inch waist, and US size 10 footwear.

100.
CHILDRENSWEAR

Until the 19th century, children wore miniature versions of adult clothing. The late 20th and early 21st centuries saw childrenswear become increasingly casual, relaxed, and fun. Comfort, safety, and durability are now key—along with, of course, design. Coupled with the fact that women now spend increasingly less time in the home and therefore have less time to make children's clothes, the childrenswear clothing market is now a mass-produced multibillion-dollar industry.

THE PROCESS

Cutting, sewing, assembling, decorating, finishing. The process for manufacturing childrenswear follows the same process as womenswear and menswear, although extra care and attention must be taken to ensure the garments comply with stringent safety regulations.

MATERIALS

NATURAL FABRICS

These are treated with fire-retardant, ecologically friendly, and chemically safe dyes. For babies' clothes and sleepwear, soft or brushed materials are most popular.

SYNTHETICS

These are extremely popular due to being durable, weatherproof, and easy to launder.

RUBBER

Rubber revolutionized childrenswear. Elastic waistbands led to increased adjustability and allowed children to dress themselves.

DESIGN DETAIL

Durability is important in children's daywear and outerwear, whereas uniqueness and decoration help sell partywear. Details such as pockets, belts, frills, closures, bows, brooches, badges, patches, and trims are increasingly more important within childrenswear than in any other sector. All of these factors, however, are usurped by branding—popularity of TV, film, and cartoon characters can sell out a range in record time.

COUNTRIES OF ORIGIN

Although a small proportion of childrenswear is still manufactured in the US and UK, the majority is made in Asia, Turkey, and Portugal.

SIZING

For childrenswear, age is generally used for sizing increments instead of height. Childrenswear can either be graded in single or dual sizes; the type of garment and market sector will determine this. Typical age groups are babywear (0–2), kidswear (3–11), and teenwear (female 12–16, male 12–20). Above the age of 2, height measurements can also be used.

CHILDRENSWEAR TRADE SHOWS

The main childrenswear trade shows are:

- **Playtime**—New York, Paris, and Tokyo: July and August.
- **LA Kids Market**—L.A.: March, June, August, and October.
- **Bubble**—London: June.

101.
FOOTWEAR

Marilyn Monroe once said, "Give a girl the right shoes, and she can conquer the world." And she was right. Shoes are the one item of clothing where comfort goes out of the window…. Because, after all, life is too short to wear boring shoes!

There are hundreds of types of footwear—the most common being shoes, boots, sandals, clogs, flip flops, moccasins, espadrilles, sneakers, brogues, creepers, and derbies. Such items are generally made of leather, wood, rubber, plastic, or jute.

Assorted embellished shoes from ASOS.com.

THE PROCESS

DESIGN AND PATTERN CUTTING
The footwear designer designs the shoe. Measurements are added to the sketch—this is called a "spec" (specification) sheet (see pages 58–59). The pattern cutter then makes a paper pattern from the measurements and specifications given on the spec sheet.

CLICKING
The clicking operative works from this paper pattern and cuts out the pattern pieces using metal strip knives. The role of the clicking operative is highly skilled, as they must place the pattern pieces in the most economical way to avoid wastage.

CLOSING
The pattern pieces that will form the top of the shoe— the upper—are stitched together, at first using a flat machine but moving to a post machine that enables the closing operative to sew a 3-D upper. Eyelets and fastenings are inserted at this stage.

LASTING/MAKING
The upper now needs to be permanently molded into a foot shape. For this, a foot-shaped "last" is used. Traditionally made of wood, it is now more common for a last to be laser cut from plastic. High-tech machinery scans the foot and makes a last that directly replicates the shape.

Once the last is approved, a left and right foot is made and all other sizes are graded up or down from this prototype. Typical size runs are US 4–10 for women and US 8–14 for men. The upper is stretched and molded over the last, and heat is applied to permanently set the shape of the shoe.

FINISHING/SHOE ROOM

Finally, the sole and heel are attached to the upper and are trimmed, buffed, stained, polished, or waxed. Any finishing treatments are applied to the upper, and laces are inserted.

MATERIALS

LEATHER

Leathers used for shoe uppers include cow, pig, box (calf), patent leather, or suede. Lining leather tends to be pig leather.

SYNTHETIC

Polyurethane (PU) emulates leather or suede and is the most commonly used synthetic for shoe uppers. Synthetic pig or goat PUs are the most popular lining materials. Unlike leather, PU is not breathable.

INSOLES

Leather insoles are preferable, as they allow the foot to breathe, although cost considerations mean PU insoles are more common within the retail industry.

SHANK

A piece of metal sandwiched between the insole and outsole to support the foot and give the shoe structure.

TOE PUFF

Stiffener sandwiched between the upper and lining material to create form at the toe of the shoe.

BACK COUNTER

Stiffener sandwiched between the heel and lining material to create form at the back of the shoe, preventing heel slip.

SOLES

Premium shoes boast leather soles, and mass-produced soles are made from reconstituted leather board.

COUNTRIES OF ORIGIN

UK

Northampton was once the heart of the UK shoe industry, and its cobblers were famous for making high-quality men's leather shoes for brands such as Trickers and Churches. In recent years, the majority of manufacturing has moved offshore.

US

As in the UK, 99 percent of shoes sold in the US are manufactured abroad.

INDIA

India specializes in leather production, leather shoe manufacture, and embellishment.

PORTUGAL AND SPAIN

Produce high-quality leather shoes with a clean premium aesthetic and premium prices.

HONG KONG, CHINA, AND TAIWAN

Asian manufacturers are experts in synthetic and non-leather products, along with embellishment, trims, and unusual materials.

VIETNAM

As in Hong Kong, China, and Taiwan, but Vietnam also produces leather.

SIZING

Industry standard for fitting purposes is US size 6 for women and US size 10 for men. All production measurements are stated in millimeters.

FOOTWEAR TRADE SHOWS

The two main footwear trade shows are:

- **Expo Riva Schuh**—Garda, Italy: every January and June.
- **MICAM**—Milan: every February and September.

102.
HANDBAGS

As with shoes, bags come in an array of shapes, sizes, and materials. Silhouettes are ever-changing, the most common being clutch, shoulder, satchel, backpack, and cross-body. Since the birth of the "It Bag" in the mid-1990s, the handbag is hands down the one accessory that can single-handedly communicate your status symbol.

THE PROCESS

If branded hardware is needed, this will be tooled up during the mock-up/sourcing period because it tends to have a lead time of four to six weeks.

DESIGN

The handbag designer sketches by hand or by using computer-aided design (CAD) (see page 53). If there is some surface detail design, this can be designed first (i.e., appliqué/print), and then a full-size spec sheet is produced with measurements (see pages 56–57).

Liquid metallic cross-body bag with pink pom-pom charm.

SOURCING

Handbags are made from different leathers, fabrics, and components. Sourcing of leathers, synthetics, and hardware is key to the design. Leathers will also need to go through a tannery to be dyed to a specific color standard.

SURFACE DETAIL

Surface design can be anything from embroideries, appliqués, quilting, studding, or printing to laser cutting. All these processes need to be considered before the bag is constructed.

MAKING

In most factories, the areas are split into sample room, tannery (leather selection), cutting, stitching, finishing, and packaging.

- Sample room—This is where a highly skilled sample maker makes the first sample.
- Tannery/leather selection—The leather/synthetic will be selected and handed over to the cutting team.
- Cutting department—This will be done either by machine (large factories producing large quantities will use a machine that cuts the patterns from a CAD program) or by hand. At this point, any required edge staining will take place before the bag is assembled.
- Stitching—Once the panels are all cut, they go on to the stitching department to be assembled.

FINISHING

After stitching, the bag will go through finishing to be inspected. It is also at the finishing stage that any labels/tags or packaging is added before the bag is boxed and ready to ship.

TYPES OF HANDBAGS

- Scoops/hobos/buckets
- Messenger/cross-body
- Grab/bowler
- Shopper/tote/shoulder
- Duffle
- Kettle
- Clutch/pouch
- Backpack
- Saddle
- Weekender
- Wristlet
- Satchel

MATERIALS

Handbags can be made of many types of materials:

- Leather
- Suede
- Snake/crocodile skin
- Pony hair

SYNTHETICS

- PU (polyurethane)—a synthetic version of leather. These are available in many types of finishes and colors.
- Satin/velvet
- Straw
- Canvas
- Felt

COUNTRIES OF ORIGIN

CHINA

For all synthetic fabrics and some leather.

INDIA

The majority of leather handbags are manufactured in India. Luxury brands look to manufacture in Italy, Turkey, and Spain because the finish will be cleaner and neater.

UK

Some designers will choose to manufacture in the UK—for example, Mulberry's factory is in Somerset.

EUROPE

Turkey is quick to market; lead times can be as short as eight weeks.

SIZING

For greater accuracy, all measurements may be given in millimeters (mm).

HANDBAG TRADE SHOWS

- **Première Vision**—Print and fabric mills, fabric trends; Paris: February and September.
- **Pure**—Accessories trade show; London: February and July.
- **London Textile Fair**—Print and fabric mills; London: July.
- **London Print Fair**—Print studios; London: April.
- **Lineapelle**—Leather fair; Milan: February and September.
- **Pool Trade Show**—Includes womenswear, lingerie, swimwear, and childrenswear; Las Vegas: August.

Chloé bag, Paris Fashion Week, Spring/Summer 2016.

103.
ACCESSORIES

Accessories are the perfect "pick-me-up." They can update an existing outfit and refresh a wardrobe instantly and without breaking the bank. As far back as the 1930s and the Great Depression, the so-called "lipstick effect" saw consumers economizing on everything but cosmetics. This pattern continues today—with global economies in downturn, the humble accessory still reigns.

THE PROCESS
DESIGN
The accessories designer sketches by hand or by using computer-aided design (CAD). For some accessories, the fabric contains the majority of the design work. With a Fair Isle knitted scarf, for example, a full-sized spec sheet with measurements and fabric references is produced after the textile is designed and a swatch is knitted to show the pattern.

SOURCING
Sourcing of materials is key to the design of accessories and occurs before the shape or style is designed. For printed scarves or hats, a specialist print designer designs the print. Print screens are then cut to facilitate production of the fabric at an acceptable cost. Digital printing a printed design can achieve incredibly graphic results but is costly. Sometimes prints are bought as stock fabric from a supplier.

FABRIC/TEXTILE CREATION/MANIPULATION
In some cases, the fabric/textile needs to be produced before the accessories are made. Textiles can also be bought as stock fabrics from specialist suppliers.

MOCK-UPS
A designer will create mock-ups if an item is complicated or to show embellishment technique and positioning. 3-D printed prototypes are produced for accessories such as sunglasses where molds are required. Protoypes are approved before going to bulk production.

MAKING
Knitting machines and looms produce textiles that are cut to shape to make knitted and woven accessories. Knitted items can be "fully fashioned"—garments are knitted to shape and size and linked to form a fully knitted garment—or "cut and sew"—a cheaper method where the fabric is produced in lengths and pattern pieces are cut, overlocked, and stitched together to create a garment.

Chunky knitted scarves and hats are usually hand knitted. Woven items always use the cut and sew method, and are finished by sewing machine. Felt and occasion hats and fascinators are shaped on a block before being finished with trims. Hand making is still key for some types of accessories—for example, jewelry.

FINISHING
Accessories are finished by hand where necessary. Trims and embellishments are added if required.

TYPES OF ACCESSORIES
- **Knitted accessories**—Hats: beanies and berets.
- **Scarves**—Knitted, woven, blanket wraps, lightweight printed scarves, and embellished boleros.
- **Woven hats**—Bucket hats and caps.
- **Felt hats**—Fedora, trilby, cloche, and beret.
- **Gloves**—Knitted, leather, and woven.
- **Belts**—Leather and polyurethane (PU), hip, waist, boyfriend, obi sash belts.
- **Sunglasses**—Acetate and metal frames. Variety of lense types including flat lenses and revo (mirrored).

- **Jewelry** — Rings, necklaces, cuffs, body jewelry, hair jewelry, and corsages.
- **Hosiery** — Socks and tights.
- **Neckwear** — Collars, bibs, and skinny scarves.

MATERIALS

KNITTED AND WOVEN SCARVES/HATS/GLOVES

- Natural yarns — Wool, cashmere, merino, angora, alpaca, cotton, linen, and silk.
- Synthetic yarns — Viscose, polyester, and 100-percent acrylic.
- Natural/synthetic mixes — sometimes yarns are mixed to create a softer feel for cheaper prices.

LEATHER GLOVES

- Leather — Pig and pig suede for cheaper gloves. Cow for premium gloves.
- Silk/jersey/fleece/wool for linings.

FELT HATS

- Wool felt.

OCCASION HATS AND FASCINATORS

- Sinamay straw, feathers/ribbons/trims/embellishments/organza/crinoline.

COUNTRIES OF ORIGIN

CHINA

Knitted and woven products, leather gloves, and occasion hats. Knit and cold weather accessories from Northern China.

INDIA

Mostly woven scarves and embellished items; also some production of leather gloves.

UK

Felt hats are made in the UK. However, much production has moved to China. Premium occasion hats are still made in the UK.

EUROPE

Turkey — Quick to market production of knitted and woven hats and scarves.

Italy — Premium woven scarves, warp-knitted scarves, and the production of premium printed fabrics.

SIZING

- Hats — Many are One Size Only, and some manufacturers use S/M/L. Traditional and structured millinery has a sizing system based on the circumference of the head.
- Gloves — Gloves are often sized S/M/L. Leather gloves have a sizing system based on a measurement taken around the four fingers just below the knuckles of the wearer's dominant hand. Finger length — from the bottom edge of the palm to the tip of the middle finger — is also used in some systems.
- Scarves — One size.
- Belts — S/M/L or waist measurement.
- Jewelry — Rings: S/M/L.
- Socks and hosiery — S/M/L.

For greater accuracy, all measurements may be given in millimeters (mm).

ACCESSORIES TRADE SHOWS

- **Pitti Filati** — Yarn and textile trade show; Florence: January and July.
- **Première Vision** — Print and fabric mills, fabric trends; Paris: February and September.
- **Pure** — Accessories trade show; London: February and July.
- **London Textile Fair** — Print and fabric mills; London: July.
- **London Print Fair** — Print studios; London: April.

104.
THE KNITWEAR PROCESS

- -

Long associated with grannies and bygone days, knitwear is being reinvented. Today's designers are bringing knitwear into the modern day by modifying garments and the knitwear process—from yarn sourcing to the shop floor and everything in between.

The knitwear design process is very much the same as fashion design in the initial design stages—first comes inspiration and concept, then comes research, experimentation, and determining color palettes before the final garment or collection is designed.

At the design phase, a fashion designer would start sourcing their fabrics to prepare for making their initial prototypes. However, a knitwear designer must "create" their fabric from scratch, so the importance of yarn sourcing and selecting the yarn of the correct quality and weight cannot be underestimated. Knitwear is a 3-D craft, and it's the combination of yarn and stitch choices that determines the shape of the garment. These elements must be given careful consideration before garment construction begins.

There are two main ways to knit—hand knitting and machine knitting (see pages 97 and 98). Hand knitting is the simpler and less expensive of the two processes. Knitting needles, a ball of yarn, and a good deal of patience are all that is needed … although the latter is required when machine knitting also!

105.
TEN BASIC KNIT STITCHES

- -

Essentially there are only two stitches used when knitting any garment—the knit stitch and the purl stitch. The knit stitch is the lower, or flat one, and the purl stitch is the higher, bumpy-looking stitch. Basic knitting involves knitting each row on the right side, then purling each row on the wrong side, known as the stockinette stitch.

1. STOCKINETTE STITCH
This is the V-patterned fabric that people tend to associate with knitting. Stockinette stitch has a smooth appearance and a tendency to curl at the edges.

2. GARTER STITCH
Garter stitch is achieved if you knit every row rather than knit one, purl one. This flat, reversible, ridged fabric stands up well to wear and does not roll at the edges.

3. RIBS
Rib stitch patterns create both texture in your knitting and elasticity in your fabric. There are many different types of rib stitches, the most popular being the 2 x 1 or 2 x 2 rib.

4. CABLES
Cable knitting is a style of knitting in which textures of crossing layers are achieved by varying the arrangement of stitches in a set sequence. It is widely associated with the Aran sweater (associated with Irish Aran Islands).

5. TUCK STITCH
This stitch creates a diamond-shaped pattern. It is most commonly associated with sweaters, socks, and gloves.

Stockinette Stitch

Ribs

Garter Stitch

Cables

Tuck Stitch

6. SEED STITCH

Seed stitch is a textured stitch created by alternating knit and purl stitches in every column and every row. Seed stitch is a highly textured stitch, in stark contrast to, say, stockinette stitch.

7. BIRDSEYE STITCH

Birdseye stitch is a graphic stitch made up of small, diamond-shaped stitches. It is commonly used in menswear for garments such as sweaters and socks.

8. INTARSIA

Intarsia is a multicolored stitch, predominantly used to build pictures and patterns. Facing and reverse show the same pattern. There are no "floats" (strands of unworked yarn) between stitches on the reverse.

9. FAIR ISLE

This stitch pattern is made up of two or more colors, with floats on the reverse. The name for this traditional hand-knitted technique is derived from a tiny island in the north of Scotland, forming part of the Shetland Islands, called Fair Isle. More recently referred to as jacquards, knit purists reserve the term Fair Isle for patterns with a limited palette of five or more colors that comply with characteristic patterns originating from the Shetland Islands.

10. JACQUARD

Single jacquards have floats on the reverse. Double jacquards have no floats on the reverse, as shown below. Instead, stitches are interlinked to form a stitch pattern, such as birdseye.

Seed Stitch

Birdseye Stitch

Intarsia

Fair Isle

Jacquard

YARN SOURCING AND TRADE SHOWS

At all levels of knitwear design, sourcing yarns can be a complicated and costly process. The main ways to go about yarn sourcing are to approach yarn companies for sponsorship, attend textile trade shows, or source firsthand or secondhand yarn. Sponsorship is the most economical approach while studying, but this can be time-consuming and there's no guarantee that you'll secure the most exciting, innovative yarns out there.

You don't have to travel the globe to source new and exciting yarns, but below are the key trade shows and suppliers that are dedicated to breaking the boundaries of knitwear yarns and design. If you're unable to travel, a phone call, email, or letter with examples of the type of yarn you're looking for is a good starting point.

TIP: Yarns do perish, so if you are buying secondhand yarns, check that they haven't become brittle.

LEADING YARN SUPPLIERS

BROOKLYN TWEED — PORTLAND, OREGON
Breed-specific yarns designed, sourced, dyed, and spun in the United States.

ROWAN — YORKSHIRE, ENGLAND
Rowan is a luxury hand-knit yarn company. They use beautiful natural fibers and offer a range of organic yarns.

TODD & DUNCAN — KINROSS, SCOTLAND
Established in 1867, this leading cashmere yarn spinner has a long heritage. They are renowned for their very high quality and supply many of the top couture houses and contemporary designers. They sponsor students at over 15 colleges and universities each year to encourage innovation in cashmere product.

UPPINGHAM YARNS — UPPINGHAM, ENGLAND
Yarns for hand and machine knitters in various fibers and limited-edition and repeated runs. Since many of the yarns they carry are made only once, they operate a free yarn-matching service.

INTERNATIONAL TRADE SHOWS

SPINEXPO — SHANGHAI AND NEW YORK
Showcase by independent textile specialists of fibers, yarns for knitting, circular knit and weaving, socks, laces, labels, and technical textiles. Shanghai in March and September; Brooklyn, New York in July.

PITTI FILATI — ITALY
The leading trade show that features new-season yarns to all levels of the knitting industry, with emphasis on technological innovation. Predominantly Italian product. Florence in January and June/July.

PREMIÈRE VISION YARNS (INDIGO AT PV) — PARIS AND NEW YORK
Presenting the latest global innovations and featuring natural and synthetic fibers, high-performance yarns and recyclable materials. Paris in February and September; New York in January and July.

TNNA, CALIFORNIA AND OHIO
The National Needlearts Association trade show exhibits the latest trends and provides an opportunity to network or buy the latest products. San Diego, California in January; Columbus, Ohio in June.

107.
YARNS

Yarn is made from strands (or "plies") of fiber that are twisted together to form a single thicker string of material. Yarn is sold in skeins or balls, which are often labeled by weight, but it's handy if they show the length too. Most shop-bought patterns specify a yarn brand, weight, and needle size, but if you're careful you can substitute for something similar. Patterns will also refer to the gauge or tension (see pages 100–101).

STANDARD WEIGHT CATEGORIES OF YARN

WEIGHTS AND COMMON USES

0 Lace or Cobweb—Only slightly thicker than thread, commonly used for lace or doilies.

1 Fingering—Still very thin, used for lace or socks.

2 Sport—Very fine, great for blankets or baby clothes.

3 DK or Light Worsted—This has a smooth and even texture. Can be "double knitted," which is knitting two strands together to create a thicker material.

4 Worsted—Thicker and warmer, used for blankets and sweaters.

5 Bulky/Chunky—Very thick, typically used for scarves and rugs.

6 Super-Bulky/Roving—Unspun and often used for felting. This can be used with very large needles, but it will be a bit difficult.

7 Jumbo—A new category of yarn that is luxuriously thick and offers a textured-stitch look. Fun to knit!

CROCHET HOOK SIZING

Steel crochet hooks, for use with crochet thread and lace-weight yarns, have a different sizing system than regular hooks—the higher the number, the smaller the hook—the reverse of regular hook sizing. The smallest steel hook is a #14 or 0.9 mm; the largest is a 00 or 2.7 mm.

YARN WEIGHT CATEGORIES

Yarn weight symbol and category name	0/ LACE	1/ SUPER FINE	2/ FINE	3/ LIGHT	4/ MEDIUM	5/ BULKY	6/ SUPER BULKY	7/ JUMBO
Yarns in category	Fingering 10-count Crochet thread	Sock Fingering Baby	Sport Baby	DK Light Worsted	Worsted Afghan Aran	Chunky Craft Rig	Super Bulky Roving	Jumbo Roving
Knit gauge in stockinette stitches per 4 in (10 cm)	33–40*	27–32	23–26	21–24	16–20	12–15	7–11	6 and fewer
Knitting needle size Metric (mm)	1.5–2.25	2.25–3.25	3.25–3.75	3.75–4.5	4.5–5.5	5.5–8	8–12.75	12.75 and larger
US	0–1	1–3	3–5	5–7	7–9	9–11	11	17 and larger
Crochet gauge in single crochet per 4 in (10 cm)	32–42 double crochets*	21–32	16–20	12–17	11–14	8–11	7–9	6 and fewer
Crochet hook Metric (mm)	1.5–2.25	2.25–3.5	3.5–4.5	4.5–5.5	5.5–6.5	6.5–9	9–15	Q and larger
US	B1	B1–E4	E4–7	7–I9	I9–K10 ½	K10 ½–M13	M13–Q	

*Lace-weight yarns are usually knitted or crocheted on larger needles and hooks to create an open, lacy fabric. For this reason, a gauge range is difficult to determine.

COLORS AND DYES

Yarns are available undyed, ready to be custom-dyed as necessary, or even left natural.

They also come ready-dyed—when buying this, pay attention to the "dye lot" to make sure you buy yarn from exactly the same batch to avoid color variation. They are available in solid colors or with different color effects. Below are some of the most popular.

1. HEATHERED OR TWEED
This contains random flecks of a different colored yarn.

2. OMBRÉ
Yarn that fades from light to dark in shades of the same hue.

3. MULTICOLORED
This yarn features two or more different colors.

4. SELF-STRIPING
This yarn has specific lengths dyed in different colors to make stripes when knitted.

5. SHIMMER
This yarn features sparkly flecks of tinsel.

6. SOCK YARN
Again, this yarn changes color to give multicolored effects without having to change to a different ball of yarn.

1 *Heathered or Tweed*

2 *Ombré*

3 *Multicolored*

4 *Self-Striping*

5 *Shimmer*

6 *Sock Yarn*

FIBERS

Wool
- Absorbent, warm, has good elasticity—it can stretch and return to original shape.
- Typical uses: sweaters and soft accessories such as scarves.

Cotton
- Soft, breathable, strong, and absorbent.
- Typical uses: socks, jersey T-shirts, and dresses.

Acrylic
- Lightweight, odor-resistant, mildew-resistant, and easy to clean.
- Melts and burns in direct flames.

Nylon
- Lightweight, strong, and resistant to mold and fungus.

Rayon
- Can imitate feel of natural fibers, such as linen, silk, wool, and cotton.
- Soft, smooth, comfortable, and highly absorbent.
- Can feel slippery to the touch, doesn't insulate body heat, and has lowest elasticity.

Polyester
- Strong, resistant to stretching and shrinking.
- Easily washable, dries quickly, and wrinkle-resistant.

Spandex/Lycra
- Great elasticity, lightweight, comfortable, breathable, and dries quickly.
- Typically used for tight-fitting clothing and underwear—socks, sportswear, and leggings.

108.
TOOLS AND EQUIPMENT

American author Wallace D. Wattles once said, "It is essential to have good tools, but it is also essential that the tools should be used in the right way." Following is a basic list of tools that is more than adequate for beginners to be able to achieve the majority of pattern-cutting techniques. Over time you'll discover new tools, develop old favorites, and determine which tools are worth investing a little more in.

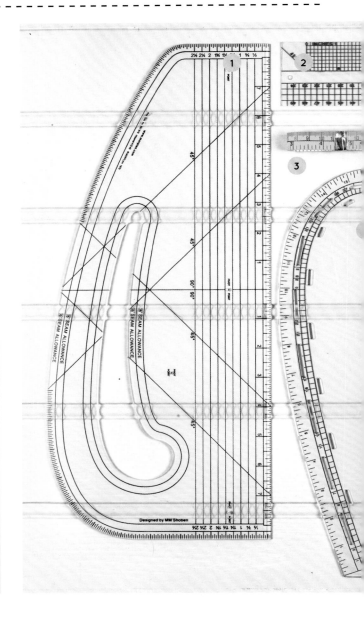

PATTERN CUTTING EQUIPMENT

1. Pattern master
2. Grading ruler
3. Tape measure (showing both metric and imperial)
4. Armhole ruler
5. Pattern hooks
6. Unpicker
7. Awl
8. Pattern drill
9. Pattern notcher
10. Set square
11. Tracing wheel
12. Tailor's chalk
13. Eraser
14. Markers
15. Dress pins
16. French curves

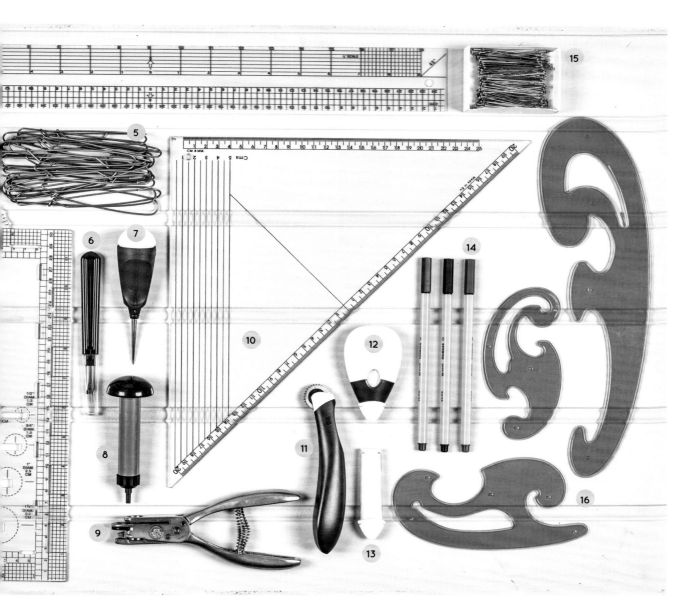

109.
PATTERN CUTTING

Pattern cutting is the skill of producing a flat paper template from which a well-fitted garment can be made. The human body is an irregular 3-D form, and no two silhouettes are the same, making the process of pattern cutting a complex one.

Creating a pattern is the stage of working out how to turn flat, 2-D fabric into a 3-D garment. One way to imagine what your pattern might look like is to think of a garment, such as a dress. Imagine you unpick all of the seams, deconstruct it, and lay the pieces of fabric flat—what you are left with is the garment in a kit form. It is this kit that you then develop for your new design.

THE PATTERN CUTTER

A pattern cutter is the link between designer and machinist or manufacturer. Besides having creative skills, a pattern cutter must understand the many technicalities of the process and work with precision and accuracy. This section breaks down the pattern-cutting process to give you an understanding of the skills needed to make a pattern or work with pattern cutters.

Experienced pattern cutters can create a pattern by chalking directly on paper or material from a set of measurements. This is an impressive skill in its own right that takes years of practice, and a designer doesn't necessarily need to be able to do it. It's also a method that can only be used to create one-off garments, since there is no record of the pattern and therefore it's unsuitable when making patterns for mass production.

COMMON PATTERN-CUTTING METHODS
FLAT PATTERN CUTTING
Drafting a pattern onto paper by using measurements of the human body and utilizing standard blocks, which are then adapted to the individual design. From this pattern, a toile—a prototype of the garment, often made in calico—is produced.

WORKING ON THE STAND
The pattern cutter works directly on the stand or mannequin with fabric and pins. No paper patterns are involved. We will look at this method in more detail on pages 170–172.

THINGS TO REMEMBER WHEN PATTERN CUTTING

It is important to bear in mind the principles discussed in the following sections, as they will all influence choices you make during the pattern-making process:

- **Grain line**—see page 159.
- **Gravity**—The way the material handles and how you want it to hang.
- **Suppression**—removing excess material to create shape is just as important as creating form and proportion.

In addition, keep the three Ms at the forefront of your mind:

- **Measurements**—You need to know the measurements from which you're working.
- **Material**—Bear in mind the fabric you'll be using because this, in turn, will affect the pattern cutting and construction methods you employ.
- **Method**—Will the garment be machine-stitched, hand-stitched, overlocked, etc.?

Consider closures, such as buttons and zippers (see pages 162–165). Finally, ask yourself if you are making a one-off piece or drawing up a pattern for mass production. This will determine if you need to keep a record of the pattern: the method you use will determine if this is possible.

110.
FLAT PATTERN CUTTING

A block is a basic, standardized pattern shape from which the pattern cutter can base and adapt their pattern. It's a basic template that covers all of the common elements you would find in a garment type. A good pattern-cutting studio should contain a set of sturdy, reusable master blocks, including at least the four basic blocks: skirt, trouser, bodice (including sleeves), and dress. Note the dress block is an amalgamation of the skirt and bodice blocks. A standardized block size within the industry is US size 6; within education it is a US size 8.

The diagram on the opposite page shows the four basic blocks used in pattern cutting. These will be modified to give the unique ingredients you need for your brand-new garment.

MAKING A FLAT PATTERN
1. Measure the block and determine how it relates to the measurements or design spec sheet from which you are working. Add any additional elements (a cuff or a collar, for example) or amend the shape (flare the pant leg, for example).

TIP: When drafting a block, start off by going larger rather than smaller. Later in the process it is much easier to remove fabric to take a garment in than to add fabric to let out. By allowing for extra fabric—known as tolerance—you will avoid the pattern piece being too tight or restrictive later in the process.

2. The master block is traced onto pattern-cutting paper (sometimes known as dot-and-cross paper due to the helpful markings it has). Lines are amended to fit the specifications you're working from.

3. When you are happy with the combination of tracing and amendments to the master block shape, you will have a temporary paper block specific to your design. Use a pen to draw around the outline, using a ruler for straight lines and a curved ruler for curves. Do not add seam allowances—these are added to your final sewing pattern. Mark center front (CF) and center back (CB) to ensure they are oriented correctly for future use. Some people annotate their blocks to include features and details such as grain line, notches, and darts (see pages 159–161), although it is perfectly acceptable to add these to your final pattern later in the process (see Annotating Paper Patterns, pages 166–167).

4. Give the block a name (e.g., Dress Front), and add any other helpful information you think you will need as you work with the pattern, including the date for reference.

5. If you make a copy of your new block from durable, heavy pattern-cutting card, you will be able to reuse the new template time and time again.

6. Cut out the pattern pieces, following the stitch lines, and also cut out the darts. Tracing the pattern and darts is easier if they have already been cut out of the block.

BASIC BLOCKS FOR FLAT PATTERNS

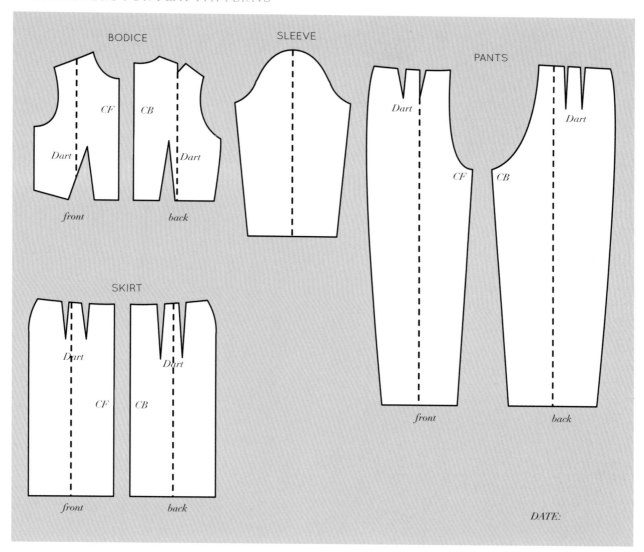

Mark center front (CF) and center back (CB) to denote the parts of the pattern that will be located on a virtual line drawn down the center of the human body to ensure the pattern is oriented correctly.

111.
CREATING PAPER PATTERNS

Armed with your block, you are now ready to create a paper pattern and compile all of the information needed by the machinist.

HOW TO CREATE A PAPER PATTERN

1. Trace around your block onto pattern-cutting paper, also known as dot-and-cross paper. Remember, the block is only a basic pattern piece—you will want to amend the pattern piece in accordance with the technical drawing or measurements that you're working from.

2. Use a tape measure or ruler to transfer the measurements you're working from onto the pattern paper, and make the shape adjustments to your pattern piece.

3. Once you are happy with your pattern piece, it is time to annotate the pattern in preparation for the machinist or manufacturer.

HALF PAPER PATTERN

If a garment is symmetrical, it is acceptable to work from a half paper pattern. In this case, the word "fold" is written along the center fold, so the machinist or manufacturer knows to place this pattern along the fold of the fabric in order to cut out a symmetrical pattern piece.

This method is only beneficial when producing one-off garments. At industry level, multiple pattern pieces are cut at the same time by layering material. It is also not advisable to use half patterns when working with delicate materials, such as silk or chiffon, as these are more difficult to fold than heavier fabrics.

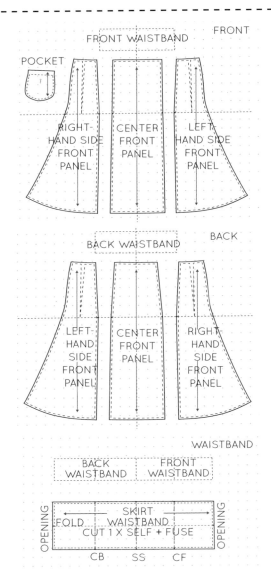

Examples of basic paper pattern pieces.

112.
UNDERSTANDING GRAIN LINES

All fabrics, whether woven or knitted, are constructed from intersecting threads. Woven fabrics are made up of horizontal and vertical threads that interlock with each other; knitted fabrics are made up of interlacing loops. For the purpose of explaining grain lines, I will use the example of woven fabrics. Woven material is the most common material used in pattern cutting because it is the most uncompromising, as opposed to, say, jersey, which stretches and fits to the contours of the body.

Fabric is woven from threads running in two different directions. These are known as the warp and the weft—the warp are the threads running up and down, and the weft are the threads running left to right. These threads react in different ways; therefore, the way a pattern is placed along the grain line of your fabric will determine how the fabric hangs. There are three types of grain:

STRAIGHT GRAIN

The straight grain is made up of the warp threads. It is the most stable grain line because the warp threads are the sturdiest fibers. Pattern pieces cut on the straight grain are least likely to stretch. The straight grain is most commonly used in garments and generally runs up the center front and center back of garments and through sleeve and pant legs.

HORIZONTAL GRAIN

When laying a pattern piece along the horizontal grain—the wefts—you are using the cross grain of the fabric. By their nature, these pattern pieces will be less stable and have more stretch in them.

BIAS GRAIN

This is when you use the grain on a 45-degree angle. By cutting across the warp and the weft threads, you are making the fabric much more unstable. Bias-cut garments are often fluid and flexible—the most common being the bias-cut dress.

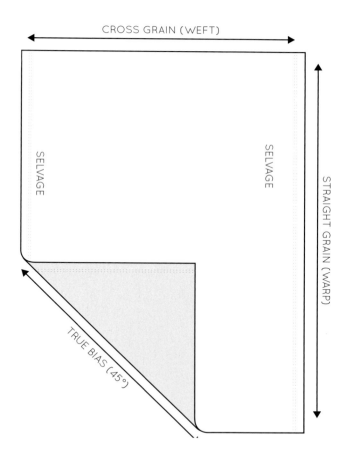

159

113.
DETAILS

It's important to familiarize yourself with some of the more common features involved in constructing garments. By doing so, you'll recognize them when following patterns and creating your own patterns. In this section, we'll look at seam allowance, darts, notches, and drill holes.

SEAM ALLOWANCE

Seam allowance is the allowance given around each pattern piece to enable pieces to be stitched together or to allow components to be attached to each other—for example, a collar on the body of a shirt.

US industry standard for seam allowance is $^3/_8$ inch (1 cm). Note that more allowance is often given on the hem of a garment. Different materials need different seam allowance—therefore it's important to toile in material as similar to the finished garment as possible.

Muslins, chiffons, and other delicate materials will need less seam allowance than heavier materials such as wool, bouclé, and padded fabrics, where up to a 1½-inch (4 cm) seam allowance is recommended. If you are using delicate materials, Vilene tape can be used to protect edges against distorting and stretching while sewing.

TIP: Until you have gained experienced making patterns, note on the pattern piece whether seam allowance has been added.

DARTS

Essentially a fold or pinch in fabric, darts are triangular shapes used to take excess material out of a garment to fit it to the human form.

Darts transform flat fabric into a 3-D shape. Most commonly used with woven fabrics, they are typically positioned in the following places on a garment: bust, back shoulder blade, back waist, front waist, back hip/buttocks, and side seam at the hip. A dart narrows to a point as it approaches the area around which the fabric is being shaped.

To sew a dart, fold the fabric and then sew down the length of the fold. Finishing the stitch line just before the tip of the dart will ensure you don't create a sharp, conical shape, which can be unattractive in areas such as the bust. Instead, aim to tease the material at the tip of the dart so that it seamlessly blends into the body of the garment.

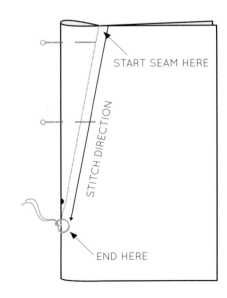

START SEAM HERE

STITCH DIRECTION

END HERE

NOTCHES

Notches are markers that indicate where two sides of a seam are to be aligned and sewn together. They are particularly useful along curved seams and to distinguish between the front and back of an armhole where one notch is used for the front and two are used for the back of the armhole. They also indicate construction points of a garment, e.g., knee level. The diagram on the right shows an example of notches on a sleeve pattern piece.

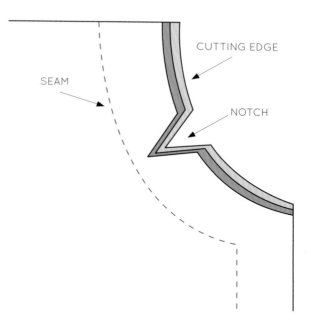

CUTTING EDGE

SEAM

NOTCH

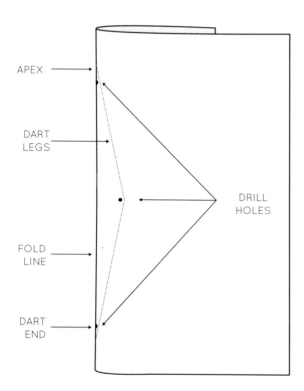

APEX

DART LEGS

DRILL HOLES

FOLD LINE

DART END

DRILL HOLES

Drill holes indicate the position of a number of details that the machinists or manufacturer must be aware of. The most common are:

• Corners and position of pockets
• Sewing/topstitching guidelines
• End of darts
• Corners to clip
• Buttons and buttonholes

The diagram to the left shows an example of drill holes on a bodice block.

114.
CLOSURES: ZIPPERS

Zippers are made up of two sets of interlocking teeth, each connected to a strip of fabric tape known as the zipper tape. The teeth are usually formed of metal, plastic, or synthetic material. The zipper tape is usually polyester, but it can be dyed or printed when used as a styling detail. A slider with a zipper pull is used to open and close the zipper. Besides being a decorative styling detail, its most common purposes are to:

- Increase or decrease the size of an opening.
- Join or separate two ends or sides of a single garment, as in the front of a jacket.
- Attach or detach one part of the garment to or from another—e.g., the hood of a coat.

TYPES OF ZIPPERS

INVISIBLE/CONCEALED ZIPPERS
Invisible zippers are most often used in dresses and skirts, or when using delicate material. The teeth are located on the back side of the zipper and usually have a dainty teardrop pull.

EXPOSED ZIPPERS
Exposed zippers are sewn onto the outside of the garment, so the entire zipper is exposed. Popularized by Herve Leger, they can also give an industrial and deconstructed aesthetic to garments such as parkas.

OPEN-ENDED ZIPPERS
These are used when both of the zipper halves are required to fully detach from each other. They are most commonly used on jackets.

METAL ZIPPERS
These have two lines of metal teeth that have been molded and placed on either side of the tape at regular intervals. They are most commonly found on jeans and accessories such as bags and can be sprayed any color.

PLASTIC ZIPPERS
Plastic zippers serve the same purpose as metal zippers and are made in the same way, although the teeth are plastic, not metal. They can be made using plastic in any color. They are a little more forgiving than metal zippers when going around corners, so they are often used in luggage.

YKK ZIPPERS
These are the industry standard and often a fit requirement within retail.

FLY FRONTS
The standard way to fasten trousers, a zipper usually starts at hip level and finishes at the waistband, allowing trousers to go over the hips and fasten at the waist. Zipper guards are stitched behind the zipper tape, as shown below, to prevent the skin from coming into contact with the zipper.

The structure of a zipper.

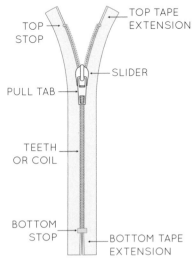

TOP TAPE EXTENSION

TOP STOP

SLIDER

PULL TAB

TEETH OR COIL

BOTTOM STOP

BOTTOM TAPE EXTENSION

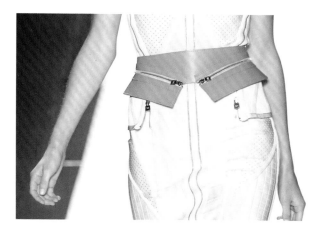

Above: *A selection of Herve Leger pieces showing exposed zips.* Below right: *Moncler Gamme Rouge, Paris Fashion Week Fall/Winter 2016.*

115.
CLOSURES: BUTTONS

When working with woven fabrics that have limited stretch, a pattern cutter must consider openings and closures. Openings through which parts of the body must pass, such as the neckline or an armhole, will more than likely need some sort of closure. Necklines, where the head has a larger circumference than the neck, will definitely need consideration, unless the garment is made from stretch material or is oversized and simply pulls on.

It is good to familiarize yourself with the most common closures and know how to select the correct one for the end use. Note that, as a rule of thumb, men's fastenings are on the right and women's are on the left. There are numerous weird and wonderful reasons as to why this is the case—ranging from the tradition that typically men dressed themselves, whereas women were dressed by servants (who found it easier to button from their right), to ease of breastfeeding.

BUTTON SIZE AND POSITION

If a garment has a Center Front (CF) opening, the buttons should be sewn on the CF. Be careful to choose the right size of button—if it's too small or too large, the closure will be useless—and consider how the button looks proportionally in relation to the garment.

The size of a button is measured using the standard of ligne (L). The button size chart below uses the internationally recognized standard of ligne (L)—the circumference of the button measured in millimeters divided by two.

SINGLE-BREASTED CLOSURES

Buttons rest in the center of all single-breasted garments, so when fastened, the button will sit half to the right and half to the left of the CF.

To avoid this placement, position the buttons as shown to make a button stand. A button stand is created by turning the material of the garment back on itself to create a panel that is two or three layers of material thick, and robust enough to sew the buttons to and create the buttonholes from. It doesn't require sewing on a separate strip.

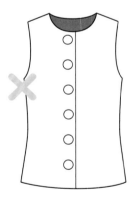 

LIGNE TO IMPERIAL AND METRIC CONVERSION TABLE									
LIGNE	18 L	20 L	22 L	24 L	28 L	30 L	32 L	34 L	36 L	40 L
METRIC	10 mm	13 mm	14 mm	16 mm	18 mm	19 mm	21 mm	22 mm	22 mm	25 mm
INCH	3/8 in	1/2 in	9/16 in	5/8 in	11/16 in	3/4 in	13/16 in	7/8 in	7/8 in	1 in

The width of the button stand should measure half the diameter of the button plus ³/₈ inch (1 cm), to ensure there is always a ³/₈-inch gap between the edge of the button and the edge of the garment. Buttonholes are on average ³/₈ inch longer than the button diameter.

DOUBLE-BREASTED CLOSURES

Predominantly used on outerwear and quintessentially linked to trench coats, in particular the iconic Burberry trench, double-breasted buttons are commonly equidistant from the CF line on the right- and left-hand sides.

CONCEALED PLACKET

A concealed placket, also known as a French front, is a self-grown piece of fabric behind which all buttons or fastenings are hidden. Self-grown means that the detail—in this case the placket—is an extension of the material used in the body of the garment. The placket extends from the CF without any seams.

Above: Single-breasted mac, Burberry, Fall/Winter 2016.
Below left: Double-breasted mac, Burberry, Fall/Winter 2016.
Below right: Loris Diran jacket with concealed placket, Fall/Winter 2016.

116.
ANNOTATING PAPER PATTERNS

Mastering the skill of annotating your paper pattern is vital. These details instruct the machinist or manufacturer on how to cut the pattern from the fabric and create the first "toile"—a prototype garment that is made to check the pattern and fit (see page 168).

Pattern cutters use a combination of symbols, color codes, and technical terms that are added to the pattern to explain to the machinist or manufacturer everything from the choice of fabric to the number of pattern pieces to be cut from that pattern. All annotations should be clear and written in upper case.

THE MOST COMMON ANNOTATIONS USED IN PATTERN CUTTING

- **Grain line**—The first and most important annotation. Marked onto the pattern piece by an arrow and usually parallel to the center back or center front seam, the grain line instructs which way the machines should lay the pattern piece onto the fabric (see Understanding Grain Lines, page 159).
- **Style name**—Written along the grain line.
- **Pattern number**—Used for identification between the designer, pattern cutter, and machinist or manufacturer.
- **Season**—For example, SS16 (Spring/Summer 2016).
- **Style of garment**—For example, dress.
- **An abbreviation of the fabric being used.**
- **Name of the pattern piece**—For example, sleeve.
- **Seam allowance**—Usually included at $^3/_8$ inch (1 cm), but if omitted write "no seam allowance."
- **Number of patterns to be cut**—Use x to represent the item to be cut followed by the number of pieces to be cut—for example, "sleeve x 2."

- **Identify fabric**—Colored pens are used to illustrate the fabric each pattern piece is to be cut from. Use pencil or black pen for the main fabric, also known as the self-fabric. Blue pen identifies if a second fabric is to be used within the same garment. Green pen is used for the lining and red pen for the interfacing.
- **Center front/center back lines**—Identified by CF/CB to identify the center lines.
- **Pleats and tucks**—Mark the direction in which the pleat or tuck should be folded using diagonal lines.
- **Gathers**—Annotated by drawing a wavy line along the length of the area to be gathered and specifying the measurement to gather to—for example, "gathering to 8 inches."
- **Right side up**—All patterns are drafted to be cut right side up, so mark RSU in red pen on each pattern piece.
- **Facing lines**—A separate pattern piece is drafted for the facing, but the facing line is annotated on the main pattern piece using a line of dots and dashes to illustrate where the facing is to be stitched to the main fabric.
- **Shading**—Illustrates details—for example, pockets. Red or broken lines are also used.
- **Seam allowance, notches, and drill holes**—See pages 160–161.

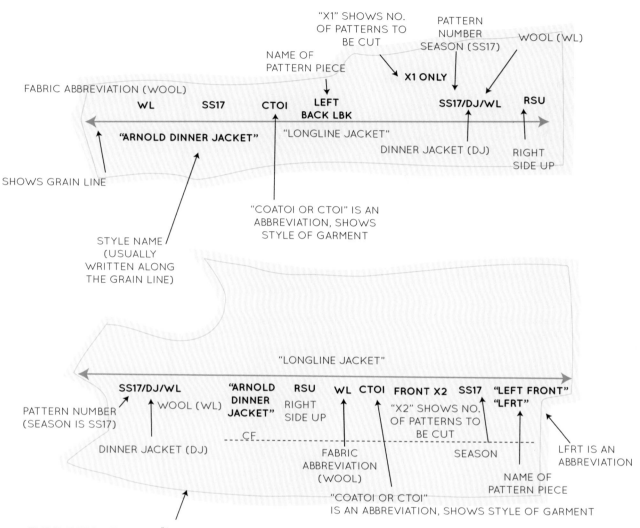

FABRIC ABBREVIATION (WOOL)

"X1" SHOWS NO. OF PATTERNS TO BE CUT

NAME OF PATTERN PIECE

PATTERN NUMBER SEASON (SS17)

WOOL (WL)

WL   SS17   CTOI   LEFT BACK LBK   X1 ONLY   SS17/DJ/WL   RSU

"ARNOLD DINNER JACKET"   "LONGLINE JACKET"

SHOWS GRAIN LINE

DINNER JACKET (DJ)

RIGHT SIDE UP

STYLE NAME (USUALLY WRITTEN ALONG THE GRAIN LINE)

"COATOI OR CTOI" IS AN ABBREVIATION, SHOWS STYLE OF GARMENT

"LONGLINE JACKET"

SS17/DJ/WL   WOOL (WL)   "ARNOLD DINNER JACKET"   RSU RIGHT SIDE UP   WL   CTOI   FRONT X2   SS17   "LEFT FRONT" "LFRT"

PATTERN NUMBER (SEASON IS SS17)

"X2" SHOWS NO. OF PATTERNS TO BE CUT

DINNER JACKET (DJ)

CF

FABRIC ABBREVIATION (WOOL)

SEASON

LFRT IS AN ABBREVIATION

NAME OF PATTERN PIECE

"COATOI OR CTOI" IS AN ABBREVIATION, SHOWS STYLE OF GARMENT

EVIDENT FROM THE LINE $^3/_8$ INCH FROM EDGE THAT BOTH PATTERN PIECES INCLUDE SEAM ALLOWANCE

Example of a typical dinner jacket block.

167

117.
LAY PLANNING

- -

Lay planning involves arranging each pattern piece prior to cutting to avoid or minimize fabric waste. It involves placing pattern pieces onto material or paper that matches the length and width of the material that will be used to make the garment to make sure it fits. It is also a good tool when pricing and working out total fabric requirements, and ensures you're placing pattern pieces in the most efficient and economical way.

TIP: It's a good idea to do lay planning on paper, which can then be placed over the fabric, to avoid making mistakes directly onto the fabric.

PRODUCING A LAY PLAN

1. Note the usable fabric width, usually 36, 54, or 66 inches wide (90, 140, or 165 cm wide).

2. Note the direction of the fabric—is it a one-way or four-way fabric? This will determine how you place each pattern piece.

3. If you are producing multiple sizes, note how many sizes you are intending to include in the lay.

4. Don't forget to allow for buffering—give yourself allowance around each pattern piece.

5. Lay out each pattern piece, noting the grain line, until you find an arrangement that you're happy with.

6. You're now ready to cut your pattern and create your first toile.

When lay planning, it is critical to understand grain lines, which, along with gravity, affect how the fabric will hang (see page 159).

118.
MAKING A TOILE

- -

A toile is a prototype made to test the fit of a garment. Besides allowing you to see if your block is working, the toile demonstrates whether the garment meets the designer's brief. But the main purpose of a toile is to allow for fit adjustments, and it is therefore one of the most important stages of creating your garment.

Select a fabric with the same characteristics of handle and weight as your final fabric. Calico is the most common material used for toiling, as it is reasonably priced, 100-percent cotton, and available in various weights—from muslin and cheesecloth to heavy calicos. When coated, it's crisp and flat, but it can also be washed to make it hang and drape.

TIP: Source secondhand materials from markets at wholesale stores for toiling. Even old bedsheets and curtains can be utilized!

THE TOILING PROCESS

The machinist or manufacturer cuts and sews the toile before trying it on a mannequin, also known as "the stand" or fit model. Then begins the adjustment process on the path to the final pattern.

Typically, adjustments are made to the first toile on the stand and then transferred to the master paper pattern. Then a second toile is produced, and the process is repeated. It may take up to six or seven toiles before the designer, pattern cutter, and machinist are all satisfied that the pattern is absolutely accurate and ready to proceed with the correct fabric.

Precision is imperative at the toiling stage. However, due to the number of toiles that may have to be made, it is not necessary to take the additional time to secure the thread ends.

Bridal gown toile on a mannequin.

119.
UNDERSTANDING THE MOULAGE PROCESS

The two most common methods used when making garments are flat pattern cutting (see pages 156–157) and moulage—working on the stand. With moulage, the designer or pattern cutter uses material and dress pins to create directly onto the mannequin. This is a more organic way of dressmaking and less technical than flat pattern cutting. Pattern pieces are traced onto paper from the finished garment in much the same way as when taking a pattern from a purchased sample.

ADVANTAGES OF THE MOULAGE PROCESS

The moulage process allows the designer or pattern cutter to instantly see the effect of gravity—the weight, handle, and behavior of the fabric, and how it hangs from the stand or human form. All garments are suspended from points such as the shoulder or waist and by working directly onto the stand; any issues around the behavior of the fabric can be more easily identified and resolved.

Ninety-nine percent of designers and pattern cutters would advocate working on a real-life model rather than a mannequin. Why? Because "a dummy can't talk back!" This is not always possible and indeed can be costly if paying for a fit model (a model of industry standard size). Predictably, mannequins are frequently used in industry and colleges.

SIZING

Before starting to create a pattern, whether flat pattern cutting or working on the stand, all designers and pattern cutters need to consider the person for whom the garment is being made. Therefore, selecting the correct mannequin is crucial. It is wise to determine a set of measurements, whether dressmaking at home, at school, or at the industry level. You can create a unique size chart by taking the following measurements:

- Bust
- Waist
- Hip
- Thigh
- Inseam
- Outseam or waist to ankle
- Circumference of the knee
- Circumference of the ankle
- Waist to hip
- Waist to mid-hip
- Waist to knee
- Nape to waist
- Shoulder (neck point to shoulder point)
- Cross shoulder at front
- Cross shoulder at back
- Cross front armhole
- Cross back armhole
- Circumference of the neck
- Shoulder neck point to bust level
- Shoulder neck point to waist at back
- Armhole
- Sleeve length (shoulder point to wrist)
- Elbow (shoulder point to elbow)
- Circumference of the wrist

KENNET AND LINDSELL'S BSD MANNEQUIN MEASUREMENTS

SIZE	BUST	WAIST	HIPS	BACK NECK WIDTH (BNW)
6 US	32 ¼ in (83 cm)	23 ¼ in (59 cm)	34 ¼ in (87 cm)	15 ¾ in (40 cm)
8 US	34 ¼ in (87 cm)	25 ¼ in (64 cm)	36 ¼ in (92 cm)	16 in (40.5 cm)
10 US	36 ¼ in (92 cm)	27 ¼ in (69 cm)	38 ¼ in (97 cm)	16 ⅛ in (41 cm)
12 US	38 ¼ in (97 cm)	29 ¼ in (74 cm)	40 ¼ in (102 cm)	16 ¼ in (41.5 cm)
14 US	40 ¼ in (102 cm)	31 ¼ in (79 cm)	42 ¼ in (107 cm)	16 ½ in (42 cm)
16 US	42 ½ in (108 cm)	33 ½ in (85 cm)	44 ½ in (113 cm)	16 ¾ in (42.5 cm)
18 US	44 ¾ in (114 cm)	35 ¾ in (91 cm)	46 ¾ in (119 cm)	16 ¾ in (42.5 cm)

Within education and industry, US size 6 or 8 is the most common size of mannequin used. This chart chart shows Kennet and Lindsell's BSD mannequin measurements of US sizes 6–18. Mannequins come in a variety of shapes and sizes to accommodate industry and customer demographic of a specific country—for example, the Japanese market would require a mannequin with a smaller hip measurement than, say, the US, to reflect the shape of their core customer.

NOTE: Most patterns and prototypes are made in a US size 6 before being graded up or down—with a 2-inch (5 cm) difference in circumference between sizes—to accommodate the size run.

120.
LEARNING TO FIT ON A MANNEQUIN OR MODEL

- -

At various stages throughout the toiling process, the designer, pattern cutter, and machinists will try the garment on either a mannequin or real-life model to check—and adjust, where necessary—the fit of the garment. It is always preferable to fit on real-life models—not only because they can give invaluable feedback about how the garment is fitting and performing, but also because changing body shapes have meant that not all mannequins accurately represent the human form.

Within the industry, fit models will be measured weekly to ensure they comply with a company's standard measurements and to accommodate any slight changes in body shapes from week to week. Due to time and cost restraints, it is not always possible to use real-life models, so being able to fit on both a fit model and a mannequin is an essential skill within the pattern-cutting process.

THE KEY STAGES OF FITTING A GARMENT

1. Look at the frame of the garment—notice the general aesthetic, and check the symmetry, that hems are even, and that the balance and proportion look right.

2. Look at the center front (CF) and center back (CB) lines and ensure they hang vertically, unless the designer or pattern cutter has intended for them not to.

3. Repeat with the side seams.

4. Check that the width of the neckline corresponds to the specifications given by the designer and that the shoulder neck points are standing at the correct distance from both sides of the neck.

5. Check the armhole. It's important that the fit model doesn't feel restricted when moving the arm up and down, and forward and backward.

6. Check that there is the right amount of suppression in the darts, and that the darts are following the contour of the body as intended. There should be no tautness or excess. If needed, let the dart out so that the garment lies flat against the body. The dart should point in the direction of the body part it is compensating for, e.g., point toward the bust.

7. Throughout the fitting process, try to pin excess fabric, rather than cutting it, because this is a more temporary adjustment. You can always take more off, but it's difficult and time-consuming to add fabric on if an incorrect cut is made. One of the benefits of working on the stand as opposed to a real model is being able to pin directly onto the torso, as the mannequin is made of compressed fibers that are then covered with a layer of cotton.

8. Note: it is not necessary to apply fastenings at the toile stage, as this is labor-intensive and has cost implications—dressmaking pins are adequate in the interim.

TIP: If you are using a real-life fit model, try to get as much feedback from the model as possible at every stage of the fit process.

172

121.
EMBRACING TECHNOLOGY WITHIN PATTERN CUTTING

As with many of the skills associated with fashion design, technology affects pattern cutting. Most students are trained to use computer-aided design (CAD) (see page 53), as well as hand drawing (see page 52) and most colleges have digital pattern software and equipment.

It is important to embrace this technology—speed and increased accuracy are just two of the benefits it brings. However, it's essential for pattern cutters to learn and understand the skill of pattern cutting by hand. Using hand and digital techniques on a project can bring about the best results—work by hand until you're happy with your pattern, then use digital techniques to complete repetitive and time-consuming tasks later in the process.

THE DIGITAL PATTERN-CUTTING METHOD

There are three methods of getting the master block onto your computer screen in order to start the digital pattern process:

1. Photograph and upload the block onto your computer—this is the easiest method.

2. Use a digitizer and digitizing table to select and click on different parts of the pattern, working in a clockwise direction to methodically trace its outline.

3. Use a scanner. This can be an expensive piece of equipment, due to it having to be large enough to accommodate the garment.

Once the block is uploaded, software is used to annotate the pattern, insert notches and pleats, add or remove seams and seam allowance, create facings and linings, and more. The fully annotated pattern can be printed and used as a paper pattern. In mass-production factories, the digital pattern is used to digitally cut the fabric for a garment. Measurements are sent to high-speed deep-ply cutting machines that are able to cut multiple layers of material.

ADVANTAGES OF DIGITAL PATTERN CUTTING

The benefits of digital pattern cutting are enormous—especially within an industry built on mass production. Even at the earliest stage of designing, spec sheets can be emailed directly to the factory, saving days in transit, reducing lead times, and increasing speed to market. Digital pattern cutting also boasts space-saving and environmental benefits—a digital library of blocks preferable to cardboard cutouts taking up space in a pattern-cutting studio.

Increased accuracy—measurements as precise as 0.001 millimeters and the speed and ease of grading patterns and producing multiple copies—all mean digital pattern is the universally preferred method.

A well-rounded fashion designer should have a solid understanding of both traditional and digital pattern-making methods. This enables good working relationships with pattern cutters and machinists alike. Technology exists as an aid to the pattern-cutting process—one of many tools, along with pencil, paper, and scissors.

122.
PLEATS AND TUCKS

Pleats are folds in the fabric of a garment, most commonly found in skirts. They can be used to add extra volume, to allow space for movement, or to control excess fabric. They are created by folding fabric back on itself and securing it into place. When sewn into place, pleats are called tucks. Pressed pleats are ironed or heat-set into a permanent crease; unpressed pleats are left to fall into soft folds.

Pleats are used to gather a wide piece of fabric to a narrower circumference and to add fullness. However, both pleats and tucks can be used purely as design details, as demonstrated by the master of pleats, Issey Miyake. Pleats are measured by degrees of fullness—the thickness or volume of pleats in relation to the original width of fabric— where "zero fullness" is flat fabric without pleats and "100-percent fullness" is fabric that measures half the width it did before pleating.

THE FIVE MOST COMMON TYPES OF PLEATS

1. ACCORDION
Narrow, heat-set pleats that create a raised zigzag pattern.

2. BOX
Fabric is folded to create a box. Most commonly found on men's shirts in the center of the back, just below the shoulder.

3. KNIFE
Pleats that all face in the same direction, 1-inch (2.5 cm) wide— e.g., the kilt.

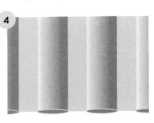

4. ORGAN
Parallel rows of softly rounded pleats.

5. INVERTED
Two folds brought to a center point and pressed—e.g., the A-line skirt.

123.
COLLARS

In its simplest form, the collar is a strip of material that wraps around the neck and is attached to the bodice of a garment at the neckline. It is most commonly made from a separate piece of material from the bodice, rather than an extension of the material used for the main body. It can be permanently attached through stitching or it can be detachable. A collar is made up of two parts—the collar and the collar stand—and the parts of a collar are shown below.

TYPES OF COLLARS

The three main categories of collars are:

- Standing/Stand-up—Standing up around the neck, rather than lying on the shoulder.
- Turnover—Standing around the neck and then folded down to meet the shoulder.
- Flat/Falling—Lying flat on the shoulders.

Collars have many weird and wonderful names, the origins of which date back hundreds of years. Below are the most common men's and women's collars.

CLASSIC

STANDARD

TAB COLLAR

EYELET COLLAR

HIDDEN BUTTON

SEMI-SPREAD

SPREAD

ITALIAN SPREAD

BRITISH SPREAD

TWO-BUTTON COLLAR BAND

BUTTON-DOWN

WING TIP

175

124.
THE ANATOMY OF A SEWING MACHINE

Sewing machines vary according to the model and
manufacturer and all have their own idiosyncrasies
when it comes to threading! Most machines share the
same basic components, so make yourself familiar with
the diagram below. Machines don't require a lot of
maintenance, but try to have yours serviced regularly
and keep it clean of dust created by fibers.

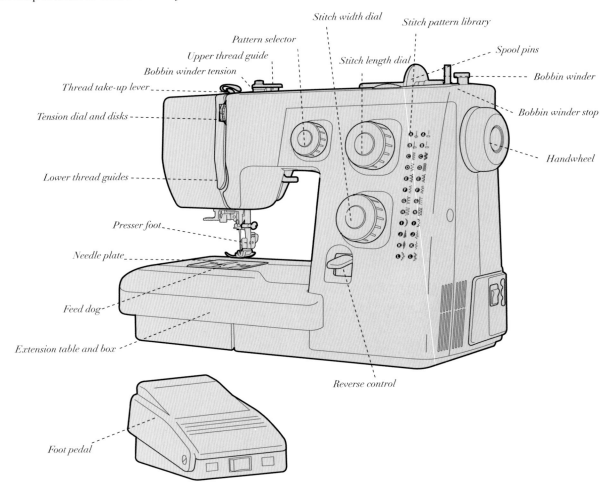

Stitch width dial

Stitch pattern library

Pattern selector

Spool pins

Upper thread guide

Stitch length dial

Bobbin winder tension

Bobbin winder

Thread take-up lever

Tension dial and disks

Bobbin winder stop

Lower thread guides

Handwheel

Presser foot

Needle plate

Feed dog

Extension table and box

Reverse control

Foot pedal

125.
WINDING THE BOBBIN

Winding the bobbin correctly takes a little practice but is an essential skill to master to ensure the smooth running of your machine. It's the first thing you'll do before threading your machine.

HOW TO WIND THE BOBBIN

1. Loosen the small wheel on the side of the machine to disengage the needle and stop it from moving as the bobbin is wound.

2. Open the bobbin cover and remove the bobbin spool from its rounded metal case. Make sure the bobbin spool is empty.

3. Place a spool of your chosen thread on the spool pin on top of the sewing machine. When the spool turns, the thread should be released counterclockwise—if it isn't, flip it upside down.

4. Pass the thread through the bobbin winder tension slot and wind the end of the thread around the bobbin a few times to secure it.

5. Place the bobbin onto the bobbin pin. Slide the pin into place so the bobbin is engaged for winding.

6. Press the foot pedal to start winding the bobbin. Continue until the bobbin is full.

7. Slide the bobbin pin to release it and lift the bobbin off. Cut the thread, leaving approximately 3 inches (8 cm) of thread trailing from the bobbin.

126.
THREADING THE MACHINE

Having wound your bobbin, it's now time to get the machine ready to sew. Make sure you switch off the power when doing this part—you don't want to stitch your fingers!

HOW TO THREAD THE MACHINE

1. Re-engage the needle by tightening the handwheel.

2. Put the bobbin back into its metal case and unwind a few inches of thread from the bobbin. Meanwhile, your other spool of thread will stay where it was at the top of the machine when you were winding the bobbin.

3. Replace the bobbin and its holder in the machine and close the bobbin cover.

4. Pass the thread from the spool on top of the machine through the thread guide.

5. Take the thread up to the take-up lever—the metal part that has an eyelet in it—and through the eyelet.

6. Pass the thread through the eye of the needle, and pull the loose end down between the two forks of the presser foot.

7. Turn the handwheel forward until thread from the bobbin is passed up through the needle plate. Pull the bobbin thread until you can see a few inches of it.

Now you're ready to sew some exciting creations.

127.
UNDERSTANDING SEWING MACHINE STITCHES

Here is a brief summary of the most common machine stitches and their uses.

COMMON STITCHES

STRAIGHT STITCH

As the name suggests, this stitch simply goes in a straight line! It's the simplest and most commonly used stitch.

The standard stitch will be aligned in the center of the sewing machine foot, but a variation of this stitch is a setting to align the stitch far to the left of the foot—this will allow you to stitch very closely to the edge of a piece of fabric.

One common use of the straight stitch is topstitching—a visible line of stitching on the right side of a garment that runs parallel to a seam and can be used to secure a hem.

ZIGZAG STITCH

Again, the name is self-explanatory. The needle moves from side to side as the fabric moves forward. Both the width and length of the stitch can be adjusted. Zigzag stitch is often used for making buttonholes and stitching around appliqué (see page 184).

THREE-STEP ZIGZAG STITCH

This can be used when a wider zigzag stitch is needed—it prevents the fabric bunching up, which can happen if too wide of a conventional zigzag stitch is used.

BLIND HEM AND STRETCH BLIND HEM

Blind hem is used for hemming woven fabrics. This stitch is practically invisible from the right side. Stretch blind hem is similar, but is used on knitted fabrics.

OVERLOCK

This stitch is used to both join and finish two pieces of fabric, preventing fraying (see Overlocking, page 180).

DECORATIVE STITCHES

All machines come with a vast array of decorative stitches, which can be used to add some excitement to a garment.

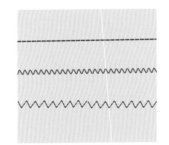

Straight Stitch, Zigzag Stitch, Three-Step Zigzag Stitch

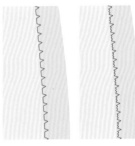

Blind Hem and Stretch Blind Hem

Overlock

Decorative Stitches

132.
EMBROIDERY

Embroidery is a way of decorating fabric by using a needle and thread or yarn. It is one of the oldest techniques of fabric decoration—examples that date back to 5th century B.C. have been found in China. Because of its simplicity, embroidery is prominent in many cultures and in many traditional costumes.

A typical use of embroidery is to produce a logo or monogram on a piece of clothing. Most commonly applied to woven fabrics where little stretch means the design won't distort, it is also possible to embroider knitted fabrics.

HAND EMBROIDERY

Special thread is usually used for embroidering by hand. The main difference between this and standard sewing thread is that it is thicker, meaning that fewer stitches have an impact.

Hand embroidery is often done with the fabric stretched and pinned over an embroidery frame or hoop. Fabric is kept taut to maintain the integrity of the design.

MACHINE EMBROIDERY

Most mass-produced embroidered garments are made using computerized embroidery machines. Embroidery software is used to program the design. The machine then uses a number of threads in different colors to quickly create the motif.

Above: *Contour Style Renata in Bloom, Dressed to Kill, 2013.* Below: *Vintage embroidered kimono.*

133.
APPLIQUÉ

Appliqué describes the process of attaching one piece of fabric to the surface of another. This can be for any number of reasons—it could be a patch, an embroidered badge, a logo, or a single part of a more intricate pattern. Sometimes appliqué is built up over multiple layers.

Appliqué can be done either by hand or on the sewing machine—the principles are the same. Most of the time, the design will be held in place with a quick and easy straight stitch, and then a zigzag or decorative satin stitch will be used around the edge of the piece to finish it neatly.

HOW TO MAKE AND APPLY APPLIQUÉS

Fusible webbing is a thin, heat-sensitive sheet used to attach one piece of fabric to another before the finishing stitches are added. The process below uses this webbing, but you could just as easily substitute a straight hand stitch to temporarily hold the fabric in place before applying finishing stitches.

1. Trace the appliqué design onto the paper side of the fusible webbing.
2. Cut around the design, leaving a margin of approximately ¼ inch (5 mm) around the lines.
3. Turn your chosen appliqué fabric to the wrong side. Use a dry iron to fuse the web onto the fabric, following the manufacturer's instructions.
4. Cut out the appliqué piece of fabric by following the lines.
5. Peel the backing paper off the fusible web and place the piece onto the garment, web side down (so that the right side of the appliqué fabric is facing up). Make sure you are happy with the placement.
6. Place a cloth over the design and use an iron to fuse the web in place, again following the manufacturer's instructions.
7. Decide if you want the edging thread match the appliqué fabric, the background fabric, or contrast with both. With your chosen thread, stitch around the edge of the design by hand or with the zigzag stitch on a sewing machine.

Above: *Gucci appliqué, Milan Fashion Week, Fall/Winter 2015.* Right: *Heavy metal denim waistcoat with appliquéd band patches.*

134.
UNDERSTANDING THE FIT PROCESS

The fit of a garment is integral to its design. It determines not only a garment's sizing, quality, and performance, but also its aesthetic. Is the skirt maxi or midi length? Should the jean sit above the anklebone or is it an ankle grazer?

How a garment fits and makes you feel is in many cases as important as the design itself. You feel different in a suit or prom dress than you do when wearing a sweater and pants or sportswear. What you wear can significantly affect both how you feel and how you're perceived. That's the theory behind the old adage, "Dress for the job you want, not the job you have!"

Fit is important from a cost perspective, for both start-up brands and retail giants. With the ongoing rise of online fashion shopping, where e-tailers are challenging traditional main street shopping, the fit process has never been more crucial to the success of a brand. From a shipping and logistics point of view, the cost of reprocessing a returned garment can be as much as twice the price of the item, so it has a huge effect on profitability. Coupled with ever-changing consumer body shapes and the fact that the average woman tries on 15 pairs of jeans before committing to buy, getting the fit right is imperative.

Most retailers and large design houses employ technologists—specialists in fitting and quality control—but it's essential that, as a designer, you also understand this process.

THE FIT PROCESS

Key to this is a prototype, which is made either by working on the stand (see pages 170–172) or from a paper pattern (see pages 156–157). The fit process is essentially the same whether you're a small brand or fitting for a bulk 10,000-unit order.

STEP 1: PROTOTYPE.

A sample is sent for comment from the supplier, or in-house pattern room, or created by your own hard work. All other sizes will be graded up or down from this prototype, so the first step is to check the fit of the sample. For details about how to do this, see the fitting guides for womenswear and footwear (see pages 186–190). The standard sample sizes for fit purposes are US size 6 for women and Medium top/32 waist and leg pants/40 inch chest for men.

STEP 2: RED SEAL

If a garment needs amending, it is "red-sealed," which means a red tag is attached to it and it is sent back to the pattern room or factory with fit comments. A second sample is made and submitted.

STEP 3: GREEN SEAL

In response to the feedback you gave with the red seal sample, an amended prototype will then be submitted for approval. The revised sample will be created in the factory in which the final production run will take place, using all of the bulk materials and methods that will be employed in the final item. If the revised sample is not right, it's red-sealed again. If it's perfect, it's approved, and it's from this "green seal" sample that all other sizes are graded and bulk production can begin.

STEP 4: GOLD SEAL

A final sample, picked at random from the bulk production run, is submitted to compare with the green seal sample. Once this is approved, the product is ready to be delivered into the warehouse or directly to stores.

135.
FITTING: CLOTHING

The fit process is essentially the same across menswear, womenswear, footwear, bags, and accessories. However, over the next few sections we'll look at fitting clothing, footwear, bags, and accessories in a little more detail, including best practices when fitting.

In all cases it's much better to fit on a real model than a stand—after all, a mannequin can't talk back to you about how something feels. Get as much feedback from your fit model as possible—from a fit and comfort perspective to personal taste. Would they buy it? How much would they be willing to spend on it?

FIRST FITS AND AMENDMENTS

Within the retail sector, it is a best practice for designers to attend all first fits, as this is where the majority of

aesthetic comments are made and changes occur. Make sure styling/fabric/trim comments are communicated before fit amendments are made.

When listing comments, start from top to bottom then back to front. When amending measurements, make sure to give the finished measurement—e.g., "reduce by ½ inch to measure 6 inches." Take and attach photos of all amendments where possible—or even better, Skype your pattern cutter or the factory with any particularly tricky amendments.

KEY MEASUREMENTS

The diagram below and table opposite shows key measurement points on the body and standard measurements for US sizes.

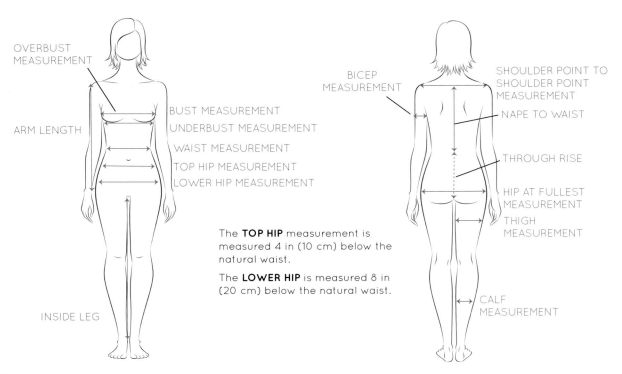

OVERBUST MEASUREMENT

ARM LENGTH

BUST MEASUREMENT
UNDERBUST MEASUREMENT
WAIST MEASUREMENT
TOP HIP MEASUREMENT
LOWER HIP MEASUREMENT

INSIDE LEG

BICEP MEASUREMENT

SHOULDER POINT TO SHOULDER POINT MEASUREMENT

NAPE TO WAIST

THROUGH RISE

HIP AT FULLEST MEASUREMENT

THIGH MEASUREMENT

CALF MEASUREMENT

The **TOP HIP** measurement is measured 4 in (10 cm) below the natural waist.

The **LOWER HIP** is measured 8 in (20 cm) below the natural waist.

QUESTIONS TO ASK YOUR FIT MODEL

- Is it easy to put on?
- Are openings/fastenings required?
- How is the general fit?
- How is the movement?
- How does the lining fit?
- Is the fabric comfortable—not itchy, etc.?
- Is the neckline sitting in the correct place?
- Is the hem the right length?
- Is the garment okay to walk in?
- Is it see-through?
- Are the shoulder seams sitting correctly on the shoulder—not too tight or too wide?
- Is there any pulling across the shoulder blades?

KEY MEASUREMENTS IN INCHES : US SIZES

MEASUREMENT POINT	4	6	8	10	12	14	16	18
Across shoulders—point to point	14 ¾	15	15 ¼	15 ¾	16 ¼	16 ¾	17	18
Sleeve length—long	23	23	23	23	23	23	23	23
Biceps at widest point	9 ¾	10	10 ½	11	11 ½	12 ¼	12 ¾	13 ¾
Bust at fullest point	30 ¾	31 ¾	32 ¾	34 ¾	36 ¾	38 ½	40 ½	43 ½
Underbust	26	27 ¼	28 ¼	30 ¼	32 ¼	34 ¼	36 ¼	36 ½
Waist at narrowest point	23 ½	24 ½	25 ½	27 ½	29 ½	31 ½	33 ½	92.5
Top hip—4 in (10 cm) from waist	30	31	32	34	36	37 ¾	39 ¾	42 ¾
Lower hip—8 in (20 cm) from waist	33	34	35	37	38 ¾	40 ¾	42 ¾	45 ¾
Thigh—1 in (2.5 cm) below crotch point	19 ¼	20	20 ½	21 ¾	23	24	25	27
Inside leg	32	32	32	32	32	32	32	32
Through rise—measured from natural front and back	25 ½	26	26 ¼	27	28	28 ¾	29 ½	30 ¼
Nape to waist	15 ¾	15 ¾	15 ¾	15 ¾	15 ¾	15 ¾	15 ¾	15 ¾
Foot size	4	5	6	7	8	9	10	11
Calf measurement	13 ¾	14	14 ¼	14 ½	14 ¾	15	15 ¼	15 ½

STANDARD MEASUREMENTS FOR KEY LENGTHS US SIZE 8

DRESS LENGTHS	From side neck point (SNP) to hem edge	Mini	33 7/8 in (86 cm)
		Short	34 5/8 in (88 cm)
		Knee	35 1/2 in (90 cm)
		Midi	43 3/8 in/45 1/4 in (110 cm/115 cm)
		Maxi	57 1/8 in/59 in (145 cm/150 cm)
SKIRT LENGTHS	Center back (CB) top edge (true waist) to CB hem edge	Micro mini	13–13 3/4 in (33–35 cm)
		Mini	15–15 1/4 in (38–40 cm)
		Midi	27 1/2 in (70 cm)
		Maxi—day	41–41 3/4 in (104–106 cm)
		Maxi—evening	42 1/8–42 7/8 in (107–109 cm)
SLEEVE LENGTHS	Overarm true shoulder point to cuff edge	Short sleeve	4 3/8–5 7/8 in (11–15 cm)
		Three-quarter sleeve	17 3/4–18 7/8 in (45–48 cm)
		Long sleeve	24 3/8 in (62 cm)
		Long sleeve—outerwear	25 1/4 in (64 cm)
LEG LENGTHS	Inseam (regular) from crotch to hem edge	Legging	28 in/28 3/4 in/30 in (71 cm/73 cm/76 cm)
		Skinny jean	31 7/8 in (81 cm)
		Boyfriend jean	30 3/4 in (78 cm)
		Flare jean	33 7/8 in (86 cm)
ARMHOLE STRAIGHT	Point to point	Jersey	7 1/8 in (18 cm)
		Woven—sleeved	7 7/8 in (20 cm)
		Woven—sleeveless	8 1/4 in (21 cm)
ACROSS SHOULDER	True point to point	Blazer—woven	15 3/4–16 1/8 in (40–41 cm)
		Blazer—stretch	15 3/8–15 3/4 in (39–40 cm)
		Woven tops—woven	15 3/8 in (39 cm)
X-FRONT (INSET SLEEVE)	5 in (13 cm) below SNP armhole seam to seam	Woven	12 5/8–13 3/8 in (32–34 cm)
		Jersey	12 1/4–13 in (31–33 cm)
		Outwear/tailoring	13–13 3/4 in (33–35 cm)

136.
FITTING: BAGS AND ACCESSORIES

- -

It may sound strange, but bags and accessories also need to go through a basic fit process. Although the majority of these items are not "fit specific"—in that one size fits all—they must be tested for functionality and aesthetics. In addition to checking that the leather, polyurethane, or yarn requested matches any swatches briefed out to the manufacturer at spec sheet stage, as a designer you need to check that you are happy with how the product looks. Below are the key points and standard measurements to check when fitting bags and accessories.

BAGS

Measure the width, depth, and height of the bag against the measurements specified on the spec sheet. Check the handle drop—imagine the bag on your shoulder, or in your hand if handheld, and measure that point to the top of the bag.

For a shoulder bag, you need to be able to get your arm through it and get the strap onto your shoulder easily—so you need a handle drop of around 9 inches (23 cm) to allow for use with a winter coat. If it's a handheld bag, you need to make sure the handle isn't so long that it drags on the floor.

It is also important to test the handle strength—at industry level this is done using scales, but you can easily do this yourself by inserting weight and checking that the pressure points, where the strap is attached to the bag, are not strained or in danger of tearing. All hardware should be nickel-free, as many people have allergic reactions to it.

BELTS

Again, all fittings should be nickel-free. To determine the correct size of the belt, measure from the end to the middle hole.

GLOVES

Take the dimension of the widest circumference of the glove. Both leather and knit gloves are measured in inches. Check that any lining is correctly attached.

CAPS AND HATS

The total circumference is the standard measurement against which to check.

SCARVES

Check that the yarn is correct and take measurements of the length and width against the spec sheet. When fitting triangular scarves, measure the longest point. Scarves are measured in inches.

EYEWEAR

Measure the temple size, temple to temple, and the lens finish—dark tint/light tint/revo (mirrored lens).

JEWELRY

NECKLACES AND BRACELETS

Check the length of the necklace or bracelet when fastened, excluding the pendant. All jewelry should be nickel-free.

RINGS

The circumference measurement is used when measuring rings, not the diameter. Measurements are taken in millimeters and attributed a numerical size.

137.
FITTING: FOOTWEAR

Arguably more important than the fit of a piece of clothing is the fit of a pair of shoes. A tight sweater is irritating, but uncomfortable shoes are agonizing. Many of us trade comfort for vanity, yet this shouldn't and doesn't have to be the case. Whether buying a sky-high 6-inch Louboutin pump or a $50 pump online, the fit of the shoe is integral to brand loyalty.

All shoes are prototyped and fitted on a US size 5.5. This dates back to when US size 5.5 was the most common shoe size. The American Academy of Orthopedic Surgeons reports that the average female adult in the US now has a shoe size of 9, yet the industry is set up and continues to sample on a US size 5.5. Lasts (see page 138) are still made in a US size 5.5.

The purpose of fitting shoes is to check, quite literally, that "the shoe fits." The designer will also check proportions, the position of the topline and straps, and that the throat of the shoe is sitting where intended (see page 130).

Shoes should be fitted on real models. It is advisable to take the the ankle circumference 4 inches (10 cm) up from the heel and the calf circumference 11¾ inches (30 cm) up from the heel.

MEASURING SHOE SIZE: TRADITIONAL VERSUS MODERN METHODS

The Brannock device, invented in 1925, is the standard foot-measuring tool for the world's footwear industry. If unobtainable, the humble tape measure can also give the numerical indication of the fitting size of your foot.

CHECK THE FOLLOWING WHEN FITTING

- **The weight of the body**—That it is equally distributed.
- **The length**—Check this by eye and by ensuring you can fit one finger in between the heel and the back counter.
- **The heel slip**—Watch the fit model walk the length of the room and note that the heel doesn't slip out of the back of the shoe.
- **Encourage wearer trials**—If there is time, encourage the fit model to wear the shoes over an extended period of time and give feedback about comfort.
- **The toe spring**—The measurement between the bottom of the sole at the toe and the toes should be less than $^3/_8$ inches (10 mm)—note this by eye.
- **The pitch of the shoe**—This is determined by the heel height and the height of the platform. If the fit model's calf contracts when wearing pumps, it is a sure sign that the shoe is too high.

138.
MAKING ALTERATIONS TO FOOTWEAR AND BAGS

Even before the fitting process begins with first samples, it's highly likely that you realize your technical drawings and spec sheets have not been interpreted exactly as you intended. Likewise, seeing your design in 3-D may highlight necessary changes that weren't obvious on the page. Alterations are therefore an important step in design development. Often these will be extremely subtle and minor alterations (a matter of millimeters) to get the product to where you want it to be aesthetically.

FOOTWEAR

With footwear, necessary alterations—the line a piece of fabric needs to take to get the correct shape, for example—are often drawn onto the sample with a special leather-marking silver pen. Alternatively, masking tape can be stuck onto the relevant part of the shoe and drawn onto. An explanatory note written onto the shoe—for example, "reduce back counter height by 2 mm," often accompanies any alterations and lines.

If any additional materials need to be added (for example, if the throat of the shoe needed to be higher), then masking tape is often stuck on the place where the additional fabric needs to be.

HANDBAGS

The process of making alterations to handbags is very similar to that of footwear. However, since bags are larger items and tend to be more malleable, there is more scope for you to affect the 3-D shape in front of you. For example, if a handle was too long, you might trim out the excess length and then tape the handle together again at the correct size. If the gusset of a bag is too wide, the excess might be trimmed away and the new edges will be taped back together.

NEXT STEPS

If any additional hardware needs to be added to both shoes and bags, it would be drawn on in the correct location. Alternatively, alterations can be listed out in an email or note; however, these are much more open to misinterpretation.

Once all alterations are marked, the physical sample is sent back to the sample-making room of your supplier or factory. They will make amendments and send a revised prototype, which is then reviewed again in the same way.

TYPICAL FOOTWEAR ALTERATIONS

- Changing the cut of the topline.
- Lowering or raising the throat.
- Moving a buckle to a new location.
- Changing the positioning of eyelets.

139.
MAKING ALTERATIONS

- - - - - - - - - - - - - - - - - - -

Once a sample is received, the only way to judge it properly is to try it on either a fit model or a mannequin. Make sure the configuration of seam lines in the pattern works for a garment, both from a functional and an aesthetic point of view. You don't want ill-advised pattern decisions to cause unsightly lumps or bumps, so you may have to reconfigure.

HOW TO ALTER THE GARMENT SHAPE

If the garment is too large or loose, fabric can be pinned to reduce volume. Alternatively, the garment can be snipped and basted back together to show how the shape should be. If it is too small or tight, cut into the fabric and add an additional panel, then either pin or stitch it in place.

Assessing the accessibility of the garment is essential at this stage; this means ensuring that it is easy enough to get it on and take it off. The placement and types of fastenings and openings should all be considered to ensure the garment is fully functional. It's always better to make these physical alterations and send them back to your supplier, since emailed notes or phone conversations are more open to misinterpretation.

TYPICAL CLOTHING ADJUSTMENTS

- Changing the position of the waist seam.
- Amending the angle of bust darts.
- Deciding whether the garment needs a yoke seam.
- Increasing the size of an armhole.

140.
CUSTOMIZATION

- - - - - - - - - - - - - - - - - - -

To customize an outfit is to make or alter it to individual or personal specifications. In an age of ever-increasing choice and variety, we all crave individuality. Long before Johnny Rotten used a safety pin in the late 1970s to prevent, as he put it, "the arse of your pants falling out," people were customizing their clothes for both practical and stylistic reasons.

Morphing items of clothing and references can be, in some respects, the purest form of fashion design. Technical design and traditional ideas give way to unconventional design methods, making customization a really exciting technique to utilize and to understand.

KEEP IT SIMPLE

Start experimenting by turning one garment into something else—a jacket into a vest, a round-neck tee into a V-neck, jeans into denim cutoffs. Simply decide on your new silhouette and get cutting!

EXPERIMENT

Aside from customizing to change the silhouette of a garment, there are endless processes that are fun to master. Try cutting and patchworking, dying, bleaching, stitching, printing, slashing, knotting, ripping, distressing, embellishing, embroidering, and appliqué (see page 184). Experiment and have fun!

REINVENT

Customizing can also be a connection to our heritage—a way of preserving history that would have otherwise been discarded by transporting it into the modern day and creating something new and original. A great example of this is the steady popularity of Army surplus stores. Garments such as parkas, bomber jackets, and military jackets—once used as functional uniform—are given a new lease of life as fashion garments. Christopher Raeburn's collections, fashioned mainly from military surplus materials—have been a defining feature of his work since he graduated from art school in 2006.

DIGITAL CUSTOMIZATION

Back in 1999, Nike introduced NIKE ID—a digital platform for designing and personalizing a pair of athletic shoes. Hundreds of brands have since followed suit, and not just fashion brands—Coca Cola and Nutella are the latest to introduce personalized packaged food. Log on and experiment with digital customization. It's a great way to practice designing and using computer-aided design (CAD) without investing in expensive software or committing to buying.

Italian blogger Chiara Ferragni wearing customized clothing head-to-toe.

141.
EMBELLISHMENTS

Customization, fabric manipulation, and alterations are not the limit of fabric reinvention. Artworking—embellishments and embroideries—is a highly skilled and intricate form of reinvention. India is the home of embellishments; their workmanship and craftsmanship is unrivaled.

Indonesia produces modern artworks on jersey, swimwear, and denim. Balinese artworking, with its strength in embroidery rather than embellishment, tends to be a more casual style.

Inspiration for artworking can come from anywhere, such as graffiti, architecture, or nature. Photograph anything you see to build a library of references and placement ideas.

Artworks must be designed with the garment they will be used on in mind—they are one and the same thing, so they cannot be designed in isolation.

PRODUCING AN ARTWORK

PAPER ARTWORKS

Draw the block of the area of your garment you're embellishing onto tracing paper. Draw freehand or trace a reference image (e.g., a dragon) onto your paper block. Now start to think about where your components—beads, sequins, studs—will go. Position components behind the paper block and trace them onto the area of artworking. For speed, any physical components can be glued directly onto the block.

Now here's the part that requires patience—draw every single component in position. If you are briefing artworking to a factory to produce a final swatch, hours spent detailing up front can save time, money, and energy if it needs to be fixed later on. Be specific—even down to the placement of beads. Specify straight rows, scattered, or chevron placement of beads within areas.

FABRIC ARTWORKS

Similar to paper artworks, draw out the block to scale and mark out your intended design. Then stitch or glue your components directly onto the fabric.

BRIEFING ARTWORK

Always work to scale for both your garment and components. You can work on a half pattern, but always mirror photocopy your final artwork and check that the mirror image works as part of the whole. If working on an asymmetrical pattern, you'll need to do a full pattern piece.

Components form a large part of your materials list. Use a key and color coding to direct the artworkers producing your swatch. The key should show each component, its actual size, and, if required, an example of the color and thread.

Add a name and description to communicate the essence of the artwork before sending it out to be swatched.

As with any form of reinvention, push the boundaries. Embellishments and embroideries have a reputation for being dainty and bridal. Think about both the components and colors you use—fluorescents and neons are current, while color flooding is dramatic.

Work on top of texture—think meshes or neoprenes (see page 109)—and play around with proportions. McQueen is an excellent point of reference for incredibly talented craftsmanship. Ashish is bringing artworking into the 21st century, while Mary Katranzou is an inspiration for both print and placement.

Reformation is a brand synonymous with ethical and sustainable fashion.

142.
UPCYCLING

Upcycling simply means changing an item to improve upon its original condition—it's recycling while elevating; refashioning a new product from something that is no longer wearable.

Upcycling can also refer to using offcuts or leftover pieces of fabric to produce a new item that is valued more highly than the materials from which it was made. Christopher Raeburn's Spring/Summer 2016 collection based on restraint and chaos saw him upcycle two-cent zipper ties into accessories that retail at $30 for three.

Upcycling uses preconsumer waste, such as fabric pieces leftover or roll ends, as well as postconsumer waste, such as garments that are torn or don't fit.

PROS AND CONS OF UPCYCLING

There are obvious ethical advantages—fast fashion dominates the main street with consumers purchasing an increasing number of items of clothing every year. The result of this is that unwanted items are increasingly less desirable as supply outstrips demand.

On top of this, it is estimated that the mainstream fashion industry discards on average 15 percent of materials en route to production. Designers who upcycle, such as Christopher Raeburn, are very few.

Increasingly, retail giants and manufacturers are looking to repurpose their own waste through collaborations and upcycled brands. Urban Outfitters and ASOS.com's "Reclaimed" collection—where preworn vintage garments are upcycled into bespoke current collections—lead the way in stores. Super-cool US brand Reformation encourages you to "Join the Reformation. From recycled fabrics to eco-friendly packaging." Mass upcycling also comes with challenges—time implications during manufacturing, inconsistencies of raw materials, and managing customer expectations being just a few.

5
SELLING YOURSELF, YOUR BRAND, YOUR PRODUCT

143.
BUILDING BRAND IDENTITY

A brand is a name, term, design, logo, or other feature that distinguishes one product from another. In a world of abundant options, brands influence the choices made by customers, employees, and investors and must be seen as your business's most important asset. Brand identity is the reputation that surrounds your brand and your product.

It's worth remembering that the origin of "branding" is the marking of livestock with a hot iron—burning a symbol into the skin to denote ownership. In fashion, too, it's a signifier of identity—people often identify themselves by loyalty to brands, and brands can be elevated by the people who wear their mark (see Securing Celebrity Endorsement, page 233).

BUILDING BRAND IDENTITY
The first step in building brand identity is creating a name and logo that will be forever synonymous with your product. It's worth spending time and, if necessary, money on developing the perfect name and logo.

Start by making a mood board of the brands that you like. Collect business cards, shopping bags, magazine pages, and online research. It might be brands that inspire you, or you might simply appreciate their logo or design. Think about what it is that makes them powerful. Is it in their simplicity, or are all of your references in the detail?

When deciding on both your brand name and logo, get some initial ideas down and take time to process them. Your ideas and preferences will evolve in very much the same way that your collection evolves, so give them time to seed and develop before committing.

Be critical and get feedback. In the same way as naming a child, all names hold connotations for people, and there may be a connection—be it positive or negative—that you have overlooked. Redesign the brand name and logo until you're 100-percent happy. Consider how the brand will look across all of your platforms—will it work just as well online as it will on physical assets, such as your business cards, letterhead, and within your lookbook?

144.
IDENTIFY YOUR NICHE

As a designer, your points of reference and influences will change daily or even hourly. Living in a digital world with a never-ending flow of inspiration is every designer's dream. Even subconsciously, we are absorbing everything around us, and in turn, these influences inspire our work. So this next skill may sound contradictory. It's about reining it in. When establishing a brand, identify your niche and work within those self-defined parameters.

Just as affiliating with the wrong brand partner can dilute your brand, so too can diversifying too soon. You want to be known for one thing: a signature style or technique that is the first thing people associate with you. It may be a type of garment—you may be known for exquisite silk dresses or a print handwriting that is exclusive only to you. It can be tempting when starting out to jump at every opportunity and to try a little of everything. Yet pretty soon you will have dissolved what it was that your brand initially stood for.

Learn from previous seasons when identifying your niche. What were your most called-in pieces by the press? Ask, "Why was that?" Identify one or two pieces that drove the brand that season and think about "move-ons" (reinventions) for the forthcoming season.

It's not about designing to order or creating collections purely to please the press. You can and will develop an aesthetic integral to your brand that will flow through seasons, while still being reactive and covering key shapes with each collection. But being mindful of the key pieces driving your brand will help you to understand what it is that people are loving about it and help you to identify your niche.

RIXO London: synonymous with printed silk dresses and bohemian style.

197

145.
PRESENTING AT THE UNDERGRADUATE LEVEL

When presenting a project, brief, or collection at the undergraduate level, you will need to talk your audience through a complete body of work, from concept stage to the final product or collection. Often your project won't involve manufacturing a finished garment, so you need to exhibit—and will be judged on—the steps you took during the creative process.

When presenting in industry, all your audience will want to know about is the final product, rather than the blood, sweat, tears, and thought processes it took for you to get there. In terms of presentation technique, the skills on page 199 all apply at the undergraduate level.

TIP: At this earlier stage of your development, it's very important to get feedback on how you carried out and presented your project so you can apply these lessons to your future work.

WHAT YOU NEED TO COVER

- **A step-by-step account of what inspired you**— What sources did you draw from for research?
- **Evidence of how you developed your ideas**— This will often mean showing your sketchbook (see page 27).
- **The experimentation stage**—Details of what you tried, along with evidence of what did or didn't work.
- **The sourcing stage**—What hurdles you overcame and why you settled on your chosen materials.
- **Product development**—Thumbnails and sketches, all the way through to your final collection designs.
- **Information about construction**—Details of how your design would be constructed.

146.
PRESENTING AT THE INDUSTRY LEVEL

If you have been asked to present—whether it be a mood board to your design team or a runway overview to a room full of directors—it means you are skilled at presenting or on your way to being so, and that you have knowledge or a skill set that others want to access. It can be nerve-wracking: "Everyone's looking at me." They may well be, but only because they're interested in what you have to say—you have a captive audience.

MASTERING THE ART OF PRESENTING

There are two elements to mastering the art of presenting:

1. Delivering the content and key messages.

2. Developing the confidence and presentation style to allow you to present successfully.

PRACTICE

The key to presenting is practice. If you had to do it every week, you'd get into the groove of it, becoming both a polished and professional presenter. However, in the design industry, presentations can be few and far between, and therefore a source of anxiety for some.

USE A PHYSICAL TOOL

You'll often have the aid of a physical tool—perhaps a trend board or an on-screen presentation—that can help you with your posture and keep your hands busy, but regardless, try to adopt and master some of the key skills below and you'll be a great presenter in no time!

PREPARE

Make time to familiarize yourself with the content of the presentation and rehearse beforehand. You may be presenting information on a completely different season from that which you're in—don't come unprepared. The skills needed when preparing for and interviewing to the media are similar to those needed when presenting (see pages 240–241).

BE CLEAR

State your subject and outline the content you're proposing to deliver. For example, "Today I'm taking you through the footwear and accessory trends for Spring and Summer. There are three trends in total, followed by a key items overview for the season."

FOCUS AND BE SPECIFIC

Think about your key messages. Identify the five things you want the audience to remember from your presentation.

INSPIRE

The trend board imagery or content of the presentation will be visually inspiring, but think about the descriptive language that you adopt. Take time before the presentation to call some key words or descriptions to mind, including descriptive color names. Consider using physical samples to further stimulate and inspire.

PROJECT YOURSELF

Talk to the back of the room. It can be tempting to look at the board and end up almost presenting to the board. If you are using samples, pass them around as a way to interact with your audience.

TRY TO ENJOY IT

Remember, people are focused on the content and are inspired by the imagery. Instill confidence in your audience by enjoying delivering both.

147.
FINDING STUDIO SPACE

So you've graduated and had an amazing reaction to your final collection. There are many exciting avenues down which you could venture—from job offers within the retail world, to freelancing, to setting up your own label. There's just one problem—studio space. Having graduated, you are now out on your own with no studio space and—perhaps even worse—no facilities. The print tables, looms, and yarns you once took for granted aren't available to you anymore.

Think resourcefully—there will be a lot of other creative people in exactly the same position. Some may have just graduated; some may be recent graduates looking to move studio space or seeking space for the first time. Sharing studio space with other designers is a great way to keep costs down and also allows you to flourish in a creative environment surrounded by like-minded people. Social media is a good starting point, as is, of course, word of mouth.

Approach universities with facilities. Start with your own before extending the search to other colleges or universities. If it's approaching the summer months, there may be a period of time when students are not in, and a group of you could negotiate using the facilities.

The end of study means losing access to studio space and facilities.

148.
MAKING A BUSINESS PLAN

If you're setting up your own brand, you will need a business plan—a strategy showing how the business will balance expenses (costs) against income (earnings). There are a few reasons for this. First, you will need to check that the numbers add up. There's no point in making product, hoping it sells and hoping you can make a living out of it. Second, you need to secure additional financial backing.

You could gain financial backing through a bank business loan, in which case the bank will need to see that your plan is realistic, both in terms of protecting their own investment and also to make sure they're lending responsibly to someone who will be able to pay them back.

The other means of financial backing is through attracting investors. This can often be a mutually beneficial arrangement—a fashion designer needs money to get their label off the ground, and a financier is able to add some glamour to their portfolio through their association with a fashion brand. Again, they will need to see that the numbers stack up and that they can expect to see a return on their investment.

PROFIT AND LOSS

Once all of the expenses are subtracted from the income, you will be left with a profit or loss. Many businesses will need to run at a loss or break even before they are established enough to turn a profit. A lot of the costs kick in immediately, but sales often take time to build up as your reputation, product, and processes are developed and honed. Most fashion brands become financially stable after trading through their third season.

It's worth getting advice from finance professionals, but it's certainly worth considering all of the factors above and listing what you know in advance to ensure a fruitful initial conversation.

KEY POINTS WHEN PREPARING A BUSINESS PLAN

We can't go through everything you will need for a complete business plan in this book, but here are some key points to consider.

INCOME

This is quite straightforward—most of the time this will simply be your sales. You need to forecast these in a realistic way, based on some tangible evidence.

EXPENSES/OVERHEADS

This will include:

- Cost of goods—Materials, labor, etc. (see Pricing a Garment, page 202)
- Distribution costs—From the factory to you; from you to shops or distributors
- Marketing
- Website—Set up and maintenance
- Payroll—Design, production, warehouse, office, sales staff
- Premises—Studio, office, warehousing, and retail premises
- Utility bills—For all of the premises
- Phone and IT costs
- Taxes

149.
PRICING A GARMENT

Once you know your target market (see Market Research, page 203) and have worked out your retail price architecture (see page 206), it's time to work out what the production cost of your garment should be. You need to base this on what you know you will be able to sell the item for, plus a margin. Elements that contribute to the cost include materials, labor costs, and hours of production, and whether a garment is produced in-house or at an external factory.

CALCULATING RETAIL PRICE

The calculations discussed here are based on retailing direct to the consumer. Selling through a wholesaler will return a smaller margin but incur lower overheads. From a business point of view, the higher the margin percentage, the better. But this needs to be realistic in terms of the retail price your customer will be willing to pay while feeling they are getting fair value. See Making a Business Plan (page 201) for more information on other costs and overheads that can influence what your target margin needs to be.

Typically, retail prices tend to be around two-and-a-half to four times higher than the production cost, but this really varies depending on your market position. Another way of looking at it is that the cost is around 25–40 percent of the retail price. You should start with the retail and work backward to find a garment's cost budget.

HOW TO CALCULATE COST FROM A TARGET MARGIN PERCENTAGE

If you have a target margin percentage and retail price in mind for a garment, you can use the following formula to work out what the cost needs to be:

Cost = retail × (100 – sales margin %)

For example, if you were going to sell an item at $30 and you wanted a 70-percent sales margin:
$30 × (100 – 70%) = $30 × 30% = Cost of $9
The following table shows the possible cost and sales margins for a $30 item:

Retail ($)	Cost ($)	Sales Margin ($)	Sales Margin (%)
30.00	7.50	22.50	75
30.00	9.00	21.00	70
30.00	10.50	19.50	65
30.00	12.00	18.00	60

RETAIL, COST, AND SALES MARGINS

Retail = the price a customer will pay for a garment.

Cost = the price you pay a supplier for a garment, or your own cost of production.

Sales margin = the amount of profit you make on each item you sell (retail minus cost).

Sales margin % = the proportion of profit made on each item expressed as a percentage.

An item with a retail of $30 and a cost of $9 would have a sales margin of $21.

$$\text{Sales margin \%} = \frac{\text{retail} - \text{cost}}{\text{retail}} \times 100$$

or

$$\text{Sales margin \%} = \frac{30 - 9}{30} \times 100 = 70\%$$

150.
MARKET RESEARCH

When establishing your brand, it's vital that you carry out market research. This gives you an understanding of the market place as a whole and helps you to understand your position in it. Thinking about your market will also help define your own brand values. Establishing these values will influence your business plan (see page 201) and the way you build your line (see page 205).

MARKET LEVEL

The market you are aiming to appeal to will affect many elements of your product, from how much you charge to where and how you sell. If you're charging thousands of dollars for each item, your business plan needs to reflect this—you are likely to sell relatively low volumes of each product, and anyone purchasing them will want a customer experience that reflects this exclusivity. You are more likely to sell through high-end boutiques rather than street markets. Conversely, if you're selling ten-dollar T-shirts, you will need to shift a high volume of units to make a profit, so you need to set up an appropriate outlet.

LOW END

Economy brands—grocery stores, low-end contemporary stores, and market traders that sell high volume at low prices.

CONTEMPORARY

These are the fashion stores you see in your local town or shopping mall. Contemporary chain stores can go from mid range to low end.

MID RANGE

Diffusion or "bridge" lines from high-end designers, intended for a wider market at lower prices. These rely

---

COMPETITORS

You will need to think about the following:

- Brands and designers doing similar work to you.
- How and where are they selling their products.
- What makes you different and how you will gain attention.
- What you can do better than anyone else.
- If there's no one else doing anything like your product, either you've made a giant leap in fashion, or (unfortunately and more likely) there isn't a market for your idea. If this is the case, think about the features or elements you can change. It may feel like a compromise, but continual refining and adjusting must happen in fashion to pave the way from conceptual to commercial.

---

on an established brand. Many designers fund their high-end projects through these lines.

HIGH END

Haute couture (custom-fitted one-off pieces) and luxury fashion brands.

CUSTOMERS

Speak to as many potential customers as you can. Show them your product and get their feedback. Would they buy it? What do they think of the price? What could be better? Who is your ideal customer? Imagine your customer and think about what they like and why.

151.
ROUTES TO MARKET

With advancements in technology and the subsequent changes to the way people shop, there have never been more ways of getting your product to your customer. The methods you choose can have a big impact on your business plan, overheads, and marketing strategy. Here are some of the main routes to market available to a fashion brand.

RETAIL

This is perhaps the most complex way of marketing your product, because you have to set up physical premises to trade from and carry all of the overheads that these require, such as rent and staff wages. Retail does, however, give you direct contact with your customers and a lot of control about the selling environment. There are also fewer middlemen, so more of the profit margin comes directly back to you.

WHOLESALE

This is designing and producing clothes and selling them to retailers who in turn sell to customers. It could be a large chain store or a small one-off boutique. Margins are smaller when working as a wholesaler, but overheads are lower. In this model you don't have to set up your own retail space; instead, you work on building relationships with buyers from various retailers.

ONLINE

One option is to sell directly to the public through your own transactional website. You won't need retail premises for this, but you will need someone to look after your website, banking support to handle sales, and a solution for the logistics of both storing your product and dispatching it to customers.

MARKETS

Most major cities have established markets that are suitable for selling your garments by taking a stall. You can start out with this, and as you see the demand and develop your product, you can work on a business plan to set up something on a bigger scale.

ONLINE MARKETPLACES

Online marketplaces, such as Etsy, eBay, Amazon, or Asos Marketplace, allow you to set up mini online stores to sell to the public.

SHOWROOM

A very popular option among young, emerging designers is to use a showroom representative. Companies offering these services act as an agent and will display your collection in their showroom space, while also offering sales, distribution, marketing, and press services. They are likely to have a lot of established connections that you may not have early in your career and can take care of elements of the business you may not have time for, giving you time to concentrate on designing.

152.
RANGE BUILDING

Once you know your target market, you need to think about how to build your clothing line strategically. If you work for a retailer or brand, they will have buying and merchandizing departments who will do the majority of the planning. However, you still need to understand the thinking behind the process, and if you're establishing your own brand, you'll probably have to do it for yourself. There are many things to consider.

PRODUCT MIX

The amount you invest in each product category reflects the volume you expect to sell. Once you have traded for at least a year, much of this is based on sales history—how things performed last year. You may want to buy more options of key best sellers. Or maybe that trend is totally over and you need to replace those sales with something new. Other items might not have worked at all—you must decide if it is time to walk away from that product type or, if you know why it failed, make changes to get it right the next time around. As a designer you also need to guide the buying and merchandizing teams on where trends are going, to anticipate and steer fashion forward (see Trend Cycles, page 36 and Runway Analysis, page 38).

DEPTH AND WIDTH

Think about product mix in this way: there will be a limited budget for your line, and you need to decide how best to break it up to get the correct depth and width of your line.

If you have an item you are convinced will be a surefire best seller, in theory you could put all your money into producing as many of that item as possible. However, this would give you an entire store full of identical products, which means too much depth.

The other extreme would be making single units of as many products as possible. This would give too much diversity and crippling development and production costs, as you would not benefit from the economy of scale, which means too much width.

You therefore need to think about customer expectations and what the minimal credible offer is. If you only sell dresses, you will need to think about different cuts, lengths, and styles, making sure you are representing current trends. If your line spreads across a number of categories—for example, dresses, T-shirts, shoes, and accessories—you need to divide the budget and options between all of these areas. If you design lines of shoes, you will need to decide how many high heels, flats, boots, sneakers, etc., you need to get the perfect line.

SIZING

Depending on the type of product, you are likely to have to produce various sizes of each option. The quantities you buy of each size need to be in line with demand. Again, sales history is very helpful here.

COLOR

You might also produce the same shape in different colorways—and end up with a matrix of multiple sizes and colors.

Depth—How many units you buy of each option.

Width—How many different options you have.

PRICE ARCHITECTURE

Your pricing needs to fit in with the market. Look at what your competitors are doing. Each product category will have its own "price architecture." This determines the lowest and highest, or "entry" and "exit," prices. So a basic T-shirt could be $10, one with a printed design $15, and one with embellishment $25. A lot of retailers think "Good—Better—Best" when planning and hope that their customers will purchase more expensive items in the line. Each of the items should represent good quality and value, and a customer should be able to see why the prices differ and the additional features and benefits that trading up gets them.

CORE AND SEASONAL PRODUCT

Your line might have a mixture of core and seasonal product, which also needs to be balanced. Core product can be sold all year round—something like a pair of jeans, some plain black pants, or a shirt. Seasonal product comes in and out of the line at different times of the year—for example, thick coats in winter and light jackets in summer; boots in winter and strappy sandals in summer; and heavy sweaters in winter and light knits in summer.

STORE GRADING

If you're working for a retailer with a lot of branches, grading needs to be considered. Similar stores are banded together based on their size and turnover. Your safest bets and anticipated best sellers should be sent to all of your stores.

The riskier pieces are often sent to top or flagship stores. You don't want to invest too much in these by sending them too far down the chain, but they're great to have in key stores to attract interest and attention (see Peacock Pieces, right).

153.
PEACOCK PIECES

One great way of really building your brand profile is through recognizing, creating, and using "peacock pieces" for press. Named after one of nature's most spectacular animals, these are the garments that capture the imagination of the press and public—those that make people stop in their tracks and say, "wow!"

Peacock pieces are often the most fashion-forward and directional pieces in a collection; they are used by even the most established brands. They can often be fairly impractical items, either in terms of end use or finding the right occasion. Most brands will only produce these pieces in small quantities, and often at a short margin (see page 202); they are items that attract attention rather than drive profit (see Key Items, page 48). Their purpose is to engage a customer with your brand and attract them to the line in the hope that they will buy items that are more wearable (for them) and more profitable (for you).

As a new brand, you will quickly gain a sense of which pieces have become press favorites through the level of coverage they receive and the number of requests for samples or images. Learn from that reaction and make sure you've got a "move-on" product. These are items that retain the essence or certain elements of a "peacock" or best-selling piece, but reinvent them to propel your line forward and freshen it up for the new season. Move-on items can often be linked to trend forecasting—last season's hit shoe with a sequin detail might have a pom-pom this season if they're trending.

154.
FINDING A GREAT PATTERN CUTTER AND MACHINIST

One of the most integral relationships you will form when developing your own collection is with your pattern cutter and machinist (or "sample hand"). Pattern cutters and machinists are some of the most highly skilled and experienced people in the fashion industry, yet they are few and far between.

A well-run sample room is one where the designer, pattern cutter, and machinist work in harmony. The machinist's role is to follow the instructions of the pattern cutter, whose job it is to realize the vision of the designer. Experienced machinists will also highlight any construction or quality issues that arise throughout the sampling stage and hopefully rectify them ahead of the production process.

Start with word of mouth when trying to find a good pattern cutter or machinist. Your college or university may have in-house pattern cutters or machinists, or friends within the industry may be able to make recommendations.

Utilize websites such as Freelancer.com and LinkedIn to advertise. Briefly detail the type of pattern cutter you require. Someone skilled in bias-cut silk dresses may struggle when asked to work on a collection made in neoprene and technical fabrics.

When you have a short list drawn up, it's important to arrange an initial meeting with the pattern cutter or machinist in person. Ideally, this will be at their studio or workplace so you can see their set up. Take examples of your work and your current collection along. Pay attention to their reaction to your work. Someone who is excited by what you show them and offers suggestions and advice on how to tackle certain pieces is already thinking about your designs. You'll know when you meet the right pattern cutter and machinist—they'll just "get you" and your aesthetic—and vice versa.

Pattern cutter's blocks hang in the studio.

155.
WORKING WITH YOUR PATTERN CUTTER AND MACHINIST

Having found your pattern cutter and machinist, the process of collaborating on your first collection begins. The experience of your debut collection will never be repeated, and this is probably a good thing. Increased time restraint and lack of experience combine to make creating your first collection a nerve-wracking and exhilarating experience with a very steep learning curve. After working together on two or three collections, the process becomes less stressful and more efficient.

Essential to surviving your first experience of working together is honesty. Giving and accepting feedback is important in any working relationship. You want to produce a collection you're all proud of, while laying the foundations for a successful relationship.

CRITICAL PATH

The following steps are those you'll work through to complete a final set of samples and patterns to be sent for production. All deadlines should be detailed and agreed on before work starts.

Using the set of master samples produced by your pattern cutter and machinist to shoot for your lookbook saves weeks of time. The master samples are sent out for production after the shoot, meaning work on postproduction for the images can happen while the production samples are being made. This is a massive time saver and preferable to waiting weeks for production samples before shooting your lookbook.

1. INITIAL TOILE

Using your designs, the pattern cutter and machinist will produce a set of patterns and toiles ready to fit. Remember to toile in as similar weight fabric to your final fabric as possible.

2. FIT SESSION

The designer, pattern cutter, and machinist fit the toile set of samples, preferably on a fit model or a mannequin, and make necessary fit adjustments. Take detailed photos at this stage.

3. SECOND STAGE TOILE AND BEYOND

Amendments are made to the pattern and new toiles are created until the designer, pattern cutter, and machinist are happy.

4. FINAL SAMPLES

Go and see the collection being created. You won't necessarily do this for future collections, but until you, the pattern cutter, and the machinist implicitly trust and understand each other's ways of working, it's worth doing. It's advisable to use locally sourced fabrics and components for your first collection. This has cost implications, but it safeguards against mistakes and accidents—inevitable when producing your first collection—and will avoid incurring long delays as you wait for replacement materials to arrive.

5. LOOKBOOK SHOOT

See the photography tips on pages 224–225 and Preparing for a Lookbook Shoot (page 228).

6. PRODUCTION

A master set of samples and patterns are sent to your supplier for production.

156.
FINDING A GREAT SUPPLIER

At the same time as developing relationships with your pattern cutter and machinist and working through the process of making your master sample set and patterns, there's another integral relationship that you need to initiate and foster—a relationship with a great supplier.

There are thousands of garment, footwear, and accessory suppliers out there, with varying levels of expertise, so choosing the right one for your brand can seem like searching for a needle in the haystack.

CONSIDERATIONS WHEN SEARCHING FOR A SUPPLIER

GARMENT TYPE

The type of garment you're producing will determine your country of origin—where your product is produced. The US, UK, Turkey, Greece, Portugal, Mauritius, Italy, India, Hong Kong, China, Vietnam, Sri Lanka, and Bangladesh are just a few of the countries that manufacture and export garments and accessories. See Womenswear (pages 133–134) for a detailed breakdown of garment type by country of origin.

FABRIC BASE

The type of collection you're producing will determine your choice of supplier or suppliers. For example, a footwear supplier or factory skilled in sneakers may find it hard to work on an order of satin-heeled shoes.

USP

Identify any unique selling points (USPs) associated with country of origin. Maybe you're producing a collection made from traditional Scottish tartan, or perhaps your brand's story centers around being proudly 100-percent "made in the USA."

RECOMMENDATIONS

As with most relationships that you'll forge, recommendations go a long way. There are trade shows where suppliers show examples of their products and pitch for new customers. These can be overwhelming and costly to travel to if you're not sure what you're looking for or who you'll find there.

Talk to friends in the industry to find out who they use. Where possible, it's best to meet potential suppliers or their in-country agents face-to-face. If this is not possible due to travel restrictions, Skype is an excellent way to make initial introductions and interview potential factories.

ETHICAL AND SAFETY REGULATIONS

There are numerous ethical and safety regulations that must be adhered to. It's your responsibility to make sure that your supplier and the factories they're using are fully compliant and hold the necessary audits.

DRAWING UP A CONTRACT

The relationship with your supplier is a partnership. When negotiating terms and conditions, you must make sure they are fair, honest, and mutually beneficial to both parties. You both need each other and need to work toward the common goal of delivering a good-quality line, within the given time period and at the agreed-upon cost. You're looking for a supplier who is above all else reliable.

It's essential to draw up a contract to protect both parties prior to starting to work together. This will formally document agreed-upon terms such as cost, production schedule, payment terms, and shipping methods.

157.
UNDERTAKING A SUPPLIER COSTING EXERCISE

When looking for a supplier and factory to partner with, the three qualities you are looking for are quality, cost, and reliability. To find these, you need to start with a discussion.

Next you'll want to undertake a costing exercise— essentially giving the supplier a garment or accessory to make and cost. Cost is the price per unit you pay the supplier for the garment. This differs from the retail price, which is the price per unit at which you sell the garment or accessory to the customer. The difference between the two figures is the margin.

HOW TO UNDERTAKE A COSTING EXERCISE

Costing exercises can be done in a couple of ways. You could give the supplier a spec sheet to follow the design and specifications, make from scratch, and then cost. This is useful for judging how they follow a brief.

You could also give the supplier an existing sample to cost. This could be a sample that your pattern cutter has made, or a sample from last season that you're looking to tweak, and for which you expect a cost similar to that of the sample.

You may also want to cross-cost—where you have a sample and cost from one supplier and you brief it to another factory to see how competitive they are on cost and quality.

You may also cross-cost from the spec stage—send the same brief to both suppliers to challenge them on sampling lead time, quality, cost, and communication throughout the sampling process. Be mindful that samples are expensive to make and cross-costing should only be done when absolutely necessary. Your

hit rate—the number of samples booked versus the number sampled—with your supplier will suffer, as will your relationship. Ultimately sampling costs get absorbed into the cost, so oversampling is a huge waste of both money and time.

A really quick way to check that your supplier is affordable, even before the spec sheet or toile stage, is to ask them to cost a bought sample or something you know the retail price of, remembering to remove all tags beforehand. This exercise will give you a rough indication of whether the supplier is affordable and competitive. When doing this, bear in mind that the retailer may have placed large quantities, which benefit from cost reductions, or they may have worked on a smaller margin.

KEY QUESTIONS TO ASK A SUPPLIER

- Could they give you a brief overview of their background? Also, give them yours.
- How many factories do they work with and where?
- What is their production capacity per year?
- What is their sampling time—the amount of time it takes to develop a first sample from receipt of sketch, paper pattern, or toile?
- What is their lead time—the amount of time it takes for them to deliver to the warehouse from the date of placing the order? Check for a new order and a repeat order—the latter should be a shorter lead time.
- Which other customers do they work with?

158.
PLANNING YOUR COLLECTION PIECE BY PIECE

Planning each piece of a collection in detail requires you to be organized, resourceful, and decisive. You will also need excellent time-management skills. A large part of the curriculum is dedicated to what is known as the "realization" of your collection at the undergraduate stage. At industry level, it's referred to as the critical path (see Critical Path in Industry, page 212). Start by separating each piece of the collection into individual garments or accessories.

Have a look at the time you have to make the collection, and decide on the order in which pieces will be made. Note how long is needed for each process of each piece—timescales will vary drastically. Prioritize the processes that take longer than others, and list processes sequentially to identify the order you need to follow; for example, you may need to get material printed before the pattern cutting can start—get that process started first.

Group processes together—shop for all of your components across multiple garments in one go. Try not to waste time, energy, or money going back twice for things or sending and receiving materials in dribs and drabs.

Give yourself a buffer—things won't always go 100-percent as planned, so factor in time to address these inevitable issues.

Manage deadlines. Give third parties deadline dates at least a couple of days before the actual final date that you need the work delivered.

You may want to get key action points down on a huge wall calendar or digital document (whichever works best for you) and then have more detail on each. Having undertaken this exercise, you'll now have a breakdown of what you need to achieve day by day. Up-front planning piece by piece will ensure you hit your deadline and will help manage your stress levels.

FOR EACH GARMENT OR ACCESSORY, YOU WILL NEED TO:

- **Produce a pattern**—see Pattern Cutting (page 154).
- **Source material and components**—see Sourcing Firsthand (page 44).
- **Experiment**—see Testing Ideas and Techniques (page 45).
- **Make**—see Working with Your Pattern Cutter and Machinist (page 208).

159.
CRITICAL PATH IN INDUSTRY

Next up, we will cover how to create a critical path (also known as time in action calendar, or flow chart) when designing within the retail industry. The key skill needed here is time management. The purpose of a critical path is primarily to ensure you hit your deadlines—if I do a certain task by this date, the design process can continue. It also allows you to plan your time and highlight key dates that will affect the design process.

Delays incurred at any stage of the design process can have massive cost implications. It will also affect your speed to market, which in an ever-competitive market is something to avoid. When devising your design critical path, you should build in buffers to allow for any unavoidable delays along the way.

Devise your critical path over a 12-month period with "week commencing" dates running along the top of the worksheet in columns. The following is a non-exhaustive list of key dates—these are the minimum requirement, but you may think of other steps. Include these by inserting them into the rows along the left-hand side of your sheet.

EXAMPLE OF A DESIGN CRITICAL PATH IN INDUSTRY

MONTH	SEPTEMBER		
WEEK	1	2	3
DATE	September 1	September 8	September 15
Trend Presentation			Present New York runway
Department Brainstorm			
Lessons Learned & Planning Volumes	Identify balance of volume Spring lines		
Key Developing Dates		Develop product for April (some May/June)	
Range Building		Range build pre-CNY	
Footwear Pre-Sign-Off			
Footwear Sign-Off and Strategy			Pre-CNY sign-off for intake end Feb/March
Development Trips	MICAM		Lineapelle (design)
Press Days			
Key Supplier Holidays			
Runways	New York	London	Milan
Festivals/Shows/Awards	Bestival	Golden Days ANZ	

	OCTOBER					
4	5	6	7	8	9	10
September 22	September 29	October 6	October 13	October 20	October 27	November 3
Update May/June & London runway	Present Milan runway	Present May/June updates and Paris runway				
		May/June		Brainstorm and shop boots ahead of India development trip		
		Develop product for May/June, including pre-season boots				
	Range build balance March/April					
		March/April				
			March/April & S/S strategy			
Asia S/S development						
			Australia S/S press day tbc		Product handover for US press day & lookbook	
				India: Diwali		
Paris						

213

KEY DATES TO INCLUDE IN A DESIGN CRITICAL PATH

- **Design brainstorm**—The start of the process from which mood and trend boards will be created.
- **Trend presentations**
- **Department brainstorm**—To further brainstorm specific ideas by department and identify key items.
- **Design or sourcing "Packs Out" dates**—Some product types are on shorter lead times than others. The lead time is the time it takes from placing an order to delivery of the product; e.g., jersey products produced in Turkey are on a four to six week lead time, while shoes imported from China will take approximately 16 weeks. You may wish to include two rows: packs out dates for short and long lead times.
- **Range building dates**—Final samples are needed for this date to start planning the range.
- **Sign-off dates**—Meetings with your heads of departments and directors to sign-off the product that you have developed before orders are placed. Include any pre-sign-off meetings you may have in preparation for your sign-off. Following sign-off stage, it's advisable for the Buying and Merchandising team to have their own critical path that covers the period from booking of the product through to delivery into the warehouse and every step in between. See Relationships Between Buyers and Merchandisers, page 254).

- **Press days**—See Relationship with Press, Marketing, and Social Media Teams, page 257).
- **Key supplier holidays**—Include Chinese New Year, which has a huge impact on production schedules. Factories close and workers can be out of the business for four weeks or more.
- **Runways**—New York, London, Paris, and Milan Fashion Weeks for Resort, Spring/Summer, Pre-Fall, and Fall, plus any other International Fashion Week dates that you want to be aware of.
- **Development trip dates**
- **Trade shows**
- **Inspiration trip dates**
- **Key shopping dates**—A reminder to shop key product at key times of year. For example, when you're heads down designing Christmas product in May, these dates will prompt you to get out and shop summer product. This can often be overlooked and if you're not careful, you could be left with only the sale rail to shop!
- **Exhibitions**
- **International key events/festivals/awards**—Anything from the Coachella Festival to Valentine's Day and Christmas.

Juana Martin runway show, Madrid Fashion Week, Spring/Summer 2015.

160.
USING A WEBSITE AS YOUR SHOP WINDOW

The rise of the Internet has given a lot of exciting options for fashion designers, as with all businesses. Instead of relying purely on "bricks-and-mortar" retail based in physical shops, and the traditional main street shopping trips of previous years, consumers and designers are able to sell online. Some people still prefer the physical experience of shopping in person and trying on before they buy, but for many, online shopping now complements—or has completely replaced—shop purchases.

Of course, there are other costs involved—namely website maintenance costs, storage of garments, and the logistics of shipping your clothes to customers. But overall it's well worth considering at least trying to trade online, as initial costs are likely to be much lower than establishing a retail store. This in turn means it might make sense to spend that little bit more to create your website to get a fully transactional interface that fits your brand and customer perfectly, which brings us onto Choosing a Web Designer, opposite.

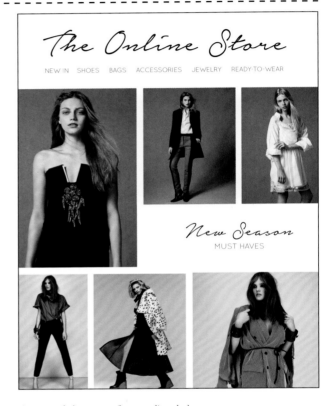

An example homepage for an online clothes store.

ADVANTAGES FOR SELLING ONLINE AS A FASHION BRAND

- **Low overheads**—Not having to rent prime real estate, heat the building, pay enough staff to keep it running to a high standard, etc.
- **Complete control over customer experience**—You don't have to worry about displays getting messed up.
- **All of your stock is in the right place for anyone to buy**—As opposed to selling out in one branch and having to move stock around your business.

161.
CHOOSING A WEB DESIGNER

- -

Whether you're freelancing, looking for a full-time job, networking, or running your own label, your website can be your shop window—and as such, you need to make sure that your digital mannequins are well dressed, squeaky clean, and standing upright. Unless you have the skills yourself, you need to find a really great web designer.

HOW TO FIND A GREAT WEB DESIGNER

- **Ask questions and listen to answers**—You need someone who is able to generate ideas and challenge you occasionally but who still listens to what you want rather than doing what they want.
- **Judge people based on how quickly they are to respond**—If they don't get back to you quickly about new business, will they really make that vital urgent amendment when you need it?
- **Look in various places**—Gumtree and LinkedIn can be great sources.
- **Look at examples of people's work**—Do they have the skills and the style you need?
- **Meet lots of candidates in person if possible**—This will allow you to compare and contrast everything from their websites to their professionalism.
- **Consider working with young and fairly inexperienced designers if your budget is tight**—They may be in the same boat as you and willing to go the extra mile to get a break and add your site to their portfolio.

162.
PLANNING YOUR WEBSITE

- -

Once you've settled on a web designer, it's important to give clear direction to avoid too much back and forth with corrections, redesigns, and amendments after production of the website, which in turn can waste a lot of time.

HOW TO PLAN YOUR WEBSITE

- **Draw up a contract to get down in writing what you want from the website**—For example, does it need to be a fully transactional website that allows people to buy directly? For this, you may need to pay significantly more. Or maybe it will be an online lookbook to showcase your product and share your contact details.
- **Send a presentation to your web designer**—Show the aesthetic of websites you like; features or tools that you want the website to have; sizes of images, fonts, and borders. It's better if you have a document like this that you can both refer to because it will ensure that the brief is being met.
- **Use presentation software such as Powerpoint**—You can use this to mock up pages even if you don't have programming skills.
- **Plan the click-through journey page by page**—Again, you can pull together a presentation on this to make sure you get exactly what you want.

163.
SHOWING YOUR COLLECTION: RUNWAY VERSUS STATIC

As part of an undergraduate course in fashion, you will have the opportunity to show your final collection. This is an extremely important event because many people from the industry (including potential employers) will attend. One choice you will face is whether to show on the runway or in a static installation or exhibition space. Much of this decision will depend on the type of product you have created. Accessories are more likely to be shown in a static show, but as an accessories designer, you could find a clothing designer to collaborate with, so you can show your work together.

Even if you have created a clothing line, a lot of runway shows will also require you to make a certain minimum number of pieces, so if your line is more of a specialist or capsule collection, you may need or prefer to create a static show.

A runway show has more of a sense of occasion and increased exposure but also demands many logistic and styling considerations. If you think you will want to contribute to a runway show in the future, you can gain invaluable experience by interning for a final-year show while you are close to the beginning of your undergraduate course.

Whether you end up with a runway or static show, this event is one of your main opportunities to raise your profile, get a reputation, and get noticed. Promote your show through any channel you can on social media. It's time to network—it's your chance to show off your really creative side and display what you can do. If people can't attend, send them images, videos, or website links to get the message across.

THE POLITICS OF SEATING AT A SHOW

Who sits where at a runway show is far from straightforward—in fact, it's a delicate, political dance.

Certain spots have prestige and connotations, so as petty as it seems, it's important to avoid inadvertently upsetting anyone and to make sure you impress the right people. You may not have A-listers in attendance at your shows (yet), but when planning the seating you need to think about who is most influential and who you want to thank and impress.

FIRST ROW

All of the most important people need to be here. They need the best view of the show, but you also need them to be seen on any media coverage of the show. Where in the front row people are seated also matters.

End—This is a prime spot, as it gets the best view of the show since the models stop, pose, and turn at the end of the runway. It is also a great spot for bloggers to take shots to upload to social media, meaning more great exposure.

Middle—Traditionally the most famous celebrities sit in the middle of the front row. This means that they are easily photographed, which adds prestige. Celebrities sometimes charge appearance fees to attend.

Base—This can be a good place to put investors. They will be happy to be in the front row but are unlikely to pick up on the finer details of the show, so they don't necessarily need the best spot.

SECOND AND THIRD ROWS

The second and third rows reflect the first, but with decreasing importance. There will also be standing room at the back of the show, by which point it's more of a free-for-all.

OTHER IMPORTANT ATTENDEES

Buyers—The people with the biggest potential to buy from the show need to be in the front row. Since they will be in competition with each other, it's important that they are spread out so each has some breathing space.

Sponsors and organizers—The people who have made the show possible need to be remembered and rewarded with a front-row seat.

Press—Press will often make up the majority of a show's attendees, so the hierarchy of influence needs to be reflected. The most important editors need to be in the front row; more junior writers from smaller publications can be further back. Some designers have been known to take revenge for bad press or a lack of coverage by banishing journalists to less-coveted rows.

Above: *Last minute backstage alterations.*
Below left: *Burberry runway finale, London Fashion Week, Spring/Summer 2015.*
Below right: *A make up artist applies finishing touches to a model.*

Selling Yourself, Your Brand, Your Product

164.
CASTING A MODEL

Models are integral to any runway or shoot. Your choice of model will affect the aesthetic of your images—maybe more so than the clothes, location, and set. It's so important to cast the right person, someone who will epitomize your brand for the season.

FACTORS THAT WILL INFLUENCE YOUR CHOICE OF MODEL

COST

Recruiting through model agencies can be expensive and involve a lot of red tape—rights to the photos, length of license to use the shots, etc. Unfortunately, modeling is an industry where you very much get what you pay for.

BE RESOURCEFUL

Don't despair. Approach model casting as you have building the rest of your team. Be resourceful and creative with the pool of talent around you. Start by word of mouth or social media, explaining your project and inquiring if anyone knows of anyone who may be interested in modeling for you.

SCOUT YOURSELF

Keep your eyes open for anyone who catches your attention. Consider using online recruitment companies over model agencies, especially when starting out. Websites such as Freelancer.com are great platforms from which to advertise your project and recruit freelancers.

ORGANIZING A CASTING

Once you have a handful of potential people, organize a casting—essentially rolling slots of 15 minutes or so to meet the models, view their book (which is their portfolio), have them try one or two pieces of your collection on, and take a headshot to remind you who you've met when making your decision.

Throughout the process, consider your audience and customer. You might meet a great girl who is sassy and carefree, but you're looking to shoot your Fall collection, which is a fierce and imposing collection centered around a dark color palette. Be selective and keep looking until you find the perfect fit for your brand.

Headshots of potential models following a casting.

220

165.
BUILDING A CREATIVE TEAM

So you've developed your collection, have a solid business plan, and have completed your market research. It's time to showcase your collection—to get it in front of the right people. You could take your physical collection to every appointment, lugging trunks of clothing across town to show magazine editors and influential bloggers, but you want to showcase the clothes in their best light—on a model as part of a photo shoot or lookbook.

A must-have asset for all brands, a lookbook showcases a collection within the context of the season; it is, in essence, a brand portfolio.

Before beginning, think about the audience for the lookbook. Will it be sent to magazines to gain editorial exposure, or to buyers to persuade them to stock your brand? Will it be an online lookbook or a physical copy?

Integral to the success of a lookbook is building the right team. You'll need to secure a model or models, a photographer, a stylist if you're not styling the looks yourself, hairstylists, makeup artists, and possibly an assistant to help on the day. LinkedIn is a great way to find people. However, I can't stress enough the importance of meeting your team in person. You'll know as soon as you meet them and see their work if they share your vision, your aesthetic, and your enthusiasm for the shoot.

Colleges and universities can be a source of enthusiastic students—of photography, styling, hair, and makeup—who would jump at the chance to be part of a lookbook shoot. Lookbooks don't need to be costly; many members of your team, especially if they're starting out, will be happy to have their expenses covered if it means they're gaining experience. Offer to share the final shots with them. Since you're financing the shoot and they're giving up their time and expertise for expenses only, it's an asset that can be shared and included in both of your portfolios.

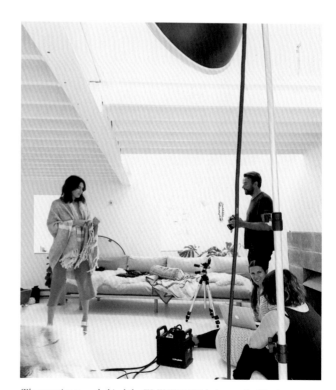

The creative team behind the ELEVEN SIX knitwear lookbook.

166.
BEING RESOURCEFUL

Your creative squad is in place—now the only thing left to do is secure a location, cast a model, source props and accessories… the list can seem endless. There is no right or wrong way to prepare for a lookbook shoot, but the golden rule is be resourceful. Break each task down and approach it as you did building your team—with creativity and a shared vision of the end result.

STUDIO VERSUS LOCATION

The key decision here is whether to shoot in a studio or on location. Both have their pros and cons.

STUDIO SPACE

Studio space can be expensive, but that's not to say you should steer away from it. Some shoots just need to be in a studio—the look that you're going for may rely on a controlled environment with backdrops and under professional lighting. Utilize your contacts—approach studios to see if there's downtime when the studio is less busy and might be available at a discounted rate.

SHOOTING ON LOCATION

The other option is to shoot on location. This can be anywhere – from your living room to a New York subway station. An online search for abandoned buildings and free space will throw up a number of potential locations.

The obvious benefit of shooting on location is cost, although it's advisable to check in advance if you are allowed to shoot in certain public spaces. The downside of this approach are factors outside of your control: hours of daylight, weather, interruptions. Maybe you want to capture that moment when the sun rises over an abandoned industrial estate—you'll need to be on location and ready to capture that 30-or-so-minute window. If you've already secured your photographer, ask for their advice and input.

PROPS

Think about the props you might need to make the poses you envision work. Identify and source any furniture or additional equipment. Again, be savvy. Source your ideal and then negotiate; props can often be borrowed if the supplier receives a credit in the lookbook. Try to approach and meet people face-to-face—you're way less likely to secure favors over email.

ACCESSORIES

Your collection may include footwear and accessories. If it doesn't, think about hooking up with an accessories designer and, again, crediting and sharing the final lookbook with them. Avoid promoting rival brands; don't include product that sells to your market or has a similar aesthetic and target customer in your lookbook. Think strategically about whom to approach to finish the look of your collection And, if you are shooting your own shoes, a good tip is to mask the bottom of the sole with masking tape to protect the sole, meaning they can be used or sold after the shoot.

Above: *A photographer at work in a studio shoot.* Left: *A model receives hair and make-up final touches on a location shoot.*

167.
CHOOSING A PHOTOGRAPHER

Photographers, like models and stylists, can make or break a photo shoot. Your photographer must not only share your vision for the shoot but also get the best out of the model on the day. A good working relationship is key—even if it is your first time working together.

Much groundwork can be done in advance of deciding on a photographer. Meet with potential candidates and talk them through your collection. Share shoot and model references with them—discuss what it is that you like and, just as importantly, dislike about these shots and looks. Have them talk you through their portfolio—take note of whether their style aligns with your vision. Ask about previous clients and shoots. You're looking for them to understand your vision, while bringing their own ideas to the project. Inspire each other—take references from each other to research further.

If shooting on location, visit it with your photographer before the day itself—a number of times if possible. Familiarize yourselves with the surroundings, and note any peculiarities or hurdles so you can work through them before the shoot day. If you have time, carry out some test shots. If you are shooting at a studio, check if the photographer has shot there before and ask if they have any advice or feedback as to how it went.

Plan how the photographer intends to work on the day. Detail the number of outfits or looks you are aiming to shoot, then agree on a realistic number and start to plan the day. Break down how long each look will take and have someone on hand—either your assistant or the photographer's assistant—who can keep track of time and be strict with knowing when to move on.

Check that the photographer is responsible for bringing all of his or her own equipment—agree to this up front.

A professional photographer's essential kit.

224

168.
CHECKING PHOTOGRAPHER EQUIPMENT AND FILE FORMATS

When you are looking for a photographer, use the Key Equipment checklist to the right, to determine that they have the basic equipment you'll need for your lookbook shoot.

TIP: Agree on all costs up front—the costs for the shoot itself and costs after the shoot. There are a lot of costs associated with photography once a shoot is over, from editing to touching up images.

FILE FORMATS

Agree on the format that you'll receive the photos in—unedited shots or polished final versions. In either case, you should request the RAW files (the original files, which are larger and more detailed to work with than JPEG), and the JPEG (files that are compatible with many more applications). You should also receive your images in both low- and high-resolution format, so you have email/website copies and bigger files to print from if you need to.

RIGHTS

Determine who owns the rights to use the photos, the timeframe of that ownership, and the terms of use. Negotiate throughout—remember that these photos can benefit both creative parties—and always draw up a contract. It sounds overwhelming, but agreeing on everything up front will save a lot of time and headaches after the shoot.

KEY EQUIPMENT

- **x2 DSLR camera bodies**—You can shoot film, but digital is cheaper. Some photographers tend to use both or Polaroid.
- **Minimum x4 SD cards**—At the very least.
- **A wide range of lenses**—To show differentiation with depth of field and outcomes of the shot. For example, 50 mm prime lenses are great for portraiture and head shots, but telephoto lenses (big, heavy white ones) would be better for the runway.
- **Tripod**
- **Camera grips**
- **Extra batteries for both cameras**
- **Battery chargers**
- **Laptop**
- **Hard drive**—To back up shoots.
- **Cleaning cloth**—To wipe dust from the lenses.
- **Stepladder**—If needed for location or studio work.
- **Flash equipment**
- **Lens hood**
- **Mood boards**—To remind you of shoot references and number of shots (can be physical or on a tablet or smartphone), so you can quickly recap in between shoots/locations.

169.
FINDING A GREAT STYLIST

The role of a fashion stylist is to combine individual pieces within a collection and highlight trends. Responsible for the final stage of the creative process, they are integral to delivering a brand's aesthetic.

Stylists are highly creative people with an inherently great sense of style. They absorb influences from multiple sources, then digest and process them to forecast the key trends. Styling is also an art form in itself. Great stylists have the ability to give different context to a collection depending on the message you and they are trying to convey. This process is called the campaign—essentially the fashion shoot.

It's integral to align yourself and your collection with a stylist who understands implicitly the aesthetic behind your collection. Ask yourself who your audience is. Are you trying to sell a collection to a potential backer or to inspire? Is the campaign part of an editorial piece for a magazine or a press tool designed to get the media interested? Ensuring your stylist is in line with your brand aesthetic will determine the success with which your collection is met.

MAKE A NOTE OF YOUR FAVORITE STYLISTS

It's a good idea to keep a list of stylists that inspire and excite you. When you see a campaign that you like in a magazine or online, jot down the name of the stylist. This will help to build up an understanding of each stylist's aesthetic.

Start a pinboard or file of visuals—tears from magazines or screenshots from online campaigns. Ask yourself what it is about the way the campaign is styled that you like, and likewise anything you don't like—this is also important.

Depending on what your project and budget is, you may be lucky enough to work with your chosen stylist.

If not, this process will allow you to find someone similar, or someone who shares your references, and it also gives you an understanding of what it is about that aesthetic that you like if you needed to style the campaign yourself.

BE RESOURCEFUL

Do you know people who have an inherent great style? Are there students in styling courses or other courses that you can collaborate with? This can benefit both parties, since workloads and costs can be shared and both can use the final photos in their portfolios.

DIRECT YOUR STYLIST

Good communication is essential. You need to be able to direct the stylist, both in the lead-up to the campaign and during the shoot itself. It's a good idea to involve the stylist from an early stage. Meet with them to present early concept boards and show them initial samples. Have regular catch-up sessions with them so that they can digest the information you're presenting. They can then go out and source clothes and accessories, and come back to you with ideas. Really focus on what you want the essence of the campaign to be. What do the final shots need to communicate and deliver?

DEVELOP A GOOD WORKING RELATIONSHIP

Develop an open, honest, and creative working relationship with your stylist. This is a skill that may be refined over time, but respect their ideas. Share openly and give a clear message when communicating your vision. It's important to both give and receive constructive feedback.

170.
INFLUENCING THROUGH STYLING CHOICES

When working on any images related to your brand—whether that's a lookbook, a promotional or marketing photo shoot, or images for an online shop—it's important to understand how your styling choices can influence the perception of your brand.

The way you combine pieces from your collection can really help to highlight key trends. How you accessorize, either from your own collection or possibly with some vintage pieces, can add an extra dimension to your brand. Choices about hair, makeup, and models can also have an enormous influence in this field (see Casting a Model, page 220).

You need to really focus on the audience and think about what they want from you. If you're designing luxury knitwear aimed at a mature customer base, you might not want to try anything too edgy or shocking in your styling; you will want to reinforce what the customer already thinks and feels about your brand. Alternatively, if you're an avant-garde label, your photo shoot will need to be similarly challenging and groundbreaking in the way you present your clothing.

In this lookbook shoot, the viewer knows that they're supposed to be looking at the coat. There are few other messages in terms of model shot, styling choices, or location. This renders the product accessible and wearable—perfect for the mainstream market.

Lady Gaga celebrating the designs of the late Alexander McQueen in V Magazine. *Posing with British artist Daphne Guinness, everything from the choice of models to directional styling makes for provocative shots with bondage undertones.*

227

171.
PREPARING FOR A LOOKBOOK SHOOT

A lot of the preparation discussed so far has involved creative skills (finding and building a creative team) and resourceful skills (negotiating, sharing assets, and keeping costs down). But the one skill that will ensure your lookbook shoot is successful is organization. Not all creatives boast organizational skills—we're generally free spirits and take it as it comes. But as the old saying goes, "Fail to prepare, and prepare to fail."

You've kept costs down to a minimum, but fashion photography and producing a lookbook is still an expensive process, not to mention the time and energy that you and your creative team have invested in the shoot. It's a highly pressurized, time-critical day. You need to ensure it runs smoothly so you get those all-important shots that you're hoping for, and for this you need to be super organized. Don't be shy about asking friends to help. The day of the shoot will see many unexpected challenges; the more help you have, the better these will be overcome.

DAYLIGHT HOURS

Regardless of the time of day or night you want to shoot, you'll have a limited window of daylight within which to do so. This, of course, will vary depending on the time of year and the country you're shooting in. This has to be your first consideration because it dictates the number of hours during which you can shoot in any given day. If you are conducting a studio shoot, it is more likely to be cost that dictates the number of shoot hours.

USING A STYLIST

Approach working with a stylist in much the same way as working with a photographer. Get them involved at the concept stage—talk them through your collection and share references for the shoot. They'll more than likely suggest accessories that you wouldn't have thought about when pulling looks together, so meeting them as many times as you can in advance of the shoot will allow you to plan and prep each look before the day of the shoot.

Of course, as with most of the creative process, there will always be changes on the day, but these should be minor—you can't afford to waste time styling the actual looks on the day of the shoot. Once you've determined each look, steam and hang everything up in separate garment covers labeled with the look number. Don't forget to consider underwear for each look (see Styling Kit, opposite).

TIP: Make provisions for your team—shoot days can be long, tiring, and exhausting. A hungry team isn't a happy team, so keep everyone fed, hydrated, and warm or cool throughout.

STYLING KIT

All good designers and stylists should carry a "styling kit"—essentially everything and anything that you'll need on the day to deal with last-minute alterations. A basic kit should include:

- **Scissors**
- **Needle and thread**
- **Dressmaker pins**
- **Safety pins**
- **Double-sided tape**
- **Bulldog clips**
- **Super glue**
- **Fusing web tape**
- **Bandages**
- **Iron/clothes steamer**—Check that you'll have electricity if on location.
- **Portable heater**
- **Underwear**—Black/white/nude thong and removable strap bra in correct sizes.
- **Blankets**

172.
PROMOTING YOUR LOOKBOOK

Having carried out a successful lookbook shoot and worked with your photographer in postproduction to select and finalize the shots, it's time to think about the format in which you'll get your lookbook out there. Is it a digital or physical lookbook? If it's digital, make sure that the file type and size can be accessed by the recipients. It's best to avoid sending high-resolution images in email; send a link instead. You will also need to include a personalized email introducing yourself and your brand.

If you are producing a physical book, use a good printer and work with them to agree on every last detail, from the weight of paper to the paper finish —a glossy finish gives your lookbook a very different feel from a matte finish.

Personally, I'd encourage you to work with physical lookbooks and always include a handwritten cover note. Unfortunately, in today's busy retail world, with the best intentions digital lookbooks can get lost in an overcrowded inbox. Delivering a physical lookbook encourages the recipient to pick it up and take a look immediately. They'll then think twice about trashing it, whereas an email can be easily and immediately trashed.

I'd also encourage hand-delivering your lookbook when possible. It is an important brand asset, and you want to ensure it gets into the right hands and stands out. If hand delivery isn't achievable, consider how it will arrive—a worn brown envelope won't turn any heads! Follow up with an email to the lookbook's recipient a week or so later.

ELEVEN SIX Fall/Winter 2016 Lookbook.

173.
SELLING YOURSELF AND YOUR BRAND

The fashion industry is highly competitive—particularly when you're first starting out and may not yet have a little black book of contacts. It can feel daunting knowing whom to approach and how. In the next few sections we'll look at keys skills needed when selling yourself and your brand: networking and making contacts, securing celebrity endorsement, and collaborating with established brands to further promote your own brand.

BE YOUR OWN BRAND AMBASSADOR

The skill that underlies all of the following skills, and is key to their success, is to be personable and charming. Your aim is to have people like your brand and to buy into it and its story. You are part of that story, so it's imperative that you live the brand and you're genuinely passionate about what you are promoting. If your brand is ethereal boho dresses, turning up in activewear en route to a workout won't do anything to cement your brand identity.

SELL YOUR BRAND YOURSELF

Press agencies exist and for a fee will use their contacts to sell your brand. Don't rush to use a press agency—no one knows your brand like you do or has the passion for it that you do. Where possible, sell it yourself.

BE AVAILABLE AND FLEXIBLE

Approach companies directly and meet people face-to-face. Be available and flexible—if, having received your lookbook, the recipient likes what they see but can only meet for a five-minute introduction at 8 A.M. next Tuesday, do it. Five minutes at their office allows them to put a face to your brand and is a great opportunity to make a lasting impression.

BE POLITE

Finally, take time after receiving any feedback or face-to-face correspondence to send a handwritten thank-you note. Little things go a long way toward ensuring you and your brand are memorable.

174.
NETWORKING AND CONTACTS

So we've extolled the virtues of selling your brand in person, being your own brand ambassador, and being available and flexible when making contacts. But what if you don't yet have any contacts? It can take years to form and build key relationships within the fashion industry, but there are ways in which you can kick-start the process and start networking almost immediately.

ONLINE RESEARCH

Simple online research is invaluable for finding generic email addresses and company structures that will allow you to build a picture of exactly who it is within that company that you need to get in front of. However, there are companies out there that have done the legwork for you, so use them!

FASHION MONITOR

Fashion and Beauty Monitor is the leading digital provider of media, public relations, and brand contacts. Boasting a global database of over 50,000 contacts, this should be your first place to start to connect with journalists, blogger influencers, and design houses, to name but a few. They offer a one-month free trial, so utilize it.

LINKEDIN

LinkedIn is another excellent platform, boasting over 300 million global members and allowing you to build and engage with your professional network. You should absolutely have a LinkedIn profile. Consider Premium LinkedIn—premium account holders benefit from advanced features. They also offer a one-month free trial.

WHEN NETWORKING AND MAKING CONTACTS, REMEMBER

- **Keep it brief**—Make sure the subject of the email is concise and get's their attention.
- **Tailor made**—You'll approach the design or buying director at *Vogue* differently from their counterpart at *People* magazine. Tailor each email to its audience.
- **Be logical and thorough**—Compile a spreadsheet of all contacts detailing whom you've approached and the method and date of approach. Use this information to make follow-up phone calls and solicit feedback after an appropriate amount of time.
- **Persistence, not pestering**—Be persistent when trying to connect with someone or receive feedback. It's important that you don't pester people, so keep your tracking spreadsheet up to date and make sure you don't contact too frequently. However, you believe in your brand and its value, so keep plugging away!

One of the great benefits of the site is that it enables you to determine email address formats. So let's say there's a company that you consider to be a great brand fit, and you really want to approach their buying team but you have no email address. Look up that company and connect with relevant people. It only takes one person to connect with you by accepting your LinkedIn request, and you've now got that company's email address. You can then insert the buyer's name once you have it.

175.
SECURING CELEBRITY ENDORSEMENT

On the road to becoming a successful fashion designer or launching a successful fashion brand, celebrity endorsement is invaluable. In an age where celebrities dominate the headlines—and increasingly where bloggers are the new celebrities of the fashion world—securing celebrity endorsement or grabbing the attention of a current blogger can be key to a brand's success. Celebrity endorsement will open doors and get your product marketed to an audience, sometimes in the millions, that you could never reach single-handedly. So how do you go about it?

INSTAGRAM

We'll talk about the role of social media in establishing a brand and securing exposure in more detail in a later section (see pages 236–237). Suffice it to say at this stage that online social platforms, in particular Instagram, should be any budding fashion designer's new best friend when hoping to secure celebrity endorsement.

Instagram is, among other things, an increasingly effective platform from which to launch a brand: a source of ever-evolving inspiration and a great way to stay abreast of new brand launches and all things fashion. But it's much more than that. It's a way of connecting with and influencing fellow creatives from global brands and industry kings to bloggers, celebrities, and perhaps—most importantly—their celebrity stylists. So get on there and get out there!

Use Instagram in the same methodical way that you approached companies and individuals when networking (see page 232). Set up your brand profile and connect with or follow as many relevant people as possible, in the hope that they in turn follow you. Upload new exciting content daily and tag people to get their attention. It's free to use, it is essentially free advertising, and what's even better is that you have complete creative control over the content you upload. Click on posts that interest you to see who they've tagged and follow them too. Again, be mindful not to pester people—instead, try to engage with them and get a relationship going.

APPROACH THE STYLIST

Now here's the important part. When trying to engage with celebrities, remember that some of them do not post content on their own account, and that they get thousands of requests a day from people wanting them to follow them or tagging them in content.

Be clever about it. Embracing your inner detective, scroll through your chosen celebrity's posts until you find one where they've tagged their stylist, and bingo—he or she should be your focus. Start following the stylist and tagging them in your Instagram posts.

Again, don't bombard them—they are the key to you securing celebrity endorsement, as they have massive influence on what their client, the celebrity, wears. Get a conversation going—introduce your brand and why you think it's a great brand fit for your chosen celebrity, and hopefully it will be the start of a relationship that works both ways. Stylists always need clothes and will welcome being approached from new, exciting brands. Offer to send physical samples over with a copy of your lookbook. Be flexible and available—don't miss the opportunity to meet and impress them.

176.
COLLABORATIONS

We've looked at the key skills needed to establish a brand and the importance of making the right brand connections (pages 231 and 232), but another route to getting brand exposure as a new and emerging fashion designer is to collaborate with existing or established brands.

Collaborations can take many forms. Back in 1993, British contemporary department store Debenhams launched "Designers at Debenhams"—a concept where prominent established designers collaborated with the store to produce capsule collections at contemporary price points, thus introducing them to a whole new target market. It is still going strong today with a rolling cast of designers. In the US, innovative retail brand Opening Ceremony hands-down boasts the most exciting collaborations out there—recently having collaborated with everyone from Rodarte to Adidas to Chloë Sevigny.

Unique multichannel shopping platform ASOS.com supports up-and-coming designers, such as Central Saint Martin's graduate Molly Goddard, in developing innovative projects and providing a launch platform.

It doesn't have to be about a retail giant, however. Maybe it's a collaboration between two start-up brands that complement each other and, in collaborating, double their reach when marketing themselves.

Being part of a designer collaboration is a fantastic catapult into unexplored markets. It's great exposure, and in most cases a highly lucrative move, with the designer securing a one-time payment at the design stage or a smaller up-front fee and a percentage of each sale. Some brands collaborate with larger, more lucrative brands to subsidize their own label trunk shows.

Just as it's important to be cautious when choosing brand partners, however, you need to be mindful that collaborating with the wrong partner or too many partners can dilute the power of your brand and be irreversibly damaging.

Above: *Fashion icon Chloe Sevigny has collaborated with numerous brands.* Below: *Karl Lagerfeld for H&M.*

177.
SECURING RETAILERS

You could have the best idea in the world, the strongest brand identity, and the most desirable product, but unfortunately, without the right platform no one will get to see it. At the very start of the design process, almost before putting pen to paper, you should determine whether a platform suitable for selling your collection exists.

Understanding your place in the market, knowing your target customer, and getting your product in front of that customer can be an intimidating task. But it doesn't have to be if you know how to go about it.

UNDERSTAND YOUR PLACE IN THE MARKET

The first thing to do when setting out to secure retailers is to compile a list of potential stores, retailers, and e-tailers that fit your brand demographic. Through completing your business plan, you'll have determined your selling prices and have a good idea of where your brand sits in the market.

Before contacting potential retailers, do your research. This could involve online research or visiting physical stores. Either way, it's important to understand not only your place in the market but also your place within the potential retailer's environment.

Study their current offer, identify what's missing, and ask yourself if your brand can fill that void. If not, maybe they are not the platform for you. Or it might be that you've pitched it perfectly, and stocking in an environment with similar brands will secure the exposure to the retailer's already established customer base. Be critical. If you were the customer, what is it about your product that will ensure it stands out on the shop floor?

LEARN FROM YOUR COMPETITORS

Who are your main competitors and where are they stocking? You won't be the first person to be breaking this ground, so utilize research already available to you. Go back to a competitor's Instagram or their blog and determine who they are tagging in posts and if that's relevant for your brand.

THINK GLOBAL

We all shop globally, so you'll need to stock globally. Research markets and retailers globally and visit them (physically or virtually) to determine your place. Identify your main competitors in those territories. Again, think smart and use research already available to you. Online e-tailer FarFetch is a pioneering online store featuring over 300 boutiques. But here's the best part—you can refine by country, so understanding, for example, Brazil's unique fashion aesthetic versus the best of US brands is only a click away.

BE PREPARED

You'll want all of this info at your fingertips before approaching potential retailers, and when you do, remember to meet face-to-face when possible to introduce yourself; be flexible and available and follow up after an appropriate amount of time. Being armed with a one-pager summarizing your research and highlighting why you think it will be a beneficial relationship can't fail to impress.

178.
USING SOCIAL MEDIA

With the rise of social media, it's never been easier to set up and promote your own brand. On the flip side, there's never been more competition. There is the potential, through essentially free advertising, to reach a worldwide audience, but there's a lot of "noise" that can threaten to drown out your message.

We have previously discussed using social media to gain press exposure by association (see Securing Celebrity Endorsement, page 233)—but this skill focuses on generating your own content. Social media presence is fundamental to creating and cultivating your brand identity. It's a way of engaging with your customers and shaping their perception of your brand and the kind of lifestyle associated with it. It's a way of having complete control of your direct communication—you can curate your pages exactly as you want them to be seen and carefully manage your public image.

Many brands employ teams of people to get people "liking" and "following" them, and those kinds of "clicks" have become an important way of measuring success and judging what customers want. The direct nature of social media also means speed; it's an incredibly quick way to connect with customers—for example, by offering a sneak peak of an item that's about to be launched.

SOME OF THE KEY SOCIAL MEDIA PLATFORMS TO CONSIDER USING

INSTAGRAM
This online and mobile and video photo-sharing app is currently the starting point for fashion social media. Its visual nature attracts creative people in search of inspiration. By selecting whom you follow, you can build a network with similar interests and taste levels. Publishing beautiful photos of your product on Instagram can really capture peoples' imagination.

TUMBLR
A simple way of creating a blog featuring images, text, video, music—anything on the web. This is a great way of building up an identity through association with other content that is in line with your brand values.

FACEBOOK
The most widely used social media platform with an enormous reach. Pages must fit within the Facebook template, so you don't have complete creative control. It is naturally a less creative platform, but it's an extremely influential one.

TWITTER
Allows users to send and read 140-character messages that can contain links to photos, videos, or other web content. Twitter is particularly good for fast communication of promotions and direct engagement, such as customer service.

Instagram, tumblr, Facebook, Twitter, and Pinterest logos.

PINTEREST

Photo-sharing and online mood board (see Online Mood Boards, page 33) that allows users to upload, collate, and curate pinboards on any topic. Good from a brand point of view to demonstrate inspiration, present your product in a particular context, and build your brand through association with other aspirational brands.

TIP: Sometimes savvy social media can be as much about what you're not doing as what you are doing. Some brands prefer to cultivate a slightly aloof approach and not engage too much with their customers. A flurry of "likes" across multiple platforms would make them seem too mainstream and accessible and dilute the impact of their brand.

BACKLASH AND CONTROVERSY

Unfortunately, these tools have their downsides. Brands can get themselves in trouble through ill-advised messages or comments being misinterpreted. Social media backlash can be immediate and fast-moving. If this happens to you, it's time for crisis management (see Media Training, pages 240–241). It's important to act in a proper and responsible manner on these platforms, or irreparable damage can be done.

Customers are also able to communicate directly with brands in a public forum, which means that complaints and gripes can hit the headlines. You must be seen to deal with this quickly and effectively.

179.
USING BLOGS AND UNDERSTANDING BLOGGERS

With millions of followers, the most successful fashion bloggers find themselves in a position of great influence.

To access this audience, brands will pay bloggers to promote their products. They are inundated with gifts, find themselves on the "A" list, and get paid to occupy the front row seats at Fashion Week. In turn, their enviable lifestyles become more and more appealing to their followers. Some are rumored to earn several million dollars per year. See Networking and Contacts (page 232) and Securing Celebrity Endorsement (page 233) for some tips on how you can try to get noticed by influential bloggers. Their recommendations can make an obscure brand extremely well known overnight.

You can use these bloggers as part of your daily research too. By following the bloggers you like most on platforms such as Instagram and Tumblr, you will receive daily updates with content that is likely to interest and inspire you. And by following the most successful bloggers, you can get a real handle on what's happening in mainstream fashion.

RUNNING A BLOG

If you run your own blog in support of your brand, you need to strike a balance:

- **Tone**—Your blog needs personality, but avoid oversharing the intimacies of your life
- **Frequency**—Blogging about the minutiae of everything that ever happens is likely to bore people. But a brand blog that is too sparingly updated can make your site feel like an abandoned building.
- **Find a niche**—Whether attempting to become an individual blogger or blogging about your own brand, you need something fresh and different to stand out from the crowd and be heard above the noise. Think of something unique you can offer, like behind-the-scenes access to your brand to give an insider's view.
- **Know your customer**—There's no point in making your content too broad. You will never appeal to everyone. Instead, think about whom your customer is and what they want to hear. Then incorporate relevant elements of fashion, culture, film, food, music, travel, interiors, lifestyle, health... anything that the customer will connect with. This sense of connection will lead the customer feeling "this brand gets me" and so "this is the brand for me."

Top left clockwise: *Blogger Giselle Oliveira in New York; securing celebrity endorsement can make or break a brand; Susie Bubble, one of the most famous and influential bloggers on the planet; Evangelie Smyrniotaki and Charlotte Groeneveld during Paris Fashion Week.*

180.
MEDIA TRAINING: PREPARATION

Now this next skill sounds a bit pretentious and self-obsessed; however, whether working as a designer in industry or setting up your own label, you are now a brand ambassador and will need to engage and interact with the media. Where possible—although they may seem daunting—opt for live interviews over pre-recorded, phone, or written interviews, as there's less of a chance of being misquoted or misrepresented in a live chat. A successful interview is dependent upon the preparation, and the following tips will help to get you ready.

1. TAKE FIVE
Switch off all devices and avoid all distractions for five or ten minutes before the interview. Think about whom the interview is with, your audience, and what key points you want to convey throughout the interview.

2. KNOW YOUR AUDIENCE
Remember, it's not the journalist. Do your homework on who the reader or viewer is and try to appeal to them in your answers.

3. WORK OUT YOUR KEY MESSAGES
List four or five key points that you want your audience to know about. When answering questions, try to look for opportunities to incorporate your key messages into your response.

4. THE THREE "Rs"
Hopefully you'll be promoting your brand, not defending it, but if you are dealing with a crisis, remember the three "Rs": regret, reason, and remedy. Begin by briefly and honestly expressing your sincere regret of the situation. Give a reason behind why it happened, being careful not to apportion blame. Finally, tell your audience what you have done and intend to do further to remedy the crisis and prevent it from happening again.

5. PREPARE FOR THE WORST
Prepare for the toughest questions you may be asked.

6. GIVE EXAMPLES
Prepare stories and anecdotes. These colorful examples stick with readers and viewers longer than statistics or regaling them with company strategy.

7. DRESS SUITABLY
Remember not to wear anything that could offend, whether conducting a filmed interview or not. The journalist could report any details within the interview.

181.
MEDIA TRAINING: DELIVERING AT INTERVIEW

Now for the interview itself. Whether it's live, pre-recorded, or over the telephone, the following skills will help you to deliver your message and conduct a successful media interview.

1. BREAK THE ICE

You'll more than likely be nervous; it would be unnatural not to be. However, so might the interviewer. Smile, have confidence, and enjoy it. You're the star—they're interviewing you because they want to hear your stories, or side of the story, and your skills and expertise. So indulge them and enjoy talking about yourself.

2. OPENING LINE

As when presenting, rehearse your opening line. Once you've delivered this successfully, you'll be on a roll.

3. ACKNOWLEDGE AND COMMUNICATE CLEARLY

Listen to the questions being asked, and engage and think about what you are going to say before responding with a clear and concise answer.

4. AVOID JARGON

Robotic responses or regaling already published company statistics or slogans can be really off-putting. Show some personality.

5. DON'T GO "OFF THE RECORD"

Unfortunately, some journalists will take a chatty, unofficial approach to the interview in order to lure you into a false sense of security and extort off-the-record information. Don't fall into this trap.

6. DON'T SAY "NO COMMENT"

Try to prepare answers for the toughest imaginable questions in advance.

TIP: When being filmed for television, try to ignore studio distractions, and unless it's "down the line"— where you're requested to talk directly to camera— look at the presenter, not the camera.

6

CAREERS AND PROFESSIONAL SKILLS

WRITING THE PERFECT RÉSUMÉ AND SECURING AN INTERVIEW

A résumé is the preferred application document in the US and Canada when seeking employment. It is most commonly a one-page document giving a brief summary of the applicant's skills and experience. It is not necessarily written in chronological order, but in an order that best highlights skills and achievements relevant to the position you're applying for.

In this section we'll look at the skills needed to not only write the perfect résumé but also to secure an interview. You'll need to be focused and professional in your approach but also inject personality into your résumé and at the interview.

WRITING THE PERFECT RÉSUMÉ

KEEP IT BRIEF
Your résumé should be no longer than one page. In reality, the person who receives your résumé will scan it for less than 30 seconds, so keep it concise.

MAKE IT ADAPTABLE
Know your audience and the role you're applying for, and tailor your résumé for that specific position.

MAKE A STATEMENT
Use a positioning statement that tells the reader what you have to offer rather than what you want—for example, "Fashion designer with eight years of contemporary market experience."

FOCUS ON THE EMPLOYER, NOT YOURSELF
You have 30 seconds to get their attention and convince them that you would be an asset to their company. Clearly state your assets and why you know you can do the job.

BE SELECTIVE

Only include relevant, targeted skills and achievements. You can elaborate on these at the interview stage. You can build up a long list of your relevant skills and experience and then pick from this for each application.

STAND OUT THROUGH LAYOUT

Again, you have less than 30 seconds to lead the reader's eye through your one-page résumé. When applying for design roles, layout is especially important because you're appealing to a visual person. Always keep the layout simple and easy to read, and highlight your key strengths.

VISUALS

Attach a one-page visual. This could be examples of your work tailored to the position you're applying to, or a one-page visual about the brand you're approaching.

HARD COPY

Send a hard copy to land on someone's desk. Emails can be quickly scanned and even more quickly trashed, so a hard copy where the employer has to think twice before physically trashing it is preferable.

OVERT ROUTES FOR GETTING TO THE INTERVIEW STAGE

AGENCIES

Sign up with retail employment agencies. They'll often want to interview you and see your portfolio before representing you to ensure they understand your style and put you forward for suitable roles. Treat this interview with the same importance as you would a job interview.

LINKEDIN

Create a profile and connect with relevant industry people or companies (see Networking and Contacts, page 232).

COMPANY WEBSITES

Go directly to the websites of companies that you're interested in working at to view their current listings.

COVERT ROUTES TO EXPLORE FOR SECURING AN INTERVIEW

WORD OF MOUTH

Fellow students or colleagues in the industry may be able to endorse or recommend you to their network of people. Let them know you're looking for a job and what type of role you'd like.

NETWORKING

From the undergraduate stage through your working life, networking is key. Believe it or not, it's a very small industry, so building relationships and reputations can be invaluable when job hunting.

TARGET COMPANIES

Even if there are no vacancies listed, you can still send your résumé and examples of your most recent work to introduce yourself and get on their radar. It's imperative that you tailor your submission—a blanket approach really isn't acceptable.

CONTENT

Consider including the following:

- Name and contact details
- Current position held and for how long
- Positioning statement—how a product/service fills a need, so identify the niche and fill it
- Compelling but brief personal profile—your chance to tell the employer why you should get the job
- Relevant career history
- Relevant achievements and accomplishments
- Education

183.
PREPARING YOUR PORTFOLIO

Within art and design careers, your portfolio is the most important body of work. It reflects your individual style, referred to as your "handwriting," your skill set, and, perhaps most importantly, your potential. It is a visual representation consisting largely of work undertaken at the undergraduate stage and is commonly your most recent work, as this tends to be the most exciting and groundbreaking. Your portfolio must be professionally arranged and presented—knowing what to include and in which order to include it is essential.

TIP: Your portfolio should be a concise body of work—don't be tempted to show too much. You will have limited time at the interview stage and don't want to overwhelm the interviewer.

1. DECIDE WHAT CONTENT TO INCLUDE WITHIN YOUR PORTFOLIO

Your aim is to take the interviewer through your thought processes, from concept, to research, and on to final design. It's important, therefore, to show development—how you got from concept to final design. This can be done through accompanying sketchbooks if preferred, but keep these brief and just highlight key pages that demonstrate your thought process or demonstrate experimentation or thumbnail designs that led to your final design.

All research included should be well-rounded and show influences from all areas of culture, not just fashion. You should aim to include four or five projects that show a variety of skills and processes, plus sketchbooks if relevant.

2. INCLUDE ILLUSTRATIONS, DRAWINGS, AND PHOTOGRAPHS

Include both fashion illustrations and technical drawings/specifications. The former should always be hand-drawn; the latter may be hand-drawn or produced using computer-aided design to show computer skills (see Fashion Illustration Versus Technical Illustration, page 78 and Spec Sheets, pages 54–55).

Photographs of the final product are also important to show, and physical swatches and samples are always nice to see in a portfolio. In an ever-increasing digital age, it's important to have hard copies—fashion and textiles is a tangible industry, so let's celebrate that at portfolio stage.

3. DECIDE ON THE ORDER OF YOUR PORTFOLIO

Reverse chronological order (most recent work first) is preferable. Place any additional projects tailored to the company you're applying to at the end.

184.
PREPARING FOR AN INTERVIEW

There are few things more nerve-wracking than interviewing for a new role, especially for that dream position that you really want. But let's turn this on its head. You've successfully secured an interview, which is no easy feat—that means that the employer has seen potential within your résumé and wants to hear more from you.

The interview stage is the time to elaborate on what you've already told the company about yourself. It's time dedicated to talking about yourself, about your assets and what you can bring to the company, and an opportunity to find out more about the company and the role itself. Really, it's just time to go in there and shine, so enjoy it.

The most important piece of work you can do in advance of the interview is to thoroughly research the brand. Visit their stores, or if they're online, know their website inside out. Know the product and reference this throughout the interview. Does the brand have a mission statement? You need to know and understand it. Read up on current news articles about the brand—what is their current position in the market? Who are their competitors?

THINK ABOUT YOUR LASTING IMPRESSION

Think about the last impression you want to leave with the interviewer. As an employer, I always look for three things:

Can the candidate do the job? I'm looking at both creative and technical ability.

Does the candidate want the job? Here, I'm looking at behavioral skills and motivation.

Will the candidate be a good team fit? This is equally as important as the previous two considerations.

PREWORK

In addition to the body of work within your portfolio, make time to pull together a couple of pages that are specific to the company at which you're interviewing. This could be a couple of mood boards for the upcoming season or analysis of current runway shows and how they relate to the brand. It could be an area of opportunity for the brand—for example, "I think your footwear line is fantastic. Have you ever thought about doing a footwear collaboration with a celebrity?" Again, this preparation and extra effort will make you stand out from the crowd.

DRESS TO IMPRESS

Know their dress code and brand aesthetic, but let your own natural style shine through in your choice of outfit.

TIP: It goes without saying, but on the day of the interview make sure you know where you're going. Arrive 10–15 minutes early and show up well prepared. It's a good idea to bring along extra copies of your résumé.

TOP 10 INTERVIEW QUESTIONS

Below are my top 10 interview questions. Prepare your responses—give yourself enough time in the days leading up to the interview to give real thought to your answers and to rehearse them, so that at the interview you're delivering your key points succinctly.

1. Can you tell us a bit about yourself and current experience?

As you did when preparing your résumé, talk about the most relevant details. You don't need to give your whole life story—just key points that are relevant to the role you're applying for.

2. Could you talk us through your portfolio?

Again, succinctly talk through this ever-changing body of work that represents you as a designer, showcasing your natural style and your skill set (see Preparing Your Portfolio, page 244).

3. What is your understanding of the job, customer, and company strategy?

Don't presume anything; after all, their strategy could have changed the day before, and how are you to know? Instead, base your answers on your research into the brand and their customer.

4. What attracts you to this job, and what could you bring to the position?

Try to think about why that vacancy exists and what help the company needs, but also layer on some personality. You're unique—what is it about yourself that the company categorically needs?

5. What do you think of the current line?

Tread carefully; be honest, but be objective. If you are identifying gaps, suggest areas of opportunities or solutions.

6. Who do you think our competitors are?

Think about both retailers and e-tailers. This is a key question used by the interviewer to ascertain if you know your marketplace. Also mention any differential points your prospective employer has from the marketplace to demonstrate that you appreciate their strengths.

7. What sort of working environment do you thrive in?

Be honest—do you thrive within a team or achieve more working independently? Think about the environment of the company you're interviewing at and how you'd operate in that environment. Give examples of where you've worked under pressure.

8. What are your main strengths and development areas?

Don't be afraid to blow your own trumpet here. Concentrate on the strengths, covering technical as well as behavioral strengths, but self-critique and identify areas where there's room for improvement. Nobody's perfect.

Ask your colleagues, friends, and family what they see as your strengths and weaknesses. They may see traits in you that you haven't identified.

9. What inspires you?

The million-dollar question! This is your time to inject real personality into the interview. Avoid generic answers and dig deep—what really excites and inspires you both in your professional life and outside of work?

10. If I gave you $1,000 and told you to let loose in Barneys, who would be your go to designer?

What seems like a throwaway, quick fire question can catch you off-guard and you can end up blurting out the first designer that comes to mind. Think about your response in relation to the aesthetic of the brand you're interviewing.

185.
SUCCESSFULLY PRESENTING YOUR PORTFOLIO

Presenting your portfolio is a key moment in an interview. Make sure you showcase your work and your potential in the best possible light by following the key points below.

CONSIDER YOUR FORMAT

It's completely up to you whether you display your portfolio in a digital format or in hard copy. Indeed, you may incorporate the two—for example, you have a website that you want to showcase and therefore use a tablet in addition to your portfolio. If you are showing a hard copy of your work, it should be no bigger than 8 ½ x 11 inches (21.5 x 28 cm) or 11 x 17 inches (28 x 43 cm) in size and in good condition.

KEEP IT SHORT

When presenting your portfolio, the golden rule is to keep it concise and edited. This not only shows respect for the viewer's time and schedule but also demonstrates that you are able to edit and curate an impactful portfolio of work from a large body of work.

LEAD THE PRESENTATION

Following the initial interview, the interviewer will ask to see your portfolio. It sounds simple, but position your portfolio facing them, not you. Indicate at this stage the amount of work that you would like to show them, including any sketchbooks or physical samples, so they have an idea of the amount of work to get through, "Today I've got four projects to take you through, one sketchbook and a couple of physical samples, plus a project that I've prepared for today's interview." It's important that you treat this as a presentation and lead the process, rather than sitting there hoping the interviewer asks the right questions to allow you to say what you want.

PRACTICE, PRACTICE, PRACTICE

Rehearse talking through your work, highlighting key moments within the research and design process that influenced your final design and allowing time for discussions around this. Highlight skills mastered and any achievements along the way. There are "master classes" that you can sign up to that review and critique your portfolio in preparation for interview stage.

186.
IMPRESSING ON THE INTERVIEW DAY

So, you've prepared for the interview, you're confident that you know the brand and it's position within the market inside out, you've got yourself there, you're dressed to impress … now all you need to do is deliver. Follow these tips to make sure that you shine.

THINK ABOUT HOW TO PRESENT YOURSELF

It sounds cliché, but eye contact, a firm handshake, a smile, and carrying yourself confidently all make for a strong and memorable first impression.

Be yourself and try to relax while being professional throughout. Try to preempt any potentially awkward periods of time—that period between being greeted and before the official interview starts. The interviewer wants to meet the real you, so show a glimmer of your personality. Likewise, at the end of the official interview, converse and show personality. Don't breathe a sigh of relief that it's all done until you're out of the office.

ENGAGE WITH THE INTERVIEWER

You'll be one of many applicants, so you want to stand out and leave a lasting impression. Prepare stories or examples of situations that you've encountered that may be relevant to the interview. A story or anecdote can make a lasting impression and is something for the employer to remember you by. At the same time, be respectful of the interviewer's time restraints.

BRING SAMPLES

I always love it when interviewees bring physical samples along. Again, it's tangible, shows foresight and preparation, and creates a lasting impression.

PREPARE QUESTIONS

Prepare questions to ask at the end of your interview. You've got face time in front of someone who is a master in his or her fields—what a great opportunity!

LEAVE EXAMPLES OF YOUR WORK

Leave the employer a copy of your résumé and printouts of any work you have prepared. This enables them to remember the content of the interview better and will help you stand out among multiple applicants.

STICK TO THE FOLLOW-UP PROCEDURE

As tempting as it might be to call for feedback, stick to whatever has been agreed on, only following up once that specified time period has lapsed. Everyone is busy and no news doesn't necessarily mean bad news—give them the time they need to interview and provide feedback to multiple candidates, but also make sure you receive adequate feedback for the time and effort you've put in.

BE PROFESSIONAL

Throughout both the preparation and the interview itself, the key word is professionalism. In an increasingly saturated industry where competition is fierce, this is a key behavioral skill to refine and display.

187.
PLANNING YOUR INTERNSHIP

In today's highly competitive retail industry, most retailers want (and have come to expect that) potential employees have undertaken some level of work experience or internship. This may be organized at the undergraduate stage through your college or university—"sandwich" courses offer the opportunity to spend the third year of your degree working in industry before returning to complete the fourth and final year of your degree.

If it's not offered through your education, it's highly recommended that you seek out this opportunity yourself—over the summer or holiday breaks. Not only does this show drive and determination, but it also allows you to get a well-rounded insight into the fashion and retail industry before committing to your chosen career path.

SECURING AN INTERNSHIP

At the undergraduate level, many colleges and universities have links to companies who offer internships. This is usually approached on a project basis, where the company will send interested students a project with the prize being securing an internship. Put yourself forward for such opportunities; even if it doesn't result in you being offered an internship, it's great to get feedback on your project.

If it's not offered though your university, you should approach securing work experience and internships as you would approach applying for a job. Some internships are paid and are therefore essentially jobs and an expense for the company. You must apply for them as you would a salaried position—impress and earn your role there.

Start by making a list of companies you really want to work for, while at the same time ensuring that you're giving yourself well-rounded experience. Also consider working abroad—although costly, this can give unrivaled experience in the fashion industry at the international level. Next, prepare your résumé and examples of your work so they are ready to send (see Writing the Perfect Résumé and Securing an Interview, pages 242–243, Preparing for an Interview, page 245, and Impressing on the Interview Day, page 248).

PLANNING YOUR TIME

The length of work experience and internships can vary from one week to one year. You won't be able to piece the internships into the amount of time you have until you have secured potential offers. It's like a jigsaw puzzle, as you must consider the dates that the companies require you to work while also ensuring that you're getting well-rounded experience from the combination of companies you're committing to.

Try to line up sequential internships to fill the time you have and avoid having to apply for your next internship while in your current role.

188.
LIVING AND WORKING ABROAD

Living and working in the fashion industry abroad can give you a real advantage when it comes to securing employment. You will experience working in a territory outside your home country and can identify differences between the two. It will also demonstrate drive and determination to prospective employers. It's not easy to plan and carry out, but it's well worth it and you'll have fun and incredible experiences along the way.

KEY SKILLS FOR LIVING AND WORKING ABROAD

ORGANIZATIONAL SKILLS
Being organized, proactive, and planning ahead are essential. Aim to go during a year that offers you diverse experiences (see page 249).

PRACTICAL SKILLS
There's an endless amount of red tape involved in living and working abroad. Ensure that you have a valid passport and the correct working visas for your intended countries. Give yourself sufficient time to secure accommodations—your employer should be able to steer you on how previous employees have tackled this and make recommendations on areas to live.

Find out the currency you'll be paid in and set up relevant bank accounts, ensuring you have enough money to see you through to your first pay check. You'll also need a cell phone and working Internet connections.

SOCIAL SKILLS
You're taking yourself out of your comfort zone—well done! You may be embarking on this adventure alone or with fellow students that you don't know too well. At times you'll feel isolated and will need to go out of your way to make friends. This will come, and remember, if it was easy, everyone would do it!

UNDERSTAND, RESPECT, AND ENGAGE IN LOCAL CULTURE
It might be your only chance to experience a country, so go for it. It's well worth considering learning the language, or at least the basics, to help you integrate and be able to say "hi," thank people, and navigate through your new environment.

PROFESSIONAL SKILLS
Use this time abroad to network, impress, and find new contacts.

189.
FIRST JOB: FREELANCING

If designing within a retailer or supplier isn't for you, you may look at becoming a freelance designer. It's an attractive proposition—from being your own boss and the freedom that it affords to working across a whole variety of briefs, projects, and brands.

On the flip side there's a little less stability than a full-time, permanent position (especially in the UK and Europe, where both designer and employee are protected by fixed-term contracts and notice periods). Freelancers can command higher daily rates but miss out on paid holidays and benefits that can make a full-time role an attractive proposition. Freelancing can sometimes lead to offers of permanent roles too—my first job started on a freelance basis.

KEY SKILLS FOR FREELANCING
The key skills you'll need when setting out on the road to becoming a successful freelance designer hinge on contacts and reputation.

BUILD A NETWORK OF CONTACTS
Ninety-nine percent of the time freelance roles or project-based freelance opportunities are filled through word of mouth rather than recruiting for the position. Try to build up a solid network of contacts from as early as the undergraduate level. Use LinkedIn to keep up to date with who's where and current roles.

BUILD UP A GOOD REPUTATION
Needless to say, your reputation precedes you, both as a designer and as an individual. A varied portfolio will showcase your talent and widen the opportunities you can put yourself forward for, while at the same time having a specialty will ensure you're in demand. A good reputation in terms of being reliable, consistent, and generally easy to work with is crucial.

SET UP YOUR WORKPLACE
Think about where you work best and where you flourish. Freelancing can be a lonely role when you're not really part of a team per se and you might spend long periods of time working from home in isolation. But again, this might suit you.

USE YOUR PRESENTATION SKILLS
As with designing for a retailer or supplier, good presentation skills are essential when delivering your project back to your employer.

190.

FIRST JOB: DESIGNING FOR A SUPPLIER

Behind every great retailer are great suppliers. We'll look at the skill set needed to develop and maintain great supplier relationships (see page 256), but first, how does the role of a designer differ when working for a supplier rather than a retailer?

Essentially, the role is very similar. Retailers will use a supplier's in-house design team primarily for two end uses:

1. To realize an idea that the buyer has had—to design, spec, and produce a sample in the absence of a design team within the retailer itself.

2. To buy product "off the shelf"—many suppliers design and develop their own trends and line to showcase and sell to their clients, the retailers.

With both of the above scenarios, your role in designing at a supplier will incorporate many of the same skills as a retail designer—from the inspiration stage and design development to writing specs. You may even attend fitting sessions at your client's office and see the product through to the stage where it's gold-sealed and ready to book.

THE DAY-TO-DAY ROLE OF DESIGNING FOR A SUPPLIER

Some of the best designers I know are supplier-trained. The crucial difference between the day-to-day role of a retail designer and a supplier designer is the increased amount of time a supplier designer spends at their desk designing. For the majority of supplier designers, there are fewer meetings and less time spent analyzing company trade. More time spent designing allows skills to develop and improve rapidly. A retail designer may have only three out of five days to work on design; the rest of their time can be taken up by meetings and managing bigger-picture responsibilities.

Although some see this as a less glamorous role, as the company you're working in is not a recognizable brand name, consider cutting your teeth at a supplier because the experience will be invaluable.

191.
FIRST JOB: RETAIL

Securing your first job can be challenging. Not only are there many routes down which you can go—from creating your own brand (see page 196), to working at a supplier (see page 252), to working within retail—but the role of a designer varies significantly within each role. In this section we'll explore the skills needed to secure, and succeed in, your first job within retail.

Having built a strong portfolio and delivered at the interview stage, you've been offered your first position. Hopefully this is your dream role. However, if it's not, don't be too quick to disregard it. The fashion industry is a small world and, unfortunately, supply for roles outstrips demand. Having graduated with a degree in knitwear, my first role was designing beach accessories. I then designed handbags before having the opportunity to incorporate footwear into my role. This then became my specialty, which it remains to this day. We all have to start somewhere—Giorgio Armani was a window dresser, while Ralph Lauren started as a tie salesman for Brooks Brothers.

BE VERSATILE

Getting a foot in the door and being prepared to work in any sector of the arena you are interested in is no bad thing. Roles evolve, particularly within womenswear design, and good designers can generally move across departments—from dresses to skirts, or from jersey product to tailoring—with ease. Footwear, bags, jewelry, accessories, swim, and lingerie designers have less scope to move due to their product areas being so technical. As you progress in these fields, you're more likely to become a specialist within your area and work your way up in that role. However, at the stage of securing your first role, be versatile and open to working across a variety of departments until you find your niche.

MANAGE YOUR OWN EXPECTATIONS

Your first role will most likely be as a design assistant or assistant designer. Both of these roles will involve a variety of duties—managing monthly magazine subscriptions, ordering supplies, completing expense claims for more senior members of the design team. There will also be more creative tasks, such as helping to compose and finalize mood boards, and compiling visuals for design packs, such as runway overviews or seasonal trend pack handouts. These tasks may feel administrative because you are facilitating rather than driving them. Persevere, remind yourself why you want to work in fashion, and see all experiences in an entry-level role as learning. There'll be opportunity to do the best part—hands-on designing. Relish the opportunity to do this under the guidance of your senior designer, and push to do as much of it as possible within your role.

NEGOTIATE SALARY

When negotiating salary, a good tip is to ask recruitment companies for a salary bracket that someone of your experience could command in that role. Think about what value you can bring to the role, what the role can teach you, and where it might lead to. Consider the whole salary package and negotiate until you settle on something that both parties are comfortable with.

ABSORB EVERYTHING

Your very first position will be one of the most exciting and informative roles of your career. You'll learn so much—from the smallest detail to global strategy and everything in between. Understand what you like and dislike about each task, each role, and each step of the design process in order to develop your natural style and discover your specialty product.

192.
RELATIONSHIPS WITH BUYERS AND MERCHANDISERS

When designing for a retailer, the most important relationships you will forge are with the buyer and merchandiser. The goal of everyone on the team you work with is to build a successful and profitable line.

BUYERS

A buyer's job is to build a successful line from the trend, color, material, and silhouette direction you give them and the designs you create. Success is measured in commercial, directional, and profitable terms. Your role is to steer the buyer toward the new and "must-have" items for the next season. Buyers are also responsible for agreeing on costs with the supplier and for placing the final orders.

MERCHANDISERS

Merchandisers control the purse strings—they are given a sales plan at the start of a season and must ensure that the company buys the correct volume and type of product at the price needed to achieve the sales plan. They ensure that the buyer is not spending too much or too little on stock. They also analyze sales history to identify what worked and what didn't, and they also manage how the stock goes out to stores.

BUILDING A RELATIONSHIP

The line that appears in store is the result of collaboration between designer, buyer, and merchandiser, and at times not everyone will agree. As is the case with so many relationships in your career, building trust is essential, and this will take time to develop. You'll spend the majority of the work week with your buyer—you should be at each other's desks numerous times a day. You'll travel the globe together on both inspiration and development trips—trips

like this can be grueling and intense, so make it fun. Designers and buyers who have great relationships on a personal as well as professional level build the best lines—you can see in the product the shared vision and the fun they had when developing it.

Trust between you and a buyer may only come after a season or two of good sales have built confidence. If you've done all of the groundwork—trend analysis, color prediction, material sourcing, and, most importantly, creatively given it your all—believe in yourself and your designs, and keep working on these relationships. You won't agree on everything, so learn to pick your battles carefully. Listen and be open to making changes when you feel that you can without compromising on the final product or line. Likewise, articulate and fight for those key pieces that you feel are integral to the collection.

TYPICAL ATTITUDES TOWARD RISK-TAKING AND DRIVING FASHION FORWARD

Designer—Push it forward; take risks.

Merchandiser—Cautious; trade like last year with improvements from lessons learned, build on best sellers.

Buyer—Strike a commercial balance between the two.

193.
RELATIONSHIPS WITH YOUR FACTORY AND SUPPLIERS

Just as a pattern cutter and machinist must work hand in hand, so must a designer and suppliers. You'll invariably have a number of suppliers—some of them key suppliers who hold a lot of business, others more fringe suppliers who you might go in and out of doing business with, depending on whether their product is relevant to that specific season. You'll either work directly with the factory or you'll work indirectly with an agent/supplier.

MEETING YOUR SUPPLIER

Once your designs are ready to brief out, schedule a meeting with your supplier. It's advisable to meet in person unless you're working directly with them, in which case designs can be emailed. Ideally, meet at the supplier's offices or showroom—seeing their in-house collections and having full access to their libraries of fabrics and trims are crucial and will further inspire you before briefing out the final design to the factory. Be flexible and use these meetings as working meetings—if they have a better pattern idea or materials you didn't previously have access to, adapt the sketch and give them a go.

SOURCING PACKS AND SAMPLES

In addition to designs and specs, brief regular sourcing packs out to your suppliers (see Sourcing Packs Within Industry, page 43). They and the factories are your connection to global fabric and trim markets when you can't visit yourself. Challenge suppliers to source the exact materials, yarns, trims, components, and constructions that you need, ideally in the country of origin to avoid excessive shipping costs.

Once the first sample comes back, the supplier will usually hand-deliver it to your office, and together you go through changes or, if there are none, request costs. Give yourself sufficient time for these meetings. The first sample stage is part of the design process, so be open to starting from scratch, morphing designs, and learning from your mistakes. Once the aesthetics of the final sample have been agreed, it's over to buyers and merchandisers to fit, gold seal, and agree on the cost, quantity, and delivery schedule.

BUILDING A RELATIONSHIP

Relationships with suppliers can be difficult for designers. In most cases, suppliers will affiliate themselves with the buyer and merchandiser as ultimately they're the people who'll place the orders. At times you can feel outnumbered, but go back to the negotiation skills learned when working with your buyer and push for what you believe to be right for the collection.

Suppliers are your eyes and ears—they'll work with an array of customers, some of whom will be your competitors, so talk trade. Ask for their take on the trade in general—best sellers—and trends or patterns coming through. Suppliers are at the hub of the fashion world—use this to your advantage.

194.
SUPPLIER RELATIONSHIPS WITH RETAILERS

When designing for a supplier rather than a retailer, you will most likely design for assigned retail accounts. The skill in working with these clients is in building relationships, understanding and responding to briefs, and designing within those parameters. This can frustrate some designers who prefer the freedom of designing a line from scratch based on their trend analysis and seasonal mood boards. However, it's an integral skill to master in it's own right—the mark of a great designer, whether within retail or supply, is someone who can design for a variety of customers within a range of price points.

Building trust between you and your client will take time, and there will inevitably be clashes of vision and arguments over creative control along the way. Keep going, listen to feedback, and work through any sticking points, and you'll get there. Some of your clients may just want the agreed-upon number of designs in a black-and-white spec format, annotated with measurements only, which they will then choose material and colorways for. At this stage, you relinquish creative control. Others may give you full creative control to design, produce a color palette, and brief out the designs, and will expect it presented back to them as a capsule collection.

Another vital part of the job is successfully presenting your designs back to your clients. This is key to giving them the confidence to commit to your designs so that they book samples and place orders. Selling yourself and your designs is crucial when designing at a supplier's.

256

195.

RELATIONSHIPS WITH PRESS, MARKETING, AND SOCIAL MEDIA TEAMS

When designing and building a line, it is paramount that designers and design teams work closely with press, marketing, and social media teams.

PRESS TEAM

The press team works with both short and long lead-time magazines and media to secure product placement and ensure brand coverage. It raises awareness of brands and collections through press events—primarily Spring/Summer and Fall/Winter press shows—to showcase the forthcoming collections.

MARKETING TEAM

Marketing teams highlight product and key messages through a number of channels, including advertising, and in the case of e-tailers, through home page and website content.

SOCIAL MEDIA TEAM

The social media team also drives product and key messages by engaging with the customer through platforms such as Instagram and Twitter. This allows them to upload unique tailor-made content. It can be particularly useful for learning what the customer likes and dislikes.

WORKING TOGETHER

Again, this stage of the process is a collaboration across all departments, so draw on the skills you would use when building relationships with any other functions— e.g., buyers and merchandisers, suppliers, clients, etc. Ultimately, however, it's the product that has to be on point before press, marketing, or social media teams will want to champion it.

Include these teams early in the process—from the trend stage onward. This could be in any forum, from scheduling a trend presentation and highlighting key items that are coming through for the season to informal infrequent chats about what you're "feeling for" and which references, exhibitions, and collections are influencing you. Get these teams excited and inspired about the upcoming season and, likewise, draw from references they have for you.

Suggest new and directional ways to showcase your product—these could be the treatment and physical props used at a press show or inspiring digital references for online content. You might know of an up-and-coming musician or celebrity that encapsulates the vision you have for the collection, or suggest a key blogger to approach to promote the line or to collaborate with.

Ultimately, you'll be asked to provide quotes or do interviews to promote a product. See the section on Media Training: Preparation and Media Training: Delivering at Interview (pages 240–241) for more information.

196.
TRAVEL TIPS

Fashion and travel go hand in hand, whether it's for shopping and inspiration, spotting trends, or visiting suppliers and factories. It's exciting and is certainly a perk of the job, but it can also be physically and mentally challenging. From jet lag to finding your way around, here are my top travel tips to help you master the vital skill of traveling well.

PREPARATION

You will quickly become a master of packing and unpacking suitcases. At certain times of the year you may be doing back-to-back trips for both inspiration and development purposes. Write a list of key things to remember—your "go-to" list—for when time is tight and you have to pack in a hurry. Remember that as long as you have a valid passport, visa, and credit card, you can pretty much pick up anything you forget when you arrive, but try to remember the essentials listed below.

PACKING LIST

- Warm and cool weather clothing
- Footwear
- Toiletries
- Underwear
- Pajamas/loungewear
- Activewear
- Headphones
- Ear plugs
- Eye mask
- Sunglasses
- Passport
- Visa
- Tickets
- Phone/tablet/laptop chargers

TIP: Check the weather forecast and ask around to see if anyone has been to your destination recently and has any tips. This will affect how you pack.

HEALTH AND STAMINA

You'll get run down from traveling through time zones, lack of sleep, and long working hours. Drink lots of water, get the right nutrients when you can, or take vitamin supplements with you, and if time permits try to incorporate physical exercise into your trip.

JET LAG

As soon as you board, set your watch to the time at your destination and eat and sleep as you would at those times. This will help to avoid, or at least minimize, jet lag. Again, lots of water, stretching, and a good moisturizer for the flight is recommended.

CREDIT CARDS AND CELL PHONES

Call both your credit card company and cell phone provider before departure to advise them of your travel dates. Even then, it's worth taking two or three credit cards because your credit card companies will inevitably decline transactions until they have ascertained that they are not fraudulent. When embarking on inspirational shopping trips, check that you have sufficient funds to buy samples. You may also need to turn on data roaming to ensure your cell phone works on arrival.

FOOD

You can experience some incredible cuisines on trips, but if you're not adventurous on the food front or have allergies, pack snacks to avoid going hungry.

197.
SHOPPING DESTINATIONS AND GUIDES

Fashion hot spots are always evolving, much like the trends we chase around the world. There are also eternal fashion capitals, which are must-visit destinations for designers. Here are some of the main destinations used for inspiration trips within the industry.

LONDON

Suggested shopping time: 4 days
London is known for its mix of high-end, contemporary, and vintage stores, and also its street style.
- Department stores include Selfridges, Harvey Nichols, Harrods, and Liberty.
- Go to Oxford Street, High Street Kensington, and Westfield Shopping Centers in Shepherd's Bush and Stratford for contemporary stores.
- East London is great for vintage and independent boutiques, particularly around Brick Lane, Hackney, and Dalston.
- High-end boutiques are mainly found in West London—particularly Kings Road and Sloane Square.
- Mayfair also has high-end boutiques, such as Acne and Victoria Beckham.
- Don't leave London without visiting Dover Street Market, a multifloor concept store created by Rei Kawakubo of Japanese label Comme des Garçons.
- The main markets are Portobello and Spitalfields.

PARIS

Suggested shopping time: 3 days
Paris is the most chic of all of the fashion capitals. High-end designers reign here, but it's also known for vintage and bustling markets.
- Your first port of call in Paris should be Le Marais, which is full of little boutiques and designer brands.
- North Marais boasts multibrands and concept stores, while Rue de Saintonge in the middle of Le Marais is an old but lively and increasingly trendy area boasting boutiques and design stores.
- Rue Vieille du Temple has a variety of footwear.
- In Bastille, head to Rue Keller for womenswear and affordable designers, such as Isabel Marant.
- Head to Etienne Marcel for the vintage scene—check out the Kiliwatch store.
- On Rue Montmarte, check out shoes and accessories at 58M.
- Huge department stores Galleries Lafayette and Printemps are both situated in Opéra.
- Avenue des Champs-Élysées is comparable to London's Oxford Street with its affordable contemporary brands.
- Look in Rue du Faubourg St. Honoré for luxury designer and the hands-down must-visit concept store, Colette.
- Madeleine—luxury designer stores, including the Gucci flagship store.
- Abbesses is a great area for unique brands, both contemporary and affordable.
- Vavin is where it's at for Parisian childrenswear.
- Flea markets: Porte de Clignancourt is good for jewelry and prints; Porte de Montreuil is good for vintage and surplus.

MILAN

Suggested shopping time: 3 days
Milan is the most luxurious of all four fashion capital cities, boasting luxury brands and department stores. Designer goods reign here, and brand outlet stores, such as Marni, are popular as a result of this. There is no real vintage or flea market vibe in Milan.
- Via Montenapoleone, part of the Quadrilatero d'Oro (Milan's golden quadrilateral), is possibly the most famous shopping street in the city. Home to designer brands Gucci and Prada and luxury leather accessory brands, including Fendi and Bottega Veneta.

- In stark contrast, Corso Como—in particular, 10 Corso Como near Milano Garibaldi—is both an eclectic and directional fashion must-see.
- Visit La Rinascente, the big department store opposite the cathedral.
- See Piazza del Duomo, Corso Vittorio Emmanuele, and Corso Buenos Aires for contemporary and midrange brands and young fashion.
- Corso di Porta Ticinese is key for secondhand clothing and independent designer boutiques and is also great for denim. It has a similar vibe to Portobello Road in London.
- The monthly vintage market on the Navigli is also worth a visit.
- Designer discounts can be found at Il Salvagente, which has designer clothing at wholesale prices. Don't miss The Highline Outlet (Corso Vittorio Emanuele, 30) for discounted menswear, womenswear, and accessories.

STOCKHOLM

Suggested shopping time: 1–2 days

Stockholm is mainly designer and mid-range fashion-led, with some independent boutiques. Immerse yourself in the cleaner aesthetic of Scandinavian style.

- Stockholm is the home of the Acne Studios brand.

ST. TROPEZ, CANNES, MARBELLA, IBIZA

Suggested shopping time: 2–3 days

All of these destinations are really useful for people watching and picking up on emerging trends, especially for swim, beach, and beach accessories. Good for all summer wardrobe and also festival trend inspiration.

BERLIN

Suggested shopping time: 1–2 days

You can get almost anything you want across all budgets in Berlin. It is deceptively spread out, so embrace bicycles—or taxis if you're loaded down with shopping—to navigate the city most efficiently.

- Mitte or Charlottenburg are the destinations for boutiques and vintage.

- KaDeWe—Kaufhaus Des Westens Directions—is the German Selfridges.
- Visit Bikini Berlin Mall, a concept shopping mall.
- Flea markets: Flohmarkt im Mauerpark (Strasse des 17.Juni, near Tiergarten)—the biggest of all the flea markets specializing in clothing and furniture. Flowmarkt, Neukölln, is the place for clothing, homewares, and accessories. The flea market at Rathaus Schöneberg, John F. Kennedy Platz, offers some clothing but specializes in housewares, books, and vinyl.

NEW YORK

Suggested shopping time: 5 days

New York has it all—a mix of high-end designer, contemporary brands, and vintage. Also an invaluable resource for street style and spotting emerging trends through people watching.

- Uptown you will find Bloomingdales, Saks Fifth Avenue, Barneys, Bergdorf Goodman, and many high-end fashion department stores.
- Most contemporary stores tend to be found Midtown.
- Visit downtown Manhattan and the Lower East Side for thriving vintage scenes.
- Brooklyn has emerged as a must-shop destination. Williamsburg and Greenpoint are a great source of vintage stores and independent boutiques stocking young designers. Brooklyn Flea Market is well worth a visit too.

LOS ANGELES

Suggested shopping time: 3–4 days

As this is the second largest city in the US after New York, you will need a car to get the most out of this vast, sprawling shopping destination. If you're prepared to drive from district to district, the rewards are plentiful, from high-end boutiques to vintage stores.

- Melrose Ave.—an array of upscale boutiques plus midrange and smaller independent stand-alones.
- West Hollywood—head to Robertson Blvd. for affordable stores such as Kitson and Madison.
- Beverly Hills—Rodeo Drive is every window shopper's delight. High-end department stores such as Barneys, Nieman Marcus, and Saks Fifth Avenue line the streets.
- Downtown—inexpensive shopping for trendsetters. Check out Friday sample sales when designers open their showrooms and sell samples for a fraction of the retail price.
- Rosebowl—vintage flea market on the second Sunday of every month. Head here for vintage clothes, accessories, jewelry, fabric, costumes, and much more.

AUSTIN, TEXAS

Suggested shopping time: 1–2 days

Encouraging visitors to "Keep Austin Weird," Austin is independent, individual, young, and casually laid back.

- Incredible vintage stores are situated on a few streets around South 1st Street.
- South 1st and South Congress—walk the blocks between the two for vintage and thrift stores.
- Great independent boutiques and local jewelry brands can be found in the 2nd Street District.
- East 6th Street—hip and creative, this is a great shopping area for one-of-a-kind accessories and jewelry.
- "The Drag"—also known as Guadalupe, the Drag is popular with students for its artistic markets full of unique accessories and jewelry finds.

MIAMI

Suggested shopping time: 2–3 days

If luxury fashion stores are your thing, Miami Design District is your place. This new, up-and-coming area features brands such as Prada, Marni, Lanvin, Rick Owens, and Louis Vuitton.

- South Beach has a mixture of contemporary, independent, and designer concept stores such as The Webster.
- For department stores, head to Aventura Mall.
- Bal Harbour Shops—there is great inspiration shopping to be had here in both the mall, which houses high-end brands, plus Neiman Marcus and Saks Fifth Avenue.
- For vintage, check out C. Madeleine's and Fly Boutique, both on Biscayne Boulevard.

BRAZIL

Suggested shopping time: 1–2 days in each

The two main shopping regions in Brazil are São Paolo and Rio.

RIO

- Rio is great for beachwear—make a point of visiting the bohemian neighborhood of Santa Teresa.
- Rua Visconde de Pirajá in Ipanema is bustling with commercial brands. Be sure to check out the surrounding commercial streets too.
- Leblon boasts chic boutiques and a designer mall, Shopping Leblon.

SAO PAOLO

- Vila Madalena is one long street full of independent brands and boutiques—a bohemian, grungy, hipster hangout.
- Iguatemi São Paulo shopping center is a diverse mix of designers and independent brands.

SEOUL AND TOKYO

Both Seoul and Tokyo never seem to sleep. Here you will find enormous, sprawling, multilevel department stores and floor after floor (and half-floors) of fashion. Some are run by independent vendors, which only close at 5 A.M. to restock for a few hours. These trips can be noisy, confusing, disorienting, exhausting … and amazing. Both cities have independent labels that you would never see stocked for retail anywhere else in the world. But beware of designer copies and counterfeit goods! Seoul has some great fabric, trim, and haberdashery markets, too.

TOKYO

Suggested shopping time: 2 days

- Shibuya 109, Parco, and La Foret are very noisy department stores, boasting floor after floor of young fashion, but beware: it's not inexpensive.
- Harajuku is the center for Japanese youth culture and fashion. Check out the back streets, Takeshita Dori and Cat Street. Opening Ceremony and Ragtime Vintage are must-sees too.
- Daikanyama has independant high-end and more affordable boutiques and vintage shops. Think of it as the Brooklyn of central Tokyo.

SEOUL

Suggested shopping time: 4 days

- Lotte department store, Hyundai department store, and Doota are enormous and sprawling—a must-shop for independent labels.
- Visit Galleria, a luxury brand fashion mall.
- Hongdae is a student area; it's worth a trip, if only once.
- Garosu-gil in the Gangnam district is a great area full of creatives and artists, morphing the old and the new. It is similar to Soho in New York. Trendsetters head here for fashion on a budget, and Gentle Monster is essential for sunglasses.
- Visit Rodeo Street for cheaper independent brands.
- Don't leave without checking out Åland; they have stores in Hongdae, Garosu-gil, and Myeong-dong.
- Dongdaemun Market is great for fabric and components.
- Namdaemun Market—one of the largest retail markets in Seoul selling various goods, from fashion to housewares.

HONG KONG

Suggested shopping time: 2–3 days

Hong Kong is full of designer and midrange brands.

- There are two enormous department stores—Harbour City in Kowloon and IFC Mall in Hong Kong. The Star Ferry will take you between the two.
- You will find lots of interesting independent stores on Granville Road, which is also the location of Rise Shopping Mall.
- Temple Street night market is interesting too, maybe more so as a tourist!

198.
SHOPPING TIPS: AN INSIDER'S GUIDE

When working for a retail brand, it's not uncommon to spend somewhere in the region of $30,000 on shopping trips, so there's a lot of responsibility. It sounds glamorous but really is hard work, with long hours and lots of miles to cover. Here are some tips to help you get it right.

RESEARCH
Budget constraints make for a packed schedule and a limited number of days. Plan each day and arrive knowing the areas you want to cover, store opening hours, and new store openings.

Downloadable "Superfuture" guides are invaluable; they are regularly updated and don't date in the way published travel guides can, and are tailored specifically to fashion and design trips. Excellent map reading skills are also an absolute must-have.

PLAN
Planning your route around a city and shopping by region is essential. Part of your route will be dictated by store opening hours, and in particular markets that might only be open on certain days of the week.

BE RESOURCEFUL
You won't be able to buy every sample that inspires you, so you will need to master the art of taking sneaky in-store photos without the sales staff realizing. Don't worry; you'll refine this skill with experience. Some vintage boutiques let you borrow pieces for a couple of months for much less than the purchase price.

BE DECISIVE
It may be only five minutes after arriving at your destination that you have to decide whether to spend $3,000 on a coat. There won't be time to visit places twice, so you need to have the confidence to buy items when you see them (see Travel Tips, page 258).

KEEP YOUR EYES OPEN—AND TAKE A LOT OF PHOTOS
Photograph as much as you can—shop windows and street style can contribute as much to the trends you take back as samples do.

PEOPLE WATCH
Notice trends emerging in youth culture. If it seems like all the kids are wearing Dr. Martens boots, decide whether this is a trend you should interpret through a version of a utility or biker boot.

REVIEW
When you get back to your hotel, take your purchases out and group them together. Notice any coherent trends emerging. If you're shopping across product categories, look for gaps that you will need to fill.

TALK TO PEOPLE
You can learn a lot from people in stores about what's trending and get recommendations of other stores. Sometimes you need to be vague about who you are and whom you work for because some brands will think you're going to copy them. Some vintage boutiques also bump up prices if they know you're spending a large company's money in their store.

DON'T HURT YOUR BACK
Use a shopping cart to avoid having to carry everything. Carrying heavy bags and spending too much time on planes is really not good for your back, so be careful.

SHOPPING TIPS: PRACTICAL SKILLS

Unfortunately, shopping trips aren't all inspiration—they require an almost equal amount of administration. Here are some tips to keep on top of it all.

BE ORGANIZED

Photograph every item at the point of purchase. This is for two reasons: first, if you need to fill in an expenses claim, you will have to submit photos, so this will already be done rather than having to unpack and photograph everything once you are home; second, if your luggage goes missing in transit, you will at least have a record of the items.

MANAGE YOUR BUDGET

Be clear what the expectation is in terms of how much you can spend. Download a currency converter to your phone so you can calculate what you're spending.

KEEP YOUR RECEIPTS

This is essential for expenses claims—otherwise you can end up paying out of pocket. I find it useful to file receipts by day as I go along. Also photograph them as you go, in case they go missing. Write a brief description of the item on the receipt as you buy it—descriptions on receipts can be unclear or can of course be in a foreign language.

As mentioned in Travel Tips (page 258), you may end up using multiple cards to pay throughout your trip, so make a note of which card was used for which item—this will allow you to match credit card statements and currency conversions back to the items.

OBEY CUSTOMS LAWS

You are essentially importing goods, so make the necessary arrangements to ensure you are declaring the goods and paying the necessary import duty when you return home.

200.
ENJOY!

When you've chosen to pursue a career in fashion design, whether you are following that dream by studying or working in the industry, things can get stressful. Pressure can get you down, and you can sometimes hit a creative block.

You should be enjoying your role, so it's important sometimes to think back to why you wanted to be a fashion designer. Here are some tips for overcoming a creative block and making sure you are having fun.

LOOK BACK WITH PRIDE

Think back to one of the earliest projects that you were proud of. Remind yourself what made it so special and gave it a spark. Remember how it made you feel. Try and harness that and apply it to your current situation.

CARRY YOUR SKETCHBOOK

Make sure you always have your sketchbook on hand, ready for whenever inspiration does take hold.

SNAP HAPPY

Always have a camera or smartphone with you, and take photos of anything that interests you visually. Flicking through these can reignite your imagination.

REVISIT OLD STYLES

Think back to your favorite outfits over the years and deconstruct them. Look at photos of outfits that five, ten, fifteen, or even twenty years ago seemed cool but now make you cringe. Identify anything that could be changed or a detail you can develop in a new direction.

TAKE A DIFFERENT ROUTE TO WORK

Take some extra time to explore and look around you. Changing routine and seeing new things really help.

DO SOMETHING NEW

Perhaps there is an element of culture you don't often partake in—maybe opera or theater. Try it. There may be ideas and inspiration those spheres take for granted but completely blow your mind with possibilities.

ENGAGE A DIFFERENT PART OF YOUR BRAIN

Do something that relaxes, distracts, and inspires you, like going to a gig. Fashion and music are a winning combination; when you see live music it will both energize and influence you, as well as enable you to let off steam.

SLEEP ON IT

Sometimes seemingly unsolvable riddles look so simple the next morning when you look at them with fresh eyes. Also, don't underestimate the impact that getting enough rest has on clearing your head and keeping stress levels under control. Staying up late battling with your muse is not always the best answer.

SOCIALIZE

Talk to people unrelated to the design world and get a different perspective. Sometimes you can get so bogged down in talking with your colleagues that this can limit your horizons.

GO FOR A RUN

Exercise can be great for relieving stress, clearing your mind, and putting things in perspective.

GLOSSARY

Abstract—Part of a design, particularly a pattern, which doesn't attempt to have a visual likeness to anything concrete.

Aesthetic—In philosophy, this is the study of what is beautiful and visually pleasing. In fashion, a "designer's aesthetic" is a set of values that they adhere to to create a coherent look; for example, a "clean, minimalist aesthetic."

Appliqué—Attaching one piece of fabric to the surface of another.

Atelier—The workshop or studio of a designer—the phrase is often used to refer to a design house.

Back Counter—The support at the heel of the shoe that sits between the outer and lining to keep the shape.

Back Neck Width (BNW)—Measurement of the gap from one side of the neck hole of a garment to the other.

Back Stitch—A strong, straight stitch that has been reinforced by overlapping loops back over previous stitches.

Bespoke—An item of clothing made to order, often tailored to fit perfectly.

Bias Grain—Positioning the grain line (warp thread) of the fabric to run at 45 degrees to the center front line of a garment. Gravity's effect on the weight of the fabric makes it stretch in length and narrow in width.

Binding—Often used in clothing, footwear, and bag construction, binding is a way of finishing two raw edges of fabric by wrapping another piece of fabric over both and sewing either side. It conceals and secures the raw edges.

Block—A basic, standardized template from which the pattern cutter can adapt their pattern.

Bodice—Main "body" section of a dress, minus sleeves.

Brief—A set of criteria that must be met by a designer. In education this could be for a project, and in industry it may be a list of required designs.

Buyers—Also called planners, they are responsible for setting budgets, forecasting sales, managing stock, and ensuring stock is in the right place at the right time.

CAD—Computer-aided design.

Calico—A type of cotton fabric, often white or unbleached. Relatively cheap and a popular choice for making toiles.

Capsule Collection—Core, essential pieces of clothing that are trans-seasonal and less likely to go out of fashion. These can be complemented with seasonal pieces.

Cast On—In knitting, this is the term for making the first row of stitches.

Casting Off—In knitting, this is making the final row of stitches in a way that means they won't unravel.

Catwalk Show—The UK term for a runway fashion show.

Color Up—To add color to a black-and-white design.

Colorways—Different combinations of colors applied to the same base design to give variation to a range. For example, a horizontally striped sweater might be available in two colorways: black-and-white, or red-and-white stripes.

Collection—A seasonal range of garments or accessories produced by a designer or label.

Color Palette—A limited and set selection of colors to standardize shades across a collection or range. This helps to avoid color clashes and to give a sense of coherence.

Concept—An idea will often be referred to as a "concept" at early stages of the design process.

Contemporary Chain Stores—The type of fashion chain stores that you would find in most towns and shopping malls. They tend to be fairly mainstream and mass-produce their garments, so they have a huge impact on major fashion trends.

Copyright—The exclusive, legal right to use a particular design. Part of the intellectual property laws that protect designers and brands and prevent unauthorized copying, reproduction, or counterfeit goods.

Cordwainer—The traditional term for a shoemaker.

Costing—The process of working out the price of producing an item.

Critical Path—A document that shows each stage of the design and production process, along with its duration and any related tasks. This is used to work backwards from product launch dates and to ensure deadlines are met. They can also be called "Time In Action Calendar" or "Flow Chart."

Cut (e.g., of a dress)—The shape or silhouette of an item.

Cut and Sew Knitwear—Garments constructed from knitted fabrics that are laid out and cut into pieces in the way that woven fabrics are normally used. Most jersey clothing is made this way. Fully Fashioned is the alternative method.

Dart—A triangular shape used to take excess material out of a garment; fold or pinch in fabric that allows the garment to fit the 3-D human form.

Design House—Term used to refer to a fashion brand, label, or designer label. Mainly used to describe purveyors of high-end fashion.

Direct to Garment Printing (DTG)—Printing directly onto ready-made garments using digital print technology. This differs from the more traditional method of printing onto fabric that garments are then constructed from.

Drape/Drapability — The way in which a garment or fabric hangs. A fabric with good drapability will hang vertically under its own weight.

Drawing Up — Sketching and committing a rough design to paper. This will often then be "penned in" — the stage where permanent ink marks are added to pencil lines.

Embroidery — Decorating fabric by stitching with a needle and thread or yarn to create a design.

Etailer — A retailer who operates solely online.

Facing — A piece of fabric applied to the inside edge of a garment to finish it.

Fashion Forward — Term used to describe directional and fast-reacting contemporary brands.

Fastenings — Features such as buttons, Velcro®, or zippers that are incorporated into a garment to make it easier to put on and keep it securely in place. Also called "closures."

Final Collection — The final range of garments produced during the final year of education. This can be on the runway or a static exhibition. Essential for building your reputation, as many people from the fashion industry attend these shows.

Fit Model — A model whose body measurements exactly match an industry standard size.

Fitting — The process of checking and adjusting a garment to ensure that it is the correct size.

Flats — Technical illustrations showing the garment as if laid flat.

Forecasting — Looking ahead and coming up with a view of what you think will happen. This can be in terms of predicting trends or estimating sales figures.

Four-Way Stretch Fabric — Fabric that stretches in both directions, both horizontally and vertically; for example, spandex or neoprene.

Freelance Designer — A designer working on a short-term contract basis. They will often have an agreed daily rate.

Fully Fashioned Knitwear — Garments constructed from pieces that have been individually knitted into the correct shape for their use. Cut and Sew is the alternative method.

Grading Up or Down — The process of increasing or decreasing the size of a pattern while keeping it in proportion.

Grain Line — The direction that the warp thread is oriented in a garment's construction. It affects the way the material behaves and how the pattern pieces must be placed onto the fabric before cutting.

Gusset — A piece of material sewn into a garment to enlarge or strengthen a part of it. In handbags, this is often the base.

Hardware — Metal components used on bags, such as clasps, buckles, rings, or logos.

Haute Couture — Translates from French to "high fashion." This is the most expensive and exclusive end of the market where items are often custom-made by the top design houses.

Hem — The edge of a garment where it has been turned under and sewn to give a neat and secure edge.

Horizontal Grain — Aligning the grain line (warp thread) at 90 degrees to the center front line of a garment—typically cuffs and yokes of shirts. The more stable warp thread runs horizontally.

Last — A foot-shaped block used in the construction of shoes.

Lay Planning — The process of working out the most efficient way of cutting pattern pieces out of a length of fabric to minimize waste. An alternative name is "marker planning."

Lookbook — A physical book or digital set of images that are produced to best sum up a brand or collection; used for promotional purposes.

Mannequin — A dressmaking stand on which garments and patterns can be constructed and refined.

Merchandiser — Also called merchants or allocators, they are responsible for deciding how the merchandiser's budget will be spent, by selecting from what the designer has produced.

Minimum Order Quantity (MOQ) — The lowest number of a garment, material, or component that a supplier will accept an order for.

Mood Board — A collection of images curated by a designer to gather ideas, themes, products, colors, and inspiration; key tool in developing and communicating design ideas.

Move-Ons — Reinventions of existing designs or products to refresh them for a new season or apply new trends to them.

Muse — Traditionally, something that inspires an artist. In modern fashion this definition has changed slightly. Some designers will associate with a model or celebrity as their "muse" to create collections based around their innate style. The muse becomes an embodiment of the spirit of a collection. In the case of celebrities, they also provide a significant boost to the profile of a range.

Muslin — A lightweight cotton fabric in plain weave, often sheer.

Options — Each unique garment in a collection or range, including instances of the same style but different colors.

Pantone — A color matching system used to standardize colors, especially helpful for communicating color requirements to suppliers.

Portfolio — A visual summary of your work used to showcase your skills to prospective employers.

Prediction—The act of forecasting trends in order to create garments that will be on trend by the time they are manufactured and in store. Often based on anticipating which high-end fashion elements will be widely adopted.

Pre-Fall—Before main Fall season shows. March: Fall shows; May/June: Resort shows (taster of Spring/Summer); September: Spring/Summer shows; December/January: Pre-Fall shows (taster of Fall).

PU/Polyurethene—A synthetic material most commonly used as artificial or faux leather for shoes and bags.

Purchase Order (PO)—A document that legally formalizes and finalizes an order placed with a supplier.

Purl—In knitting, this is a stitch constructed in the reverse way of a regular stitch. Combinations of knit and purl stitches can be used to create textured patterns.

Realization—Planning your collection piece-by-piece in the final year of education.

Right Side—The side of a fabric that is intended to be visable when the garment is worn. The other side of the fabric will often be less attractive due to the way it has been constructed.

Red-Sealed—A sample of a garment with a red tag attached to it, meaning that amendments are necessary. This is sent back to the pattern room or factory with fit comments.

Seam Allowance—Refers to a thin strip of fabric between its edge and the stitches that are used to make a seam with another piece of fabric.

Season—The period that a range or collection is designed to be sold and worn. The majority of design houses and brands have two seasons per year: Spring/Summer and Fall/Winter.

Selvage—The edges of a piece of woven fabric that are finished in a way that prevents unraveling.

Soft Accessories—Knitted or woven accessories, including hats, gloves, scarves, and hosiery.

Sourcing Packs—A physical or digital collection of images or references that your supplier can use to source the correct materials or components for a particular garment.

Spec Sheet—Abbreviation of specification. This is a technical document sent to suppliers giving key details about the design and materials required.

Straight Grain—Aligning the grain line (warp thread) parallel to the center front line of a garment. The warp thread runs vertically, which gives stability, and the weft runs horizontally, which gives a degree of stretch.

Supplier—The manufacturer from which you source garments or components. This will often be an agent who in turn has links to production factories.

Swatch—A sample piece of fabric. Typically a cutting of a fabric used to communicate requirements to a supplier. Also, in knitting, a small "swatch" is produced to measure gauge.

Tears—Images torn from sources such as magazines and newspapers, usually to use on a mood board.

Tension—In knitwear, this is the number of stitches per inch. Technically abbreviated to GG, it is also referred to as gauge, and affects both the appearance and behavior of the fabric.

Throat line—The part of a shoe that attaches the vamp to the quarters.

Thumbnail—A small sketch of an idea or collection of ideas.

Toe Puff—Stiffener sandwiched between the upper and lining material to create form at the toe of a shoe.

Toe Spring—The curve of the sole of a shoe from the ball of the foot to the toe.

Toile—An early test version of a garment made in a cheaper material than the finished product. Used to perfect the design without wasting more expensive fabric.

Tolerance—The amount of variation allowed from the measurements or quantities of an order. This will often form part of a contract and be expressed as a percentage.

Topline—The opening in the upper of a shoe through which the foot enters.

Topstitching—Stitching that is visible on the top or "right" side of the fabric. Often decorative but can also be used near hems to add definition.

Two-Way Stretch Fabric—Fabric that stretches in one direction—usually along the weft from selvage to selvage.

Undergraduate—A student actively working toward a degree.

Unique Selling Point (USP)—The distinguishing feature(s) that make your product or brand different from anything else.

Visuals—Images or pictures.

Warp—In a woven fabric, this is the thread stretched across the loom, which runs along the length of the fabric. It is more stable and doesn't stretch much.

Wearer Trial—A way of testing clothes by arranging for people to wear them in everyday circumstances and giving their honest feedback.

Weft—In a woven fabric, this is the thread that passes across the warp at right angles to interlock with it. The weft has more stretch and "give."

Work Into—Develop an idea.

INDEX

ACKNOWLEDGMENTS

Thank you to the incredibly talented people who contributed to this book: Dennic Chunman Lo, Hayley Pritchard, Linette Moses, and Orlagh McCloskey for all of your help and valuable insight. Catherine Carnevale, Jane Haigh, Leandra O'Sullivan, Maria Robinson, and Rebecca Owen for your specialist knowledge. Fergus McKeefry, Jo Hunt, Nicola Rolston, Rowena Chalmers, Sian Ryan, Andy Grant, and Vanessa Spence for answering questions at lightning speed. Debbie Shasanya, Ema Excell, and Sophie Rhind—Instagram Queens!—for your unique photos and for inspiring the reader.

Mark Searle for this great opportunity and for years of friendship. Caroline Elliker for your expertise, endless dedication, and commitment to this book. Jo Turner for your inspiring, elevating influence, guidance, and great humour. Steven Faerm, US Content Advisor, for your kind words and knowledge.

Thanks to London, New York, Victoria Park, and music for endless inspiration.

Mum, Dad, Sinéad, Gráinne, Fergus, and Ursula—thank you for your encouragement and enthusiasm and for instilling independence and uniqueness in us. To the Wee Ones: Stevie, Posy, Molly, Malachy, Monty, Sebastian, Alex, and Bridget Gráinne—the next generation—here's to seeing your names in print, and to being whatever you want to be! For Auntie Eileen, Auntie Tina, and a lineage of seamstresses and talent. Chris, Alan, and Emma—thanks for your support, laughs, encouragement, and interest throughout.

Matt—without whom this book wouldn't and couldn't have been written. Where do I start? Co-author doesn't do you justice. Incredibly intelligent, ever modest, and the patience of a Saint—and always with humour! Thank you.

We wrote this book for Gráinne, and with her encouragement to "make it count."

PHOTO CREDITS

t = top, b = bottom, l = left, r = right, m = middle.

Alamy: EDB Image Archive 108tl; PHOTOTAKE Inc. 115b; david pearson 184; Image Source 200

Getty Images: Victor VIRGILE 6; Francois Durand 9t; Bertrand Rindoff Petroff 9b; HUGO PHILPOTT 10t; Steve Pyke 10b; Eamonn M. McCormack 15tb; Kay-Paris Fernandes 19; Virginia Turbett 25t; KAMMERMAN 25b; Pascal Le Segretain 27l; Jacopo Raule 27tm; Victor Chavez 27bm; Victor VIRGILE 27brx2; Stefan Gosatti 27tr; Tristan Fewings 29; iconogenic 31tr; Naomi Yang/Figarophoto 31tl; Justin Hollar 31ml; Philippe Biancotto/Figarophoto 31br; Andrea Klarin/Figarophoto 31bl; Paul Rousseau/Figarophoto 31bm; Michael Tran 33tl; kyphoto 34; Mike Marsland 37(3); Stephen Lovekin 38; Kirstin Sinclair 50; Ethan Miller 61l; Asia Images 75; Morsa Images 87b; Laetitia Hotte/Figarophoto 91bm; Timur Emek 95tl; Stefania D'Alessandro 103; Atlantide Phototravel 105; Shana Novak 106t; Thomas Northcut 106m; Rocio Dominguez/EyeEm 106b; Ben Monk 107t; John Phillips 108br; David M. Benett 109bl; Victor VIRGILE 109tr, br; Rasmus Mogensen/Figarophoto 109tl; Randy Brooke 110tr; Victor VIRGILE 110tl; Daniel Zuchnik 113; Antonio de Moraes Barros Filho 111l; Daniel Zuchnik 113; Antonio de Moraes Barros Filho 115t; Antonio de Moraes Barros Filho 117tl; Naomi Yang/Figarophoto 117tr; Julian Ungano 117m; Arkan Zakharov 117br; Stuart C. Wilson 121tr; Steve Granitz 121bl; Samir Hussein 121tl; Norman Wong 145tr; Paul Farrell 145tl, bm; Jacopo Raule 145br; Benni Valsson/Figarophoto 145bl; Christophe Cufos/Figarophoto 146tl; Vittorio Zunino Celotto 146b; Arun Nevader 146tr; Wendelin Spiess/Figarophoto 146rm; Victor VIRGILE 146lm; Andrew McCaul 148; C. M. Kimber 150t; Lew Robertson 155; Victor VIRGILE 163br; Emulsion London Limited 165t; Victor VIRGILE 165bl; Don Freeman 169; Malina Corpadean 183t; Venturelli 184t; Timur Emek 193; Richard Drury 207; Naomi Yang/Figarophoto 216tl, tm, tr, bl, br; Magnus & Mads/Figarophoto 216bm; Gallo Images 219br; J. Clarke 219tr; Samir Hussein 219bl; Ian Gavan 220; GM Zimmermann/Figarophoto 222; Willie Maldonado 229br; Olivier Saillard/Figarophoto 229t; Sean Gallup 234bl; Monica Mcklinski 239br; Daniel Zuchnik 239tl; Christian Vierig 239bl; Thomas Barwick 264

iStock: David_Ahn 24

Shutterstock: Dahabian 22; Yulia Reznikov 26; FashionStock.com 28; Evgeniya Porechenskaya 31m; FashionStock.com 31rm; FashionStock.com 32tl, tlm, trm, br; enchanted_fairy 32tf(back); Maxim Kovich 32bl(back); Chirkov 32br(back); Marilyn Volan 32tm(back); Nata Sha 32trm; Thanwa Intasen 32bm(back); Aepsilon 32tl(back); Photoman29 32bl, bm; Gromovataya 32tr; Flat Design 33; Elaine Nadiv 33tr; Dmitry_Tsvetkov 33bl; coka 33br; RaSveta 34; 1000 Words 37(1); ishkov sergey 37(4); FashionStock.com 37(2l, 2r); eClick 37(6); Christos Siatos 37(5); a katz 37(1b); Hadrian 37(1m); taviphoto 37(back); Anna Chelnokova 44r; Dragon Images 52b; Comaniciu Dan 52t; Asia Images 75; Lole 80; sylber 80; Eternalfeelings 87t; FashionStock.com 88t; dvoevnore 89t; YamabikaY 89b; conrado 91tm; Evgeniya Porechenskaya 91bl; FashionStock.com 91tl; Fresh Stock 91tr; indira's work 91br; Mykola Komarovskyy 93l; liviatana 95bl; ultimathule 96; sspopov 105b; FashionStock.com 108tr, bl; Photoman29 108bm; Ovidiu Hrubaru 110b; FashionStock.com 116t; Savvapanf Photo 116b; FashionStock.com 117bl; V.Kuntsman 121br; Catwalk Photos 135; andersphoto 141; Greenseas 150m; Vlad Ozerov 150b; Sergey Goruppa 151t; tdee photo cm 151b; Neo Tribbiani 151m; Ovidiu Hrubaru 163tl, tr, bl; FashionStock.com 165br; catwalker 215; wrangler 227t; Carsten Reisinger 229bl; Charts and BG 230; Everett Collection 234t; Featureflash Photo Agency 239tr; Songquan Deng 250l; Ditty_about_summer 250r; Kiev.Victor 260; Northfoto 261l; Alberto Stocco 261r

Also: Will Anderson 88b, 95br, 221, 230; Julie Eilenberger 111r; Ema Excell, One Vintage Day Photography 224; Neal Grundy 69, 91 (swatches), 108 (swatches), 109 (swatches), 110 (swatches), 140, 152–153; Steven Klein/V Magazine 227br; Aisling McKeefry 21bl, 49tr, bl, br, 51, 62, 63, 107b, 138, 183b, 250m; Reformation 2, 195; Sophie Rhind 21tl, tr, br, 44; RIXO London 197; Debbie Shasanya 49tl, 138; ELEVEN SIX 223; Oliver Wien of european pressphoto agency b.v. 61r

All trademarks, trade names, and other product designations referred to herein are the property of their respective owners and are used solely for identification purposes. This book is a publication of Quintet Publishing Limited, and has not been authorized, licensed, approved, sponsored, or endorsed by any other person or entity. The publisher is not associated with any product, service, or vendor mentioned in this book. While every effort has been made to credit contributors, Quintet Publishing would like to apologize should there have been any omissions or errors, and would be pleased to make the appropriate correction for future editions.